Budgeting for America

Second Edition

John Cranford

Congressional Quarterly Inc.
1414 22nd Street N.W.
Washington, D.C. 20037

59180

HJ
2052
C73
1989

Congressional Quarterly Inc.

Congressional Quarterly Inc., an editorial research service and publishing company, serves clients in the fields of news, education, business, and government. It combines Congressional Quarterly's specific coverage of Congress, government, and politics with the more general subject range of an affiliated service, Editorial Research Reports.

Congressional Quarterly publishes the *Congressional Quarterly Weekly Report* and a variety of books, including college political science textbooks under the CQ Press imprint and public affairs paperbacks on developing issues and events. CQ also publishes information directories and reference books on the federal government, national elections, and politics, including the *Guide to Congress*, the *Guide to the U.S. Supreme Court*, the *Guide to U.S. Elections*, *Politics in America*, and *Congress A to Z: CQ's Ready Reference Encyclopedia*. The *CQ Almanac*, a compendium of legislation for one session of Congress, is published each year. *Congress and the Nation*, a record of government for a presidential term, is published every four years.

CQ publishes *The Congressional Monitor*, a daily report on current and future activities of congressional committees, and several newsletters including *Congressional Insight*, a weekly analysis of congressional action, and *Campaign Practices Reports*, a semimonthly update on campaign laws.

An electronic online information system, Washington Alert, provides immediate access to CQ's databases of legislative action, votes, schedules, profiles, and analyses.

Printed in the United States of America

Library of Congress Cataloging-in-Publication Data

Cranford, John, 1952-
    Budgeting for America / John Cranford. -- 2nd ed.
        p. cm.
    Bibliography: p.
    Includes index.
    ISBN 0-87187-441-5
    1. Budget deficits--United States. 2. Program budgeting--United States. 3. Government spending policy--United States. 4. United States--Economic conditions--1981- I. Title.
HJ2052.C73   1989   88-14998
353.0072'2--dc19   CIP

For my mother and father

Table of Contents

Tables and Figures

Tables

Figures

Preface

Much has happened since 1982, when the first edition of *Budgeting for America* was published. The previous year, Ronald Reagan and his Capitol Hill disciples had transformed congressional budget making, using for the first time five-year-old legislative tools to attack entrenched domestic spending (while protecting and even enhancing the Pentagon). At the same time they sought to remake the economy by slashing personal and corporate income taxes.

The adherents of supply-side economics believed in their vision, but before that first year was out even true believers like Reagan's budget director David A. Stockman knew it was a formula for disaster. The editors of Congressional Quarterly undertook then to explain just what was happening.

Few people assumed at the time that President Reagan, the supposed slayer of deficits and wasteful federal spending, would eventually preside over a period in which spending rocketed completely out of control, leading year after year to the largest deficits on record and the near tripling of the national debt. But that was the case. Few believed that deficits could become as large as they have without wrecking the economy on the shoals of high inflation, high interest rates, and, ultimately, recession. That, fortunately, did not happen. But many still fear that the ship of state is headed for the rocks.

The congressional budget process is now more than a decade old. When it was conceived in 1974, Congress did not intend the process to be a surrogate for the will to act responsibly on the deficit, which at the time was relatively small. Over time, however, the budget process has acquired the cloak of deficit-cutter, which does not fit it well. And like the budget itself, the process is in near tatters. The budget process consumes Congress, just as the deficit threatens to consume the budget.

The second edition of *Budgeting for America* looks beyond the Reagan presidency to illustrate the difficulties facing his successors and future Congresses as they try to wrestle the budget under control, in hopes of preventing an economic crisis. It does so by explaining first how the nation got to where it is and then the ways in which both domestic and international factors influence the federal budget.

The book examines the procedures that Congress has created to retain a measure of authority in the constant political tug-of-war with the president and to cope with the political pressures within itself. It looks at the Gramm-Rudman solution to the deficit problem, which simultaneously avoids and exaggerates those pressures. Finally, the book outlines the tough political and economic choices Congress has faced and will continue to face in the coming decade. Throughout, the book makes evident how economic policy intersects political considerations, and how difficult it is to understand, much less direct, the flow of the economy.

Like its predecessor, this edition leaves much unsaid. It provides details of how Congress makes its spending and taxation decisions, but it takes a long view, focusing on broader questions and efforts in Congress to make big-picture budgeting decisions. However, much of Congress's work is fine-tuning federal programs through the authorization and appropriation processes. Those actions have as much consequence for the budget—and the deficit—as do the annual budget resolutions or the bottom lines of spending bills that have much greater visibility.

Attention is paid in this book to the enormous political demands put on individual members of Congress by their constituents or by interest groups. Every grand-scale budget decision made—whether to cut total spending or to increase revenues—can be undone in the course of writing authorization and appropriations bills by the crafting of compromises, the granting of small favors to win a few votes, or the changing of circumstances.

Other writers, such as Aaron Wildavsky in his regularly revised *Politics of the Budgetary Process,* take a more thorough look at the politics. Stanley E. Collender's annual *Guide to the Federal Budget* may be a more complete technical explication of each step of the process. But *Budgeting for America* strikes a middle ground, detailing the process while mapping the political topography and providing a historical context. Although more could be said, this book offers a beginning.

I must acknowledge the contributions of others to this enterprise. The editor of the first edition, Martha V. Gottron, and its chief writers, Thomas J. Arrandale, Christopher J. Conte, and Margaret C. Thompson, built a sturdy foundation for the second edition. In addition, I drew heavily upon the reporting of my past and present colleagues at Congressional Quarterly, in particular, Elizabeth Wehr, Pamela Fessler, Eileen Shanahan, Jacqueline Calmes, and Dale Tate. Their comprehensive, authoritative accounts of the workings of Congress's budget and tax machinery are the best in print.

I offer deep gratitude to my colleague David Rapp for his careful reading of the manuscript, and for the insights that he provided from his vantage as CQ's current budget reporter. I thank Stan Collender and my former colleague Ann Pelham for their suggestions for revising and refining parts of the manuscript, and Mary Cohn for her timely advice and encouragement. And I especially thank Colleen McGuiness, who edited the book and kept it alive when I was despairing of finishing it.

Most of all, I thank my wife, Sharon H. Cranford. She, too, offered sound criticism of the manuscript, and her perseverance, good humor, and love kept me going through it all—all the while she was being mother and sometimes father to our two sons, Sean and Colin.

Those named above—and those unnamed—who brought so much to this book deserve credit only for its assets. Blame for any errors—be they factual or interpretive—belongs to me alone.

Budgeting for America

1

The Deficit Crisis

Jimmy Carter was elected president in 1976, promising—vainly—to balance the budget before he finished his first term. His fiscal failure was overshadowed, however, by an economy gone awry on his watch. Soaring deficits alone were not responsible for Ronald Reagan's election in 1980 and Carter's early retirement from the White House. But they did provide an obvious target for those critical of how Carter and the Democrats managed the economy.

Republican Reagan, too, promised a balanced budget and did not deliver. But his good-times politics and the relative prosperity that came toward the end of his first term helped to guarantee him a second.

Yet, where Reagan inherited enormously high inflation, rising unemployment, budget deficits measured in the tens of billions of dollars, and a coming recession, the unpredictable and largely uncontrollable nature of the U.S. economy meant that his successor's fate would be either considerably better or much worse.

It was possible that the next administration would enjoy continued prosperity. In 1988, inflation was down—it hit a twenty-year low in 1986—though it was threatening to creep upward. Unemployment, which crested at a post-World War II high during Reagan's first term, was down to its lowest point since 1974. Most significantly, the

economy had been on a path of sustained growth since November 1982, a point never overlooked by Reagan administration partisans, who attributed it entirely to their economic foresight.

But a time bomb threatened whoever captured the White House in 1988. Annual budget deficits had exceeded $200 billion and promised to stay above $100 billion into the next decade. A recession was lurking; if not in 1989 or 1990, then soon thereafter. Not even Reagan could repeal the business cycle. Deficits would only get worse when the economy turned down; that was the way the federal government was structured, even after eight years of "Reaganomics." And the nation was in deep, deep debt—approaching $2.8 trillion in federal government debt alone by mid-1989. That debt was the sum of decades of deficit spending and had nearly tripled in size while Reagan was in office. The net cost of paying interest on that borrowing was expected to approach and even exceed the size of the deficit itself in fiscal 1989.

Another factor was the collapse of the stock market. The nation's largest one-day fall in stock prices in both absolute and percentage terms occurred Black Monday, October 19, 1987. Over the one-week period leading up to and including that day, the Dow Jones Industrial Average, a leading measure of stocks, lost a third of its value, representing a loss of wealth of $1 trillion.

The consequences for the economy of the crash were not readily apparent. In fact, the market closed out 1987 at almost exactly the level at which it had begun the year. The loss of wealth was all on paper—theoretically. However, drops in the market of historic proportions almost always coincided with economic turndowns. The economy continued to grow at a good clip in the last three months of the year, but much of the rise in gross national product (GNP) was due to a large increase in business inventories—double the inventory increase of the previous quarter. That meant that more goods were backing up in warehouses and not being sold to consumers. In fact, consumer spending fell during the quarter for the first time since the expansion began.

Since consumer buying had fueled the economy's five-year climb, the postcrash numbers worried some economists that the growth spurt might be over, plants might start laying off workers to allow inventories to decline, and 1988 might bring with it a recession. Such concerns were exaggerated; in the first quarter of 1988 the economy grew at an inflation-adjusted rate of 2.3 percent. Though hardly spectacular, the first quarter was anticipated to be the worst. And though early projections about 1988 from administration and Congressional Budget Office economists were gloomy, by October the economy's growth was expected to average 2.8 percent for the year.

But public focus was not diverted from the crash, its implications for the economy, or the need to rethink priorities. Many, but certainly not all, market observers laid the crash at Washington's feet. The enormous budget deficit and equally large trade deficits made economists, politicians, and Wall Street anxious. Most of all, the crash concerned those in Europe, Japan, and elsewhere overseas who had benefited from American consumers' deep pockets and who

were helping significantly to finance the budget deficit. The concern also affected ordinary Americans. A nationwide poll conducted in mid-1988 by the Gallup Organization for the Times Mirror Corp. showed that 59 percent believed the budget deficit to be a "bad thing"; 20 percent did not.

It is not easy to understand the correlations between government spending and the economy. Large deficits can cut into domestic credit markets, reducing money for business expansions or increasing interest rates. Often, foreign investors must take up the slack. Meanwhile, demand for dollars overseas to make those investments increases the rate of exchange, drives down more expensive exports, drives up cheaper imports, and makes the trade deficit worse. Thus more dollars are spent abroad than foreign-held dollars are spent in the United States, and the difference, called the current account balance, must be borrowed overseas. And all along interest rates must stay high enough to attract and retain foreign investors. But higher interest rates in turn can be a drag on the economy and a precursor to recession.

The upshot of the crash was a historic turnabout for the Reagan administration. Despite repeatedly rejecting calls from Capitol Hill for a "budget summit" to address the nation's fiscal ills, Reagan agreed the day after the crash to meet with congressional leaders to set a new agenda for deficit reduction. Those in Congress who previously had tried to bring Reagan to the bargaining table were cheered in those first, worrisome days. "There are 20 different reasons" the market collapsed, said Senate minority leader Robert Dole, R-Kan. (House 1961-1969; Senate 1969-). "But for those of us concerned about the deficit, this won't hurt."

The results of that parley were mixed at best. Economically, the summit made a marginal difference in the scope of congressional budget cutting already planned for fiscal 1988 and 1989. In political terms, it was less important. The summit disappointed those on Wall Street who had hoped for significant changes in taxing and spending policies. And its carefully crafted terms left politicians free of the need to make tough election-year decisions in 1988. That year, for the first time in the Reagan era, Congress and the White House engaged in almost no budget fights. All the decisions necessary for fiscal 1989 that ordinarily would have been made in calendar year 1988 were instead embodied in the summit agreement of late 1987. But the fact that legislative and executive branch policy makers were able to avoid tough decisions for a year provided no end to concerns about the budget. The "historic" budget summit merely put off the pain for a new president and a new Congress in 1989.

What Deficit Problem?

For decades, even before the deficit grew into a stubborn creature of uncontrollable spending, presidents and Congress have fought—mostly with each other—to bring the federal budget into check. Except for the Vietnam War and the Watergate scandal, no other issue since World War II has so divided Congress and at times paralyzed government decision making. Directly or indirectly, congressional historian George B. Galloway noted in 1955, "perhaps nine-tenths of the work of Congress is concerned . . . with the spending of public money."

The government has run chronic deficits since the mid-1960s because of expanding financial commitments to defense and domestic programs and a reluctance to raise taxes. Continuous deficits fed inflationary fires and made fiscal policy an ineffective, often counterproductive, tool for managing the U.S. economy.

For most of the 1970s, the struggle for spending control dominated congressional deliberations. In a direct challenge to the Democratic Congress, President Richard Nixon made sweeping claims that he could refuse to spend money appropriated by Congress; to restrain growth in total outlays, Nixon believed he could ignore congressional directives. Out of that confrontation came a realization that Congress had lost control over budget decisions. As a result, lawmakers devised a new budgeting process in 1974 and put it into use in 1975 (for the fiscal 1976 budget), regaining a measure of influence over the White House, if not the budget.

Before Reagan took office in 1981, however, Congress had shied away from the politically tough task of cutting back federal spending. Yet the political momentum of Reagan and the Republicans' ascendancy changed all that. Early in his first year Reagan joined with the Republican-controlled Senate and conservative Democrats in the House to cut $35.2 billion from the fiscal 1982 budget, and progressively more from future years. A few small programs were ended; others were lumped together into "block grants" to the states with less money than the sum of the original programs combined; some entitlements—programs whose beneficiaries are "entitled" by law to the money they provide—were cut back. Meanwhile economic conditions and demographic trends pushed spending ever upward anyway, seemingly beyond control by either the legislative or executive branches.

Simultaneously, Congress went along with a tax cut that reduced revenues $35.6 billion in 1982 and, again, significantly more in later years.

But the first spending cuts were so sweeping, the tax cut so deep, and the deficit such a yawning gulf that Reagan's call for further spending reductions went unheeded later in the year. And, although deficit reduction has become an annual Capitol Hill ritual, Congress since 1981 has not taken such a meat-ax to spending. Even the two-year budget summit agreement in November 1987 yielded less in one-year spending cuts, though it incorporated a large tax increase (the fourth since Reagan engineered the 1981 tax cut) and for the first time ever enacted a two-year ceiling on appropriations. Together, the package of cuts and new taxes promised to reduce the fiscal 1989 deficit by $45.9 billion if the agreement were not breached.

For some economists—but few politicians in the 1980s—the issue was not elimination of the deficit, but instead managing and understanding it. In a 1986 book challenging conventional deficit wisdom, Robert Eisner, a Northwestern University economist, offered a compelling argument that "hysteria," not science, propelled the concern about deficits. Although he did not believe any deficit was acceptable, Eisner complained in *How Real is the Federal Deficit?* that the accounting for the deficit overlooks the fact that state and local governments, businesses, and individuals borrow all the time for "capital" improvements—building roads, investing in new machinery, buying houses. So, he wondered, why should the federal government behave any differently?

There are obvious benefits to deficit spending, Eisner noted. Casting his lot with twentieth-century mainstream economics and the theories of John Maynard Keynes, he contended that one person's debt is another's wealth, with borrowing providing a strong stimulus to the economy. He made a special point about adjusting the way deficits are viewed to account for inflation—which, he said, tends to make deficits appear larger than they really are. And he said deficits ought to be discounted to take into consideration the fact that often there are more persons unemployed than there would be if the economy were performing at

capacity. Eisner disputed the notion that government borrowing always "crowds out" private investment. "That might occur in a full-employment economy," he wrote. "Over the last 30 years of usually less than full employment though, we find that the stimulus effects of real federal deficits are dominant."

Eisner is not alone in arguing against a wholesale assault on the federal budget simply to eliminate the deficit. But even he agrees that the deficit has grown out of hand. Because the economy has grown so much over the years, and the dollar's relative value has diminished due to inflation, figures are difficult to compare. One consistent approach, however, is to look at the deficit as a share of the national economy, as measured by GNP. From the end of World War II through 1974, the annual federal deficit did not exceed 2 percent of GNP, except on four occasions. Since 1975 it has been below 2 percent only once, in 1979. The deficit's share of GNP was 6.3 percent in 1983 and stayed in the 5 percent range through most of Reagan's presidency.

Most economists contend that a deficit that is more in line with historic trends—2 percent of GNP—is serviceable and acceptable, and perhaps even desirable. But the deficit is not the only measure of the budget. Spending and taxing have political and economic consequences well beyond the bottom line of the deficit.

Expansion of Federal Outlays

The new national government spent a total of $5 million in fiscal 1792, its fourth year in operation. The United States then had four million people, most living on farms or in small towns. The government grew—and its outlays increased—as the country acquired new territories, settlers moved west, and the nation fought wars.

"The original role of the federal government was limited both by the precise language of the Constitution and by the prevailing social consensus that powerful central governments should be avoided," noted Donald G. Ogilvie, associate dean of the Yale University School of Organization and Management, in a 1981 study entitled *The Congressional Budget Process after Five Years.*

"As a result, federal activities were restricted to those traditional 'public good' functions such as the maintenance of national security forces, management of the monetary system, and the operation of the executive, congressional and judicial branches of the government."

Annual federal outlays reached the $1 billion level only in 1865, the last year of the Civil War, then subsided below that mark for the next fifty-two years, until the nation entered World War I. The government spent $18.4 billion in fiscal 1919, incurring a $13.4 billion deficit. But just as in the decades after the Civil War, outlays once again fell off in the peacetime following World War I, holding between $2 billion and $3 billion a year during the 1920s. (See Table 1-1.)

But the nation was undergoing rapid change. Its population had soared, and its economy had grown vastly larger and more complex. People crowded into fast-sprawling metropolitan regions and moved more often from one place to another. Life expectancies lengthened, and families lived apart. Those changes "combined to produce new requirements for federal programs," Ogilvie suggested, and "complicated and expanded the role of the public sector in social, economic and political affairs."

The nation's federal system reached a turning point in the 1930s during the Great Depression. President Franklin D. Roosevelt and Congress launched massive federal programs to pull the economy out of the worst downturn in U.S. history. Spending for domestic assistance programs jumped to $7 billion by 1939 as outlays for civil needs

surpassed spending on the military, veterans, and interest on the war-incurred debt. During World War II federal spending multiplied tenfold, reaching $92.7 billion in fiscal 1945. Postwar spending declined but stayed well above previous peacetime levels. The Korean War buildup doubled outlays from less than $30 billion in fiscal 1948 to $76.1 billion in fiscal 1953. Spending fell below $70 billion for fiscal 1955. But the budget has grown steadily since then in every year except fiscal 1965.

It has been a steep climb since the American Revolution. "It took 186 years for the federal budget to exceed $100 billion," Ogilvie wrote. "It took only nine more years to reach $200 billion; four more to exceed $300 billion; two more to reach $400 billion; and an additional two years to go to $500 billion." Government spending continued to increase at the rate of $50 billion a year until 1987, when the brakes were finally applied and spending grew by only $14 billion. That limited restraint notwithstanding, spending jumped $60 billion in 1988 and projections were for spending to increase at that rate well into the future.

A Fiscal Constitution

There is no limit in the Constitution on how much the government can spend, tax, or borrow. Before the Great Depression of the 1930s, government spending was limited by general concurrence that outlays should not exceed revenues except in times of war. Political economists James M. Buchanan and Richard E. Wagner have written that this understood "fiscal constitution" in the past constrained the government's impulse to launch new spending programs. "Barring extraordinary circumstances," according to Buchanan and Wagner, "public expenditures were supposed to be financed by taxation, just as private spending was supposed to be financed from income."

Table 1-1   Federal Government Receipts, Outlays, and Deficits (in billions)

Fiscal year	Receipts	Outlays	Surplus or deficit
1789-1849	$ 1.2	$ 1.1	$ 0.1
1850-1900	14.5	15.5	−1.0
1910	0.7	0.7	−0.1
1920	6.6	6.4	0.3
1929	3.9	3.1	0.7
1932	1.9	4.7	−2.7
1940	6.5	9.5	−2.9
1943	24.0	78.6	−54.6
1945	45.2	92.7	−47.6
1950	39.4	42.6	−3.1
1951	51.6	45.5	6.1
1952	66.2	67.7	−1.5
1953	69.6	76.1	−6.5
1954	69.7	70.1	−1.2
1955	65.5	68.4	−3.0
1956	74.6	70.6	3.9
1957	80.0	76.6	3.4
1958	79.6	82.4	−2.8
1959	79.2	92.1	−12.8
1960	92.5	92.2	0.3
1961	94.4	97.7	−3.3
1962	99.7	106.8	−7.1
1963	106.6	111.3	−4.8
1964	112.6	118.5	−5.9
1965	116.8	118.2	−1.4
1966	130.8	134.5	−3.7
1967	148.8	157.5	−8.6
1968	153.0	178.1	−25.2
1969	186.9	183.6	3.2
1970	192.8	195.6	−2.8
1971	187.1	210.2	−23.0
1972	207.3	230.7	−23.4
1973	230.8	245.7	−14.9
1974	263.2	269.4	−6.1
1975	279.1	332.3	−53.2
1976	298.1	371.8	−73.7
1977	355.6	409.2	−53.6
1978	399.6	458.7	−59.2
1979	463.3	503.5	−40.2
1980	517.1	590.9	−73.8
1981	599.3	678.2	−78.9
1982	617.8	745.7	−127.9
1983	600.6	808.3	−207.8
1984	666.5	851.8	−185.3
1985	734.1	946.3	−212.3
1986	769.1	990.3	−221.2
1987	854.1	1,004.6	−150.4
1988	909.0	1,064.1	−155.1

Source: Office of Management and Budget.

Note: Totals may not add due to rounding. Transition quarter between fiscal 1976 and 1977 excluded.

When the government began new spending programs to counter the depression, however, strict adherence to balanced budgets was impossible. During the same period, economists advising the government gave theoretical support to deficit spending during peacetime years to stimulate production. The old link between taxes and spending gradually gave way as Congress approved new programs that spent federal money for broad and innovative national purposes.

It is argued that ending the balanced-budget consensus in the 1930s was a direct stimulus to new spending programs because there was no longer the direct need to burden taxpayers with their cost. In the process, Ogilvie said, "government lost its only yardstick by which to determine how many worthy federal programs the country could afford."

The shifting national priorities resulted not only in increased spending but also in changed spending patterns. Federal outlays grew rapidly for tasks, notably national defense, that the federal government traditionally had performed. But as new social programs came on line they absorbed more and more of the government's resources; the share that the government poured into defense declined as a proportion of the budget.

Annual U.S. military spending reached a high of $82.9 billion during World War II and of $52.8 billion during the Korean War. Defense outlays fell off in the mid-1950s but climbed back above $50 billion in fiscal 1962. In the 1960s, during the Vietnam War, defense spending climbed steadily, reaching $82.4 billion in 1969. Thereafter, it declined slightly, and then grew at a slow pace. As the country sought to upgrade its military capabilities, however, beginning in 1980, military spending accelerated. Defense outlays nearly doubled under Reagan from $157.5 billion in 1981 to just under $300 billion in fiscal 1989 projections.

After Korea and except for three years during the Vietnam buildup, however, defense purchases of goods and services accounted for a declining share of federal spending as measured against GNP. By the early 1980s, defense outlays were rising again and expected to reach 6.1 percent of GNP in 1988, down from the 9.3 percent average just prior to Vietnam.

At the same time, federal government payments to individuals—the poor, the sick, the elderly, retired government workers—exploded. From $32.7 billion in fiscal 1966 (when they comprised 4.4 percent of GNP) such payments rose to an estimated $437.9 billion in fiscal 1988 (9.3 percent of GNP), accounting for two-fifths of all outlays (half again as much as defense). And federal grants to state and local governments—for purposes such as highways construction, mass transit, sewage treatment plants, job-training, revenue sharing, community development, and welfare services—escalated from less than $2.2 billion in 1950 to more than $116.5 billion thirty-eight years later.

The Enormous Debt

Congress not only rode a domestic economic roller coaster in 1987—thanks to the stock market—but an international one as well.

For most of the year, the dollar had continued to decline in value compared with the Japanese yen and West German mark—the currencies of the United States' most competitive trading partners. The fall had begun apparently on its own in February 1985 but had been sustained by administration and foreign government policies designed to force a change in the world trade picture. Ultimately, by the end of 1987, foreign governments were intervening in currency markets to shore up the dollar, to keep it from falling too far.

Yet the nation's imbalance of imports over exports continued to worsen in dollar terms in 1987—yielding a record "merchandise" trade deficit of $177.6 billion for the year (up from $166.3 billion the year before and $39.7 billion in 1981). There were signs that the dollar's fall (by the end of 1987 it was worth half its 1985 peak against the other two major currencies) had begun boosting exports. But ever-more-costly imports were still quite high, offsetting export gains.

Another measure is the "current account" deficit—more important because it includes trade in services and investment, which have long been strong points in the U.S. economy to the simpler measure of merchandise trade. The current account deficit hit a record $160.7 billion in 1987. It was the sixth deficit year in a row and the fifth straight record; in 1986 the current account deficit was $141.4 billion.

And for the third straight year the United States was a net-debtor nation. Foreigners owned more in the United States than U.S. citizens owned abroad, and for the first time in history foreigners earned more here than U.S. citizens earned overseas. The country slipped more than $368 billion into the red as it borrowed heavily abroad to finance the budget and trade deficits. In 1986, the nation was a net debtor by $263.6 billion, a reversal from 1981 when the United States was a net creditor by $141.1 billion. (See Figure 1-1.)

Consequences for Growth

These deficit numbers were not worrisome for everyone. They did, however, become the fulcrum for political debate on the economy in 1987 and the national election year of 1988.

As congressional Democrats saw it, the nation was headed for a serious calamity without a change in direction of government economic policy. For the Democrats, the central issue was debt—government and private. Republicans instead hailed Reaganomics, claiming that, risen like the phoenix from the ashes of the 1982 recession, the economy was cruising along nicely with no end to the good times in sight. For them, debt was not a big thing, or at least not in relation to the happier aspects of the economy. (That, in itself, was a big switch. It was Republicans in the 1970s who refused to vote for increases in the statutory ceiling on the federal debt, complaining that such votes were an endorsement of the Democrats' deficit spending.)

Worry about the government's debt grew loud—possibly because it was a creature of public policy (though many economists credit tax policy and other government actions for private debt as well). Federal borrowing was also growing in the 1980s at a much more rapid rate than it had in the previous decade.

Historically, the debt had grown by less and less each year, at least since World War II when federal borrowing was larger than the economy's total output. That portion of the national debt owned by the public fell from 113.6 percent of GNP in 1946 to 24.4 percent in 1974. (A significant part of the debt is also "owned" by government trust funds, such as those for military retirement and Social Security.) In fact, throughout the 1970s, publicly held debt was relatively constant as a percentage of GNP. Then it began a sharp rise upward in 1983, as a result of record, Reagan-era deficits. In 1987, a year of modest economic growth, the public debt reached 43.0 percent of GNP. (See Table 1-2.)

But federal borrowing was not the only issue confronting policy makers in the 1980s. Corporate and consumer debt has been counted as at least as serious to the long-term health of the economy. For example, most economists credited the economic growth since the 1982 recession as largely

Figure 1-1 Budget and Trade Deficits

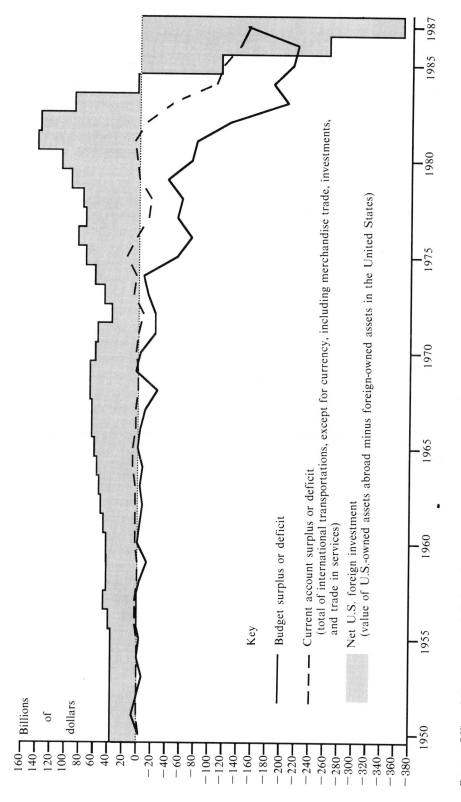

Sources: Office of Management and Budget, Commerce Department, Treasury Department.

Note: Budget is fiscal year; others, calendar year.

Table 1-2 The National Debt

Fiscal year	Total federal debt (in billions)	Debt held by the public [a] (in billions)	Public debt as percentage of GNP
1940	$ 50.7	$ 42.8	44.6
1941	57.5	48.2	42.7
1942	79.2	67.8	47.6
1943	142.6	127.8	72.7
1944	204.1	184.8	91.5
1945	260.1	235.2	110.7
1946	271.0	241.9	113.6
1947	257.1	224.3	100.3
1948	252.0	216.3	87.3
1949	252.6	214.3	81.2
1950	256.9	219.0	82.1
1951	255.3	214.3	68.0
1952	259.1	214.8	62.7
1953	266.0	218.4	59.7
1954	270.8	224.5	60.8
1955	274.4	226.6	58.6
1956	272.8	222.2	53.2
1957	272.4	219.4	49.8
1958	279.7	226.4	50.3
1959	287.8	235.0	48.8
1960	290.9	237.2	46.8
1961	292.9	238.6	46.0
1962	303.3	248.4	44.5
1963	310.8	254.5	43.3
1964	316.8	257.6	40.9
1965	323.2	261.6	38.9
1966	329.5	264.7	35.8
1967	341.3	267.5	33.7
1968	369.8	290.6	34.2
1969	367.1	279.5	30.1
1970	382.6	284.9	28.8
1971	409.5	304.3	28.8
1972	437.3	323.8	28.1
1973	468.4	343.0	26.8
1974	486.2	346.1	24.4
1975	544.1	396.9	26.1
1976	631.9	480.3	28.3
1977	709.1	551.8	28.5
1978	780.4	610.9	28.1
1979	833.8	644.6	26.3
1980	914.3	715.1	26.8
1981	1,003.9	794.4	26.6
1982	1,147.0	929.4	29.6
1983	1,381.9	1,141.8	34.4
1984	1,576.7	1,312.6	35.6

Table 1-2 *Continued*

Fiscal year	Total federal debt (in billions)	Debt held by the public [a] (in billions)	Public debt as percentage of GNP
1985	1,827.5	1,509.9	38.3
1986	2,130.0	1,746.1	41.6
1987	2,355.3	1,897.8	43.0

Source: Office of Management and Budget.

Note: Data are as of end of fiscal year. GNP = gross national product.

[a] Debt held by the public is a measure of all federal securities (including those held by the Federal Reserve System), except those held by federal government accounts, such as civilian and military retirement funds and the Social Security and Medicare trust funds.

the result of consumer spending. That growth is reflected in such disparate mirrors as the studied affluence among young professionals and the trade deficit, which was exacerbated by such "yuppie" purchases as BMW cars from Germany.

But if consumer purchases aided the economy in the short tun, they might ultimately prove ruinous, since much consumer spending was financed through credit cards and other forms of consumer debt. Annual borrowing by consumers, businesses, and state and local governments grew at triple the rate of inflation from 1972 through 1986. And, though federal borrowing comprised a smaller share of total borrowing in the United States in 1986 than it did fifteen years earlier, when it was relatively small, the trend since 1974 has been that private borrowing (including that by states and localities) has grown at a faster rate than federal borrowing. No doubt, a significant degree of the growth of private debt is attributed to increased demands on state and local governments, as the federal government has pulled back from financing some domestic programs. But the fact remains that the federal government was not the only contributor to the economy on a debt binge. (See Table 1-3.)

Ultimately, most economists agree, that level of debt growth is not sustainable.

But questions remain: Whose belt gets tightened, and at what cost?

Politics Provides an Answer

A clear vision of the political perceptions on the issue of debts is found in the twice-yearly reports of the Joint Economic Committee of Congress. Markedly different and partisan views came from the Democratic and Republican flanks of the committee, which maintained a Reagan-years tradition of producing separate reports on the nation's fiscal health.

As the president's second term drew to a close, the Democrats pushed harder to stake out a position contrary to the administration's, while the Republicans clung to a continuation of Reaganomics—principally an aversion to taxes—to keep the United States prosperous into the 1990s.

Particularly in their August 1987 and February 1988 reports, the Democrats focused on Reagan's "Legacy of Debt," as their 1987 report was titled. While acknowledging that unemployment, inflation, and economic growth were registering in the healthy range at the beginning of 1988 (the stock market's convulsions notwithstanding), Democrats complained that the country had ignored "insistent warning signals beneath the surface" that could lead to big troubles ahead.

Table 1-3 New Borrowing: Government and Private (in billions)

Year	Net federal government borrowing	Net private nonfinancial borrowing [a]	Net annual increase in domestic debt
1972	$ 15.1	$157.7	$172.8
1973	8.3	188.0	196.3
1974	11.8	164.8	176.5
1975	85.4	107.6	193.0
1976	69.0	174.5	243.5
1977	56.8	260.2	316.9
1978	53.7	318.2	371.9
1979	37.4	348.4	385.7
1980	79.2	262.5	341.7
1981	87.4	288.5	375.9
1982	161.3	227.6	388.9
1983	186.6	363.6	550.2
1984	198.8	555.1	753.9
1985	223.6	631.1	854.8
1986	215.0	614.9	829.9

Source: Board of Governors of the Federal Reserve System.

[a] Includes state and local governments, households, and nonfinancial businesses.

"The economy has been increasingly resting on the shifting sands of debt," said the panel's chairman in 1988, Sen. Paul S. Sarbanes, D-Md. (House 1971-1977; Senate 1977-).

For their part Republicans chose to accentuate the positive, crediting in 1987 "the free enterprise foundation of our economic system and the Reagan administration's adherence to sound economic principles." They totally ignoring the question of too much debt.

In early 1988, GOP optimism was unshaken, although the subject of debt was no longer ignored. "I don't disagree that the debt is too high, and we have to come to grips with it," said Rep. Chalmers P. Wylie of Ohio (1967-), the committee's ranking Republican. But where Democratic interest was directed toward the problem, Republicans struck it a glancing blow, arguing that a constitutional amendment requiring a balanced budget would do the trick.

The Democrats tied the nation's debtor status to its weakened trading posture, and said, even in the best case, if the nation's

trade balance showed steady improvement and a surplus by the mid-1990s, the net foreign debt would reach $700 billion or more.

Extracting the nation from that predicament would require the country to reverse its trend of consuming far more than it produces, which could lead to a significant decline in the national standard of living, the Democrats cautioned. That would be particularly true if economic growth slowed and the nation entered a recession.

"Once you get inside the box, it's hard to get out of the box," Sarbanes said.

But the Republicans sniffed at that conclusion and argued that Democratic attempts to throw cold water on "the Reagan experiment" were misplaced and counterproductive. To them, talk of a reduced standard of living evoked memories of President Carter's failed attempts to battle the "energy crisis" and to overcome inflation. It sounded entirely too much like Carter's July 1979 televised energy crisis address that complained of a national "crisis of confidence." That speech was widely derided later for its attack on American "malaise."

"The [Reagan] experiment has worked out well," Wylie said. "We regard this as more of the 'malaise' type of conclusion, which we think has a negative psychological effect."

Surging Foreign Investment

The conflicting—and no doubt confusing to many—partisan views of the debt were not clarified much when the equally divided views of economists were taken into account. Depending upon which "side" an economic argument was presumably supporting, it took on the appropriate political shading. For instance, in February 1988 the president's Council of Economic Advisers took sharp issue with Democratic and nonpartisan complaints about the size of foreign investment in the United States, and the significance of that debt.

"This is not a dire threat to our future," argued council chairman Beryl W. Sprinkel. In its annual report to the president and Congress, the council analyzed the debt question in great detail. The report pointed out that the United States' net debt abroad—including foreign ownership of land and buildings in this country, as well as investments such as bank accounts and Treasury securities that paid dividends— was, at about $400 billion, less than 10 percent of GNP.

The cost of "servicing" or paying the interest and dividends on that amount of borrowing to foreign investors would be about one-half of 1 percent of GNP annually—in essence a pittance, according to the council.

But, even in the scenario of the Joint Economic Committee Democrats, it was not just the cost of the interest payments on a foreign debt cresting toward $1 trillion that was scary. What was also frightening was the possibility that foreign investors might retreat.

Foreign investment in the United States was perceived as both a blessing and a curse. Without it, domestic investors would have to take up the slack, a dubious prospect in the spendthrift 1980s when the domestic savings rate—always low—was falling. At 3.8 percent, the amount of disposable income devoted to savings struck a forty-year low in 1987. Yet if the dollar were to continue its downward slide in relation to other currencies, dollar-denominated investments, such as Treasury bonds, would lose value. Interest rates would then have to climb to keep foreign investors interested.

At the same time, the cheap dollar was making U.S. assets a bargain for foreign investors and was causing some commentators to worry. "It's one thing for the Japanese and Germans and others to buy U.S. government bonds to finance our huge trade imbalances with them," wrote magazine publisher Malcolm S. Forbes in January 1988. "But it's a whole and totally impermissible other thing for them to use their vast billions of dollars to buy great chunks of America's big businesses."

The Commerce Department reported in March 1988 that the growth in "direct foreign investment" in the United States— defined as ownership of 10 percent or more of an asset—was outpacing the growth of direct U.S. investment abroad. The numbers still favored the United States, but the gap was about to be closed with foreigners holding a direct stake in U.S. assets worth about $250 billion and U.S. citizens having a corresponding stake overseas of about $300 billion.

The paradox for policy makers was how to encourage some continued foreign investment without setting off either an interest-rate spiral that might have both inflationary and recessionary implications, or further alarms about foreigners buying up the United States.

More and more the answer was to work to reduce or eliminate the budget and trade deficits. First, that would take pressure off the dollar. Second, the worldwide economy would be better balanced. Many economists noted that the United States had enjoyed higher economic growth in the 1980s than had Europe, especially Germany; the developing countries saddled with huge loans to Western banks; and, to a lesser degree, Japan. (See Table 1-4.)

This imbalance, in part traceable to the large trade surpluses and deficits that had developed in different countries, had to be corrected if the trade picture and the dollar's value were to stabilize. But foremost was the cost of borrowing to finance the activities of the U.S. government.

In an unusual move, thirty-three well-known international economists issued a report in December 1987 calling for greater effort to reduce the federal budget deficit. The group, which included two Nobel laureates and fourteen former government officials from thirteen countries, denounced the just-completed budget summit agreement between Congress and the White House as "grossly inadequate" to prevent a worldwide economic collapse.

The public show put on by the group was a bit of an oddity for economists, as was its ideological breadth—though it had no representatives of the far right or left. Assembled by the Washington, D.C.-based Institute for International Economics, the group called on the United States to make an even more substantial reduction in the budget deficit—the "structural deficit" to be precise, defined as the deficit that would occur when unemployment is reduced to the lowest possible point. Elimination of the structural deficit by the early 1990s was seen as a desirable goal. A tax increase and cuts in both entitlements and defense spending were seen as probably necessary to make a sufficient reduction in the deficit.

Rudolph G. Penner, former director of the Congressional Budget Office, was one of the thirty-three economists. His experience with Congress and the administration did not lead him to believe the kind of tough decision making needed would be forthcoming. "Six months ago," Penner said in December 1987, "I would have said a 500-point fall in the stock market would probably get everyone's attention. It did not."

Consequences for the Government

Even if there were no dire international repercussions from the growing national debt, its effects on the budget itself and the domestic economy promised to be difficult to manage well into the future. Not only will efforts to reduce the deficit impinge on other spending, but the long-term cost of paying for the accumulated deficits of a generation will soak up a major portion of available resources. And, until the political assault on the deficit ends—presumably by eliminating or diminishing it—there will be little opportunity to expand government programs, even where there is broad consensus to do so.

The budget deficit in 1971 was $23 billion and net interest payments on the national debt were $14.8 billion. In 1987, the deficit had increased more than sixfold and the interest payments almost tenfold. Where net interest costs amounted to 7.0 percent of the $210 billion budget and 1.3 percent of the $1.1 trillion economy in 1971, interest was the third largest slice of the budget pie in 1987 behind defense and Social Security—consuming 13.8 percent of the $1 trillion budget and 3.3 percent of GNP. (See Table 1-5.)

The political cost of servicing the national debt was also high. More than a third of the revenue from individual income taxes in fiscal 1988 was used to cover net interest payments. It cannot be easy to increase taxes when the money will go not for new programs or for deficit reduction, but

Table 1-4 World GNP

| Country | Annual average | | | | 1981 | 1982 | 1983 | 1984 | 1985 | 1986 | 1987 [a] |
	1961-1965	1966-1970	1971-1975	1976-1980							
United States	4.6%	3.0%	2.2%	3.4%	1.9%	-2.5%	3.6%	6.8%	3.0%	2.9%	2.9%
Canada	5.3	4.6	5.2	3.7	3.0	-3.4	3.7	6.1	4.3	3.0	3.7
Japan	12.4	11.0	4.3	5.0	3.7	3.1	3.2	5.1	4.7	2.5	3.6
European Community [b]	4.9	4.6	2.9	3.0	0.2	0.8	1.5	2.4	2.6	2.6	2.3
France	5.9	5.4	4.0	3.6	1.2	2.5	0.7	1.4	1.7	2.1	1.6
West Germany	4.7	4.2	2.1	3.4	0.0	-1.0	1.9	3.3	2.0	2.5	1.7
Italy	4.8	6.6	2.4	3.8	1.1	0.2	0.5	3.5	2.7	2.7	2.7
United Kingdom	3.2	2.5	2.1	1.7	-1.2	1.0	3.7	2.2	3.7	2.3	3.5
Developing countries	5.3	5.8	5.7	5.0	2.2	0.9	0.5	2.8	1.7	4.0	3.3
Communist countries [b]	4.4	5.0	4.2	2.8	2.0	2.6	2.7	2.3	2.3	4.1	c
Soviet Union	4.7	5.0	3.0	2.3	1.3	2.7	3.2	1.5	0.8	3.8	1.0
Eastern Europe	3.9	3.8	4.9	1.9	-1.0	0.9	1.9	3.5	0.5	2.7	2.0
China	-0.2	8.3	5.5	6.1	4.9	8.3	9.1	12.0	12.0	7.5	9.5

Sources: Commerce Department, International Monetary Fund, Organization for Economic Cooperation and Development, Council of Economic Advisers.

Note: Percentage change from previous year; adjusted for inflation.

GNP = gross national product.

[a] Preliminary.
[b] Includes other countries not shown separately.
[c] Not available.

Table 1-5 Deficits and Net Interest Payments (in billions)

Fiscal year	Budget deficit	Interest payments
1971	$ −23.0	$ 14.8
1972	−23.4	15.5
1973	−14.9	17.3
1974	−6.1	21.4
1975	−53.2	23.2
1976	−73.7	26.7
1977	−53.6	29.9
1978	−59.2	35.4
1979	−40.2	42.6
1980	−73.8	52.5
1981	−78.9	68.7
1982	−127.9	85.0
1983	−207.8	89.8
1984	−185.3	111.1
1985	−212.3	129.4
1986	−221.2	136.0
1987	−150.4	138.6
1988	−155.1	151.7

Source: Office of Management and Budget.

merely to pay the costs of old borrowing.

This growth in interest costs has been steady and shows no signs of letting up. It could worsen, in fact, if another bout of high interest rates like that in the late 1970s and early 1980s were to strike. And threats of continued high deficits could frighten foreign investors enough that higher interest rates would be required to keep them from unloading their Treasury securities.

Net interest costs are one thing, but gross interest costs are another. Net interest costs were $151.7 billion in 1988, but total interest payments by the federal government were $214.1 billion. The difference, oddly enough, was earned by the government itself.

Federal government trust funds—separate accounts with their own sources of revenue that paid for Social Security, highway construction, and military and civil service pensions, among other things—are required by law to invest their surpluses in Treasury securities. The Social Security

trust funds in particular were enjoying ever-growing surpluses in the late 1980s, and by some projections could hold trillions of dollars in the early part of the twenty-first century, before "baby boomers" begin to retire and draw down the surplus.

That fact had some people predicting a partial if not complete solution to the debt problem. Sen. Bob Packwood, R-Ore. (1969-), the ranking Republican on the Finance Committee, in early 1988 propounded a novel theory that at some point the entire national debt could be owned by these trust funds, eliminating the need for foreign or even private domestic investment in government securities. Packwood's point, however, did not address the problem that when the trust funds begin to be depleted, the rest of the budget would have to be running a surplus to retire the trust-fund-owned debt. And that surplus might have to be quite large.

Finally, it has even been suggested that some in the Reagan administration might actually have designed huge budget deficits because they kept up the pressure to reduce spending, and, by extension, the overall size of government. Sen. Daniel Patrick Moynihan, D-N.Y (1977-), harbored such suspicions. But in his Reagan-years memoir, *The Triumph of Politics,* David A. Stockman, Reagan's first budget director and a former Republican House member from Michigan (1977-1981), denied that anyone in the administration had been so cynical.

Even so, as long as the deficit is a political problem, an economic problem, or both, worthy government activities will be squeezed as tightly as those that are not so worthy. And adherents of the notion that government has a role in providing services to the nation will be straightjacketed—forced to scrap with others similarly inclined over limited slices of the budget in the name of deficit reduction.

"It is shameful," wrote Brookings Institution economist George L. Perry, "to deplore drugs and withhold the funding to combat them, to finance AIDS research by cutting cancer research, to ignore the homeless because poverty funds are limited, to choose between plane crashes and train wrecks, and to penny pinch the essential housekeeping chores of government to levels not befitting a wealthy and proud nation."

Searching for Political Will

The budget process enacted into law in 1974 was designed to give Congress a measure of control over the president and itself. The 1974 Congressional Budget and Impoundment Control Act was not the first such effort, nor will major revisions to it enacted in 1985 and 1987 be the last. The first of those two revisions to the budget law, named for its sponsors the Gramm-Rudman-Hollings antideficit law, was supposed to enforce a deficit-reduction discipline on Congress that the 1974 law could not. The 1987 revision was designed to correct constitutional defects in the 1985 law.

Not surprisingly, Gramm-Rudman (as it is most often called) proved to be almost as toothless as the earlier law in its first few outings. As former representative Richard Bolling, D-Mo. (1949-1983), a framer of the 1974 budget law has noted, the congressional budget process "could be viable, if the will is there."

But congressional will is a difficult thing to find, much less to harness. The government and its spending power are great and in heavy demand. Within a decade of Franklin Roosevelt's election as president and the beginning of activist domestic government, the United States was a global military power, taking on far-reaching responsibility for the world's and the

nation's security. Twice since then the country has fought wars overseas—in Korea and in Vietnam. And at the same time that it was mired in Vietnam, the nation launched President Lyndon B. Johnson's War on Poverty to improve the welfare of its own citizens.

And if finding the will to control such a machine would challenge any institution, Congress also managed—intentionally and otherwise—to forfeit most year-to-year budget control. To ensure that recipients of many of the new domestic programs would be guaranteed their benefits, Congress created entitlements that were effectively removed from the annual appropriations process. Little more than one-quarter of any year's total spending is nowadays subject to appropriations that may be reduced relatively easily if Congress so chooses; some of the rest may be cut, but only through difficult and time-consuming political fights over the intent and structure of programs. Such cuts require the underlying laws governing the programs to be changed, not just the spending levels.

Reagan budget director Stockman warned before he left office that such loss of budget control could reduce Congress to "a green eye-shaded disbursement officer who totes up the bill, writes the check and then trundles off to the chapel to mourn."

The Deficit's Downward Path

Congress spends money—whether for battleships and bombers or domestic social programs—because a majority of senators and representatives believe there is a national consensus for federal action. The deficit has grown because in many cases Congress badly underestimated, or paid no attention to, the future costs of social and military programs. And most programs, notably widely disbursed entitlements like Social Security, enjoy such broad popular support that few have dared suggest cutting them back.

Other than reducing spending, the route to reducing the deficit—increasing taxes—is no less daunting a political task. Efforts to reduce the deficit through tax increases have met in recent years with only slightly better success than entitlement cuts. Yet as Penner, the former Congressional Budget Office chief, put it in December 1987: "Through polls and other sources, it is clear that a vast majority of the American people really do demand a level of services that cannot be met by current tax law."

For all that, the deficit appears marginally more under control as the nation heads for the 1990s than it did in the mid-1980s. Following enactment of the 1981 tax cut, and Reagan's failure to persuade Congress to continue the severe domestic-side budget cutting that began that same year, the deficit began ratchetting up at an alarming rate. High interest rates and the 1982 recession contributed, as did an enormous build-up in defense spending.

Congress took some steps to limit the growth of spending during the mid-1980s—restraining, for instance, spending on local water projects and on Medicare, the health care program for the elderly—but it used the occasion to expand some aspects of Medicaid, the health program for the poor. Then, with the peak 1986 deficit still unforeseen, Congress took two steps in 1985 aimed at putting the brakes on an out-of-control budget: It put an end to the Reagan administration's defense increase, which more than doubled military spending from 1980 through 1985. In the fiscal 1986 budget, Congress actually cut a small amount from that appropriated for the Pentagon the year before. And it enacted Gramm-Rudman.

The effect was a momentary downward dip in the deficit, and—absent a serious economic downturn—probably an end to the threat that deficits will continue to grow forever. Gramm-Rudman had the nominal effect in fiscal 1986 of lopping $11.7 billion off current-year spending—and reducing the "baseline" for future budgets by the same amount. But the Congressional Budget Office and other observers credited the defense cuts as the real reason for the deficit's shrinking from $221.2 billion in 1986 to $150.4 billion in 1987. (An unintended, one-time windfall of $21.5 billion from the 1986 tax law also helped in 1987.)

But Gramm-Rudman is viewed as less an act of political courage than a means for Congress to take cover from the heat of politically unpopular budget decisions. The law supposedly requires the government to keep its deficits to a declining path of targets that, if exceeded, must be met through a process of automatic, across-the-board spending cuts. The Supreme Court struck the law a blow in 1986, declaring the automatic spending cut process unconstitutional. But in 1987 Congress repaired the unconstitutional automatic cutting procedure, and it relaxed Gramm-Rudman's deficit targets for future years in an acknowledgment that the law's aim of bringing the budget into balance by 1991 was impossible. The law now does not require a balanced budget until 1993—but, unless economic growth booms and inflation stays low, significant cuts and tax increases will be needed to reach that goal based on expected levels of spending. (See Table 1-6.)

Some close observers of Congress, like Penner, do not believe that legislators will allow themselves to be blamed for across-the-board cuts. But at the same time there is serious doubt that Congress can find the will to cut deeply enough—or raise taxes enough—to keep the deficit on the Gramm-Rudman track. In early 1988, when it was unclear that the terms of the budget summit agreement would yield a deficit smaller than the Gramm-Rudman target for the year, Penner offered what was then—and remains—a common assessment of the political attitude toward the antideficit law.

Table 1-6   Gramm-Rudman Deficit Targets versus Actual Deficit (in billions)

	1986	1987	1988	1989	1990	1991	1992	1993
Gramm-Rudman deficit targets (1985 law) [a]	$171.9 [b]	$144.0	$108.0	$ 72.0	$ 36.0	$ 0.0	—	—
Revised Gramm-Rudman targets (1987 law) [a]	—	—	144.0 [c]	136.0 [d]	100.0	64.0	$ 28.0	$ 0.0
Actual or projected deficit	221.2	150.4	155.1	176.0 [e]	167.2 [e]	157.6 [e]	151.0 [e]	133.7 [e]

Source: Congressional Budget Office.

Note: Fiscal years.

[a] For every fiscal year except 1986 and 1993, the law allowed Congress and the president to miss the deficit target by $10 billion before automatic cuts would be ordered. Therefore, in effect, the deficit targets for each year were $10 billion higher.

[b] Automatic cuts put into effect for fiscal 1986 were limited by law to $11.7 billion.

[c] Automatic cuts that would have been required for fiscal 1988 were limited by law to $23 billion; the law allowed the automatic cuts to be voided by enactment of at least $23 billion in spending cuts and new revenues through the ordinary legislative process.

[d] Automatic cuts for fiscal 1989 were limited by law to $36 billion.

[e] Congressional Budget Office February 1988 estimates, assuming that no budget policy changes are made after fiscal 1988.

"My own gut feeling is that they'll get around Gramm-Rudman," he said. "How they bury that critter, that's what's unclear."

Awaiting a New President

Left for the new president and a new Congress is the same devilish political problem that Reagan and four Congresses occasionally confronted and more often dodged for eight years.

In a speech to the Cleveland City Club in January 1988, Reagan invoked the credo of his presidency—that taxes are bad for the nation's economic health and that Congress has not exercised the will to control spending: "The deficit has not been caused by the cut in taxes. The deficit would increase if we yielded to those who want us to increase taxes," he told his audience. And without acknowledging the cuts in his own prized defense program, he said there had been real progress made on the deficit. But, he said, the deficit is still "an embarrassment and a shame, most dangerous perhaps because it signals the complete break-

down of one of the most basic functions of the United States government."

That last theme—that the budget process itself is broken—has also been a Reagan battle cry. But it can be heard just as often from frustrated liberal Democrats as from thwarted conservative Republicans. "I think we need a new budget act. We need a new process. What we have is a mess," is how Rep. David E. Bonior, D-Mich. (1977-) put it in late 1987.

The two sides would never agree, however, on what about the process is broken, or how to fix it. Members of Congress are mostly frustrated at the time involved in budget decisions and the intractability of the deficit. Reagan has been blocked in his desire to further cut the size and role of government. And Bonior and his more liberal allies would never grant Reagan what he wanted, a constitutional amendment that would ban deficit spending or authority to veto individual items in appropriations bills, instead of the entire bill.

Neither Republican vice president George Bush nor Democratic Massachusetts governor Michael Dukakis—the major party contenders for president in 1988—offered much in the campaign about their own fiscal visions. Bush did adopt Reagan's vehement antitax stance, taunting those who questioned his sincerity to "Read my lips: No new taxes." And Dukakis did not adopt the failed Democratic approach of the 1984 presidential campaign, in which former vice president Walter F. Mondale promised that he would increase taxes. Neither even mentioned a growing crisis facing the government fund that insured deposits in the nation's savings and loan institutions. That fund was technically bankrupt in 1988 and faced obligations estimated between $50 billion and $100 billion to deal with more than five hundred financially troubled savings institutions. It was a cost that taxpayers almost assuredly would have to bear, adding significantly to the difficulties of reducing the deficit. And while both Bush and Dukakis promised spending restraint, neither offered details.

The newly elected president could get some help from a fourteen-member National Economic Commission, appointed by Reagan and the congressional leadership in the aftermath of their 1987 budget summit. Chaired by former Democratic National Committee chairman Robert Strauss and Reagan's former transportation secretary Drew Lewis, and populated with the likes of AFL-CIO president Lane Kirkland and former Reagan defense secretary Caspar W. Weinberger, the commission was expected to report to the new president perhaps by March 1989 on ways to confront the deficit crisis.

It was also hoped that consensus recommendations from a bipartisan commission would carry sufficient weight to overcome political outcry against painful options.

But many conservatives feared that the commission was unbalanced, dominated by liberal Democrats and Republicans who could not be counted on to flatly oppose a tax increase—which many believed the commission ultimately would recommend.

Others, including commission member Sen. Pete V. Domenici, R-N.M. (1973-), hoped that it would look beyond the question of the deficit to the budget process itself. Domenici, a long-time member of the Senate Budget Committee, and its chairman during Reagan's first six years, was a strong advocate of budget process changes—including a two-year budget cycle. Changes in budget process were often touted by frustrated members of Congress who believed that they and their colleagues would never take seriously the need for reducing the deficit. The experience of 1988, when a de facto two-year budget dating from the previous year helped alleviate political pressures on congressional budget making, was fresh in Domenici's mind. Whether he could persuade his fellow commission members to tackle that task remained to be seen.

2

An Economic Primer

By the time Ronald Reagan was elected president, a half century had passed since one theory of economics had so dominated political decision making in Washington. Not since the 1930s, when President Franklin D. Roosevelt propelled the nation out of its deepest economic mire using principles espoused by John Maynard Keynes, had economists' views been thrust onto center stage.

Roosevelt, using Keynes's ideas of federal spending to encourage production and thereby stimulate growth, sparked an extraordinary expansion of the federal government for combined economic and social purposes. But eventually the costs of that government grew out of control. And the economy, suffering stagnant growth and rising inflation and interest rates, seemed unresponsive to government stimulus, alarming economists, political leaders, and ordinary people of nearly every ideological stripe.

By the late 1970s, Keynes's "demand-side" economic model found a competitor, one that emphasized savings and investment to promote growth—the "supply side" of the economic equation. It focused on shrinking government's claim on revenue and was neatly married to a political view that saw government's role chiefly as the defender of the nation's external security, not as a redistributor of wealth.

In the early 1980s, the supply-side beliefs of the president and his chief lieutenants sparked dinner table debates in a country where the subjects of politics and economics often were ignored.

The tenets of supply-side thinking swept down Pennsylvania Avenue from the White House to the Capitol at the start of 1981, burning through traditional Democratic party alliances and exciting members of Congress to endorse Reagan's determination to effect an about-face in the growth of government. Historic spending and tax cuts were enacted in the first seven months of his presidency— an overnight miracle compared with the usual pace of congressional budgeting.

But the promises of those heady days have gone unfulfilled, and the legacy has been mixed. Government has not shrunk. It has continued to grow faster than the overall economy, although perhaps not as fast as it might have. However, through the end of 1988, the nation's economy enjoyed sustained, albeit weak, growth, following a brief but deep recession in 1981-1982. While the onset of that recession was largely attributable to monetary, not fiscal, policy, it remained to be seen if that period of growth ultimately would be given a Keynesian or supply-side explanation. Most likely adherents of both points of view would claim success.

The use of deficit-spending as a spur to the economy is a well-established Keynesian principle. Government spending led all other major categories in contributing to the growth of the economy between 1980 and 1987. "There are a number of lessons to be learned from the Reagan years," said Lawrence Chimerine, chairman of Wharton Econometrics Forecasting Associates, a private consulting group. "The first is that Keynes is alive and well."

Personal consumption was close behind government spending as a component of gross national product (GNP), the total output of goods and services in the economy. But supply-side theory stressed savings and investment, and private investment grew slower than the economy as a whole during the period. Personal savings was lower on average than any period since that immediately following World War II. "The most disappointing result of the [1981] tax cut was that economic growth was not robust," conceded William A. Niskanen, chairman of the libertarian Cato Institute and a member of Reagan's Council of Economic Advisers from 1981 to 1985.

But supply-siders argued that positive effects of the tax cut and other supply-side incentives could not be overlooked. And it is fairly clear that the supply-side's central tenet—low tax rates—had become conventional wisdom by the mid-1980s. If stimulative tax cuts were anathema to Keynesians—unless, for example, they were needed to climb out of a recession—by 1986 they were not so bad. "Supply-siders worried . . . about how to generate wealth. The question they raised is an important one to which not sufficient attention was paid before," agreed Harvard University economist Robert B. Reich, an avowed Keynesian.

The huge income tax cut Reagan demanded and got in 1981 was opposed by most Democrats. Reagan's tax reform proposal enacted in 1986, which hung on even further reduction in tax rates (and elimina-

tion of tax breaks that were favored by conservatives and liberals alike), survived because of Democrats' support. Part of that was because the measure further rescinded corporate cuts enacted in 1981 and later rolled back. Part was because it promised to take millions of poor persons off the tax rolls altogether. Another factor was that it was not supposed to be a tax cut at all. By balancing cuts for individuals with increases for corporations, the measure was carefully designed to be "revenue-neutral."

The supply-siders who in 1981 pressed chiefly for a cut in overall taxes had turned their focus to rates—and the depressing effects of higher rates on incentives to earn. The size of the nation's tax bill itself became less of an economic concern.

Supply-side thinking had earned a place in the economic debate—and in policy. But despite its dominance in 1980, when the congressional Joint Economic Committee's Democrats joined with Republicans to produce a report, "Plugging in the Supply Side," it fell out of the political debate. Rep. Jack Kemp, R-N.Y. (1971-1989), was an original supply-sider, author of a precursor to the 1986 tax law, and the only credentialed member of that corps to seek the presidency in 1988. But his campaign's failure to catch fire was not a ringing endorsement of further supply-side thinking.

Kemp's dropping out of the race in early March 1988 may have guaranteed Reagan's place as the only supply-side adherent to occupy the White House. Or, perhaps, it was just further evidence of the economic theory's assimilation into the political mainstream.

Through an Economist's Eyes

Economics tends to look either at the very large or the very small in its attempts to understand and explain events. Macro-economic theories, when applied to the government's influence on the economy, focus on aggregate amounts of spending, taxes, and borrowing. Macroeconomists concern themselves with cycles of growth and recession, and such measures of the economy's health as employment, productivity, prices, and interest rates.

Microeconomics, on the other hand, looks more closely at individual programs, such as targeted public works jobs, or price- and income-support payments to corn farmers.

Both aggregate spending and corn price-supports (which help make up that aggregate) may have discernible effects on many levels of the economy; both could affect inflation, for instance, and in opposite ways. If government spending soars, the resulting demand increase could stimulate job growth, higher wages, and higher prices all around. If farmers are paid by the government the difference between a set price for their crops that is artificially low and some higher "target" price, the lower market price for the corn (and lower prices for hogs that feed on it) can buffer some of the macroeconomic inflationary pressure.

Where the federal budget is concerned, macro and micro concerns often collide. A member of Congress from Nebraska, say, might well favor a reduction in the deficit, but not through reduced farm payments. Likewise, job training programs are sacred in urban districts, even those represented by members who call themselves fiscal conservatives.

But to the degree that the government bases its policies on real economic, rather than political, concerns, the macro view tends to prevail.

Political Views of the Economy

Widespread unemployment during the Great Depression had shaken the confidence of Americans in their own economy. Out of that experience, and the remarkable economic prosperity that resulted from the government-led war effort of the 1940s, a postwar consensus emerged that the government should play a central role in the nation's economic life.

"From our earliest days we had a tradition of substantial government help to our system of private enterprise," said Roosevelt. "It is following tradition as well as necessity if government strives to put idle money and idle men to work, to increase our public wealth and to build up the health and strength of the people—and to help our system of private enterprise to function."

It was that philosophy—and its alleged consequences—that Reagan directly challenged. "The people have not created this disaster in our economy," Reagan said in announcing his candidacy for president in 1979. "The federal government has. It has outspent, overestimated, and overregulated. It has failed to deliver services within the revenues it should be allowed to raise from taxes."

President Jimmy Carter's chief economist, Charles Schultze, acknowledged in 1979 the change in the public mood that would sweep Reagan into office the next year. "One of the things that a democratic, civilized government has as its objective is to give its citizens . . . a condition in which they have some sense of control of their own future," Schultze said. "The future is always uncertain, but when the measuring rod by which we do our planning shrinks—not only shrinks, but shrinks in unpredictable amounts—it weakens significantly people's control of their own future."

In 1988, there was no national consensus on the economy—or on whether there needed to be a change. Reagan could trumpet the seventy-plus months of relatively inflation-free growth since the 1982 recession as evidence that things were fine. Democrats could raise fears of recession in the aftermath of the October 1987 stock market crash, continuing high budget deficits, and an expanding national debt that voters' great-grandchildren would ultimately inherit. But the economic debate was largely removed from questions of fiscal policy—that is, where the government chose to spend taxpayers' money.

Competitiveness—fear that the United States was bowing to new industrial giants in the Far East and evolving into a nation of hamburger-flippers—was the dominant theme of economic debate. And while there was an element of fiscal policy in that fear (economists connected the need to finance the budget deficit overseas with an inflated dollar, rising imports, and depressed exports), there was not much call for a return to intense government stimulus. Reagan had not swept government away, yet the conventional view remained that government was big enough.

Obeying the Business Cycle

The essence of a relatively free economy is that it has ups and downs, the bigger downs being recessions. And the design of economic policy since World War II has been to counter both the negative and positive effects and flatten what is known as the business cycle. From time to time, chiefly during recessions or other periods of high unemployment, or during bouts of severe inflation, there are efforts at directing government resources right at pockets of trouble. But most so-called countercyclical government policy—like that embodied in the supply-side tax cut of 1981—seeks to achieve longer term goals.

Postwar economic policy succeeded to an impressive degree in tempering recessions and unemployment. Previously, from 1854 to 1937, business activity expansions lasted an average of twenty-six months, while the average recession ran twenty-two months. But from 1945 to the end of the

1982 recession expansions averaged forty-five months and recessions only eleven months. The economy spent only 19 percent of the time in recession since World War II, compared with 46 percent in the earlier period. It was on the basis of that experience that some postwar economists proclaimed that activist government policy had "tamed" the business cycle. (See Table 2-1.)

The 1960s were a case in point. It was a period that saw wholesale growth of government assistance and a long and expensive war in Vietnam; and the economy responded with vigor.

The nation enjoyed its longest nonstop economic expansion in history—106 consecutive months—from February 1961 through February 1969. The GNP rose from $1.7 trillion in 1961 to $2.4 trillion in 1969, adjusted for inflation and measured in constant 1982 dollars. About eleven million jobs were created, permitting the unemployment rate to drop to 3.5 percent by 1969. Disposable personal income per capita—after taxes and adjustment for price increases—increased by 33 percent in the same period. And corporate profits doubled.

But those successes were clouded by steadily worsening inflation. Consumer prices increased 2.9 percent in 1966 and 1967, and then jumped 4.2 percent in 1968, 5.4 percent in 1969, and 5.9 percent in 1970, a recession year.

Critics of the post-Depression stabilization policies contend that the Vietnam episode was just an extreme example of the inability of government to take fiscal actions when they are needed. Even analysts sympathetic to the goals of stabilization policy concede that these critics have a point. They acknowledge that while the automatic stabilizers in the budget respond instantly to changes in economic currents—unemployment insurance will prop up incomes and the tax code will take less money out of the economy during downturns—discretionary policies do not.

Table 2-1 Economic Growth and Recessions in U.S. History

Trough	Peak	Length of expansion (in months)	Length of previous recession (in months)
December 1854	June 1857	30	—
December 1858	October 1860	22	18
June 1861	April 1865	46 [a]	8
December 1967	June 1869	18	32 [a]
December 1870	October 1873	34	18
March 1879	March 1882	36	65
May 1885	March 1887	22	38
April 1888	July 1890	27	13
May 1891	January 1893	20	10
June 1894	December 1895	18	17
June 1897	June 1899	24	18
December 1900	September 1902	21	18
August 1904	May 1907	33	23
June 1908	January 1910	19	13
January 1912	January 1913	12	24
December 1914	August 1918	44 [a]	23
March 1919	January 1920	10	7 [a]
July 1921	May 1923	22	18
July 1924	October 1926	27	14
November 1927	August 1929	21	13
March 1933	May 1937	50	43
June 1938	February 1945	80 [a]	13
October 1945	November 1948	37	8 [a]
October 1949	July 1953	45 [a]	11
May 1954	August 1957	39	10 [a]
April 1958	April 1960	24	8
February 1961	December 1969	106 [a]	10
November 1970	November 1973	36	11 [a]
March 1975	January 1980	58	16
July 1980	July 1981	12	6
November 1982		71 [b]	16

Source: National Bureau of Economic Research.

[a] Wartime expansion or postwar recession.
[b] Through October 1988.

Looking back over the previous four decades, economist Arthur Okun noted in 1980 that no significant discretionary stimulative fiscal action was adopted while the economy was still in recession. "Most of the strongly stimulative fiscal actions were taken in the first year of recovery," he said. "On occasions, these worked effectively to promote the restoration of prosperity; on others, they may have overdone the job—providing a stimulus that was too much too late."

Government's Successes and Failures

Whether government policies have been activist or not, the very size of government made an enormous difference in the economy after Roosevelt. The portion of GNP attributed to all government purchases rose from 13 percent in 1929 to about 20 percent in 1987. Of that, the federal government's share climbed from less than 3 percent of GNP in 1929 to 17 percent in 1987. (See Table 2-2.)

But the bad experience with inflation in the 1960s has only worsened. Prices had been remarkably stable prior to World War II. The consumer price level in 1940, for instance, was no higher than the price level in 1778. But the price level in 1987 was more than 700 percent above the 1940 level.

In part, the miserable record of postwar policy on inflation reflects the greater stress the government placed on fighting unemployment during much of the period. In addition, the government sometimes found itself politically unable to use the policies necessary to restrain demand and thus curb inflation.

In most cases, the failure reflected a political reluctance to take purchasing power away from the American public. Other times it resulted from a deadlock between liberals and conservatives over what to sacrifice in the interest of restraint or over whether to brake the economy by raising taxes or cutting spending. Even when restraint was applied, the public reaction was usually so negative that policy makers were unable to hold the reins long enough to slow inflation.

By the late 1970s, the nation found it increasingly difficult to strike a politically acceptable balance between unemployment and inflation. Rapid inflation had become deeply ingrained in the economy, and it resisted conventional methods to defeat it at acceptable political cost. It appeared increasingly that demand restraint would bring inflation down only at the cost of high and sustained joblessness. At the same time, soaring energy prices and a perplexing slowdown in productivity threatened to prevent the rapid economic growth and resulting low unemployment that Keynesian policies were designed to promote. "The new reality . . . is the re-emergence during the 1970s of the economics of scarcity—a progressive imbalance between the demands we have

been placing on our economy and our capacity to satisfy them," wrote Alfred Kahn, a Cornell University professor who served as Carter's chief inflation adviser.

Keynesians worried that the only solutions required long-term sacrifices, and few politicians enjoy carrying such a message to the public. "To materially reduce standards of living as compelled by low productivity is unthinkable for a Democratic government in peacetime," declared Sen. Jacob K. Javits, R-N.Y. (House 1947-1954; Senate 1957-1981), in 1979.

"It is not clear," observed economist Robert Solow of the Massachusetts Institute of Technology, "that our political process can deal with solutions whose horizon for success might be 10 years away."

Supply-siders countered that the problem was nothing more than government excess. But they had no opportunity to test their theory. As Reagan was taking office, the Federal Reserve Board employed a classical technique to drive down inflation. Under the leadership of Paul A. Volcker, a Carter appointee, the Fed tightened the money supply, bringing on a deep recession. Inflation was beaten, leaving Reagan to worry about the resulting unemployment. Such is the interplay between monetary and fiscal policy.

Perspectives of Different Schools

Before Keynes, economists generally viewed the economy as a self-adjusting mechanism that naturally tended to provide full employment. That happy result was produced by the free workings of wages and prices, which were thought to balance supply and demand.

Under this "classical" view, if workers are unemployed (because the supply of workers exceeds the demand for them), wages will fall. Lower wages in turn will

Table 2-2 Components of U.S. GNP (in billions)

Year	Total GNP	Personal consumption	Private investment	Government purchases	Net exports
1940	$ 100.4	$ 71.0	$ 13.4	$ 14.2	$ 1.8
1941	125.5	80.8	18.3	25.0	1.5
1942	159.0	88.6	10.3	59.9	0.2
1943	192.7	99.5	6.2	88.9	−1.9
1944	211.4	108.2	7.7	97.1	−1.7
1945	213.4	119.6	11.3	83.0	−0.5
1946	212.4	143.9	31.5	29.1	7.8
1947	235.2	161.9	35.0	26.4	11.9
1948	261.6	174.9	47.1	32.6	7.0
1949	260.4	178.3	36.5	39.0	6.5
1950	288.3	192.1	55.1	38.8	2.2
1951	333.4	208.1	60.5	60.4	4.5
1952	351.6	219.1	53.5	75.8	3.2
1953	371.6	232.6	54.9	82.8	1.3
1954	372.5	239.8	54.1	76.0	2.6
1955	405.9	257.9	69.7	75.3	3.0
1956	428.2	270.6	72.7	79.7	5.3
1957	451.0	285.3	71.1	87.3	7.3
1958	456.8	294.6	63.6	95.4	3.3
1959	495.8	316.3	80.2	97.9	1.5
1960	515.3	330.7	78.2	00.6	5.9
1961	533.8	341.1	77.1	08.4	7.2
1962	574.6	361.9	87.6	18.2	6.9
1963	606.9	381.7	93.1	23.8	8.2
1964	649.8	409.3	99.6	30.0	10.9
1965	705.1	440.7	116.2	138.6	9.7
1966	772.0	477.3	128.6	158.6	7.5
1967	816.4	503.6	125.7	179.7	7.4
1968	892.7	552.5	137.0	197.7	5.5
1969	963.9	597.6	153.2	207.3	5.6
1970	1,015.5	640.0	148.8	218.2	8.5
1971	1,102.7	691.6	172.5	232.4	6.3
1972	1,212.8	757.6	202.0	250.0	3.2
1973	1,359.3	837.2	238.8	266.5	16.8
1974	1,472.8	916.5	240.8	299.1	16.3
1975	1,598.4	1,012.8	219.6	335.0	31.1
1976	1,782.8	1,129.3	277.7	356.9	18.8
1977	1,990.5	1,257.2	344.1	387.3	1.8
1978	2,249.7	1,403.5	416.8	425.2	4.1
1979	2,508.2	1,566.8	454.8	467.8	18.8
1980	2,732.0	1,732.6	437.0	530.3	32.1
1981	3,052.6	1,915.1	515.5	588.1	33.9
1982	3,166.0	2,050.7	447.3	641.7	26.3
1983	3,405.7	2,234.5	502.3	675.0	−6.1
1984	3,772.2	2,430.5	664.8	735.9	58.9
1985	4,010.3	2,629.4	641.6	818.6	79.2
1986	4,235.0	2,799.8	671.0	869.7	−105.5
1987 [a]	4,486.2	2,966.0	716.4	923.8	−119.9

Sources: Commerce Department, Council of Economic Advisers.

Note: GNP = gross national product.

[a] Preliminary.

make it profitable for business to hire more workers, and unemployment thus will be eliminated. Similarly, prices rise and fall according to demand, so that everything that is produced is consumed.

Interest rates play a key role in classical theory. Analysts believed that they assure a balance between savings and investment, and thus guarantee that whenever people choose to increase the amount of money they set aside no drop in economic activity will occur.

Under classical theory, an increase in the amount of money people save expands the supply of money available for investment. That in turn reduces the price investors have to pay for money, which is the interest rate. But a drop in interest rates increases the incentive for investment so that higher investment takes the place of laggard consumer spending, assuring (in the classical view) that economic activity continues at a pace guaranteeing full employment.

Classical economics explains recessions as part of the economy's inherent self-adjusting abilities. During boom periods, the classical economists argued, prices or wages sometimes accelerate more quickly than is justified by the underlying relationship of supply and demand. Recessions reduce demand, and thus bring them back into line.

Recessions also were thought to occur when the supply of money gets out of line with the demand for it. If the supply of money falls short of what people want at full employment, it was believed there would be a temporary decline in economic activity, forcing prices to decline. But the drop in prices causes a given amount of money to rise in value, restoring production to its natural state of full employment.

The Depression shattered the confident optimism of classical economics. For the decade of the 1930s, an average of 18 percent of the work force was unemployed. In 1933 the jobless rate totaled 24.9 per-

cent. In 1936, seven years after the onset of the Depression, 16.9 percent of the labor force—nine million people—were still out of work. Those statistics raised serious doubts about the validity of arguments that the free-market behavior of wages and prices can assure economic self-adjustment and full employment.

Keynesian Economics

In 1936 Keynes offered an explanation for why the economy appeared stuck in a condition far short of full employment. The explanation, he said, lies in fluctuations in income, not prices, wages, or interest rates. Keynes noted that incomes decline when wages drop because of unemployment. As people lose income, they spend less and production is cut back in an adjustment to reduced demand for goods. That in turn leads to more layoffs, causing income and then demand to drop further in a frightening downward spiral.

Keynes said the classical economists were wrong to assume that reduced interest rates could come to the rescue in such a situation. He argued that interest rates might never drop low enough to prompt the level of investment needed to start the economy growing again.

Interest rates, he maintained, represent the price people receive for exchanging cash for other kinds of assets, such as bonds. Because cash is preferable to other kinds of assets, there is a "floor" for interest rates below which people will be unwilling to exchange their cash for securities, he said.

Keynes concluded that using monetary policy to increase the supply of money and drive interest rates down is like pushing on a string. It will not necessarily bring the economy out of a recession, he argued, because it will not necessarily increase investment.

Moreover, he warned that a drop in incomes could cause savings to dry up so there would be no money available for investment in any case. And he also noted that businesses would be reluctant to invest anyway if consumer income is so diminished that people might be unable to buy whatever is produced.

Keynes's theory suggested that the economy could fall into a recession and stay there. In such circumstances, Keynes said, the only way back to full employment is for the government to bolster consumer purchasing power enough to guarantee sufficient demand. The rub, according to Keynesians, is that the government cannot add to consumer demand if it insists on balancing the budget.

A balanced budget requires that any income pumped into the consumer sector through higher federal spending or lower taxes be offset by the higher taxes or lower spending. Otherwise, to increase income, government has to incur a deficit.

In Keynes's view, President Herbert Hoover made a terrible mistake in 1931 by pushing for a big tax increase to balance the budget despite a painfully high level of unemployment. The tax increase, according to Keynes, merely reduced already low income further, compounding the economy's weakness.

Focus on Employment

Keynes argued that joblessness results from inadequate demand, which in turn reflects insufficient income in the hands of consumers. The Keynesian remedy for this problem is to increase demand, either by cutting taxes or increasing spending. Once people start spending their additional income, Keynesians said, the demand for goods and services will rise, production will increase, and the unemployed will be offered jobs.

The focus of Keynesian theory on unemployment is not surprising considering that joblessness was a chronic problem in the 1930s. Later, when inflation also came

to be recognized as an economic worry, Keynes's successors said demand-oriented policies could correct that, too.

They argued that, just as unemployment occurs when demand falls short of the economy's productive capacity, inflation results when demand exceeds economic capacity. If everybody is producing as much as they can, increasing incomes merely compel consumers to bid up the prices for the limited quantity of goods and services that can be produced, according to this theory. The Keynesian cure for inflation is thus to restrain purchasing power, either by cutting back government spending or raising taxes, until demand again comes into line with supply.

Policy makers found in the 1950s and later that it was not easy to strike a perfect balance between unemployment and inflation. Policies to cure one of those economic ills generally produced at least some of the other. Much of the history of postwar economic policy consisted of a debate over what the balance between the two should be.

Conservatives generally were willing to accept a higher level of unemployment to keep prices stable. That fit with the conservative belief that the economy tends to stabilize itself at a high level of unemployment anyway. Conservatives argued that there is a "natural" rate of joblessness. Some people simply choose not to work, and efforts to eliminate all unemployment are thus futile, they said.

Liberals, on the other hand, could not accept the notion that some degree of unemployment is voluntary. They argued that the private economy does not automatically perform to its full capacity, and that government policies to assure full employment are much more important than perfect price stability.

Inflation or Unemployment?

The economic statistics for 1970 proved to be doubly disappointing. Recession drove the unemployment rate up to 4.9 percent. And at the same time, consumer prices continued to rise. The failure of economic slowdown to cool inflation significantly during the 1969-1970 downturn raised one of the central problems on which postwar economic policy foundered.

As the president's Council of Economic Advisers noted ruefully in February 1971, "Sophisticated econometric analysis of the relationship between the behavior of prices and a large number of variables that might explain it ... did not generally predict the rate of inflation experienced in 1970, given the actual conditions of 1970." Inflation, it seemed, had a momentum of its own.

The classical economic view assumed that wages and prices respond primarily to supply and demand. Economists who held this view assumed that fiscal or monetary restraint would slow the rate of price and wage increases by reducing demand for goods and services. Thus, lower demand for goods was thought likely to lead to price cutting, and lower demand for labor to wage reductions.

By the end of the 1970s many economists contended that the see-saw process had been short-circuited by the success of postwar economic policy, which had managed to avert prolonged recessions. "In the bad old days, any hesitation in economic growth might have been the beginning of a real depression," Solow noted in 1980. "Only a brave or overconfident seller of goods or labor would maintain prices and wait for things to improve. In an economy whose recessions are infrequent, mild and short, prices are less likely to plummet when demand weakens. Sellers are more likely to stand pat and cover their costs. If the upturn arrives on schedule, their strategy is vindicated for next time."

As the break between unemployment and inflation became increasingly obvious through the 1970s, economists developed more elaborate theories to explain the independent behavior of wage and price setting. Arthur Okun, for instance, came to explain wage and price behavior as being governed by an "invisible handshake" that prevented either from turning down.

Okun said there is a tacit agreement between business and consumers that prices will be related to costs instead of market forces. The modern marketplace has become so complex that it no longer pays consumers to shop for the best bargains. Thus, for business, it is now more important to build up consumer loyalty than to try to compete by offering the lowest prices. That loyalty has been established by guaranteeing that prices are related to costs.

Okun concluded that businesses have become reluctant to cut prices during periods of economic weakness because they know that such a strategy at best will win them only the temporary loyalty of customers, while price increases following slumps may anger customers. Basing prices on costs prevents sharp price-cutting during recessions, although it may help moderate price increases during periods of economic strength.

Similarly, employers are reluctant to cut wages during a slump because they need to maintain the long-term loyalty of their employees. That is especially true, Okun argued, where employers are eager to keep workers who already have the training and experience that makes them highly productive.

Cutting wages at the first sign of a slump would be harmful in the long run because it would undermine the implicit trust between employer and worker, according to Okun. It could lead workers to resign at the first opportunity. Thus, employers tend to maintain wage rates and keep more workers than they need during the early stages of a slump. If the downturn gets worse, they tend to lay off workers according to seniority rather than cut wages generally.

Finding a Solution

The difficulties economists had figuring out the connection between employment and inflation had political fallout. In capitalizing on President Gerald R. Ford's administration's inability to find an acceptable combination of the two, Carter spoke of a "misery index" that added the unemployment and inflation rates. Under Ford, Carter said, the "misery index" stood at an all-time high in nonrecessionary times of 13.5 percent. That ploy was to embarrass Carter four years later when candidate Ronald Reagan noted that the "misery index" had climbed above 20 percent during Carter's presidency.

Some economists wondered just how deep or prolonged a recession would have to be to drive out inflation. "The most reasonable reading of the evidence is that it might take a rather long time, maybe more like five years than one or two years," concluded Solow. "During that time, the economy would be depressed, probably severely. A more gradual approach, which would lead to less damage to production and employment, would, naturally, take even longer."

That view was vigorously disputed by a group of conservative economists who in the 1970s developed a theory known as "rational expectations." Led by University of Chicago economist Robert Lucas, they argued that wages and prices would adjust rather quickly, with fairly little effect on production and employment, once workers were convinced that the government will not step in to prevent a recession.

Liberals replied that it would be impossible for government to convince the public that it will keep its hands off the economic system. "It is, after all, a political system," noted Brookings Institution economist Barry Bosworth, who served as director of the Council on Wage and Price Stability

under Carter. "People do understand now that the competitive market is not a religious theology. It's simply a set of rules that we put together to try to govern behavior in as fair a fashion as we can. We've changed the rules repeatedly, and it's bound to happen in the future. You just can't partition the economic arena from the political arena and keep them separate."

The back-to-back recessions of 1980 and 1981-1982 provided an answer, but at a classical price. Inflation, measured by consumer prices, went from 13.5 percent in 1980 to 10.4 percent in 1981, then plummeted to 6.1 percent in 1982 and 3.2 percent in 1983. Unemployment, however, behaving according to the theory that you cannot help one without hurting the other, shot from 5.8 percent in 1979 to 9.7 percent in 1982.

The Productivity Puzzle

What came to be recognized as one of the economy's most serious problems was largely overlooked until the mid-1970s. And it was one that not only Keynesians, but others, found difficult to explain. Over time, the nation's productivity was falling.

Productivity is defined as output per hour of labor. And it is the basic source of increases in income in the long run. When productivity improves, wages can increase without cutting into profits or raising prices. But when productivity fails to improve, wage increases either eat away at profits or force businesses to boost prices to protect profit margins. A drop in productivity normally leads to higher labor costs. Because most businesses set prices by adding certain markups to costs, the result often is higher prices for consumers.

Productivity tends to be cyclical, a leading indicator of the direction of economic growth. It normally rises during the later stage of recessions and the early part of economic recoveries. Typically, businesses are slow to lay off employees at the beginning of recessions because they are reluctant to lose workers and because it takes them some time to be convinced that a downturn is occurring. Thus, in the early phases of recessions, output drops but the level of employment holds fairly steady. As a result, productivity, or output per worker, drops.

As recessions advance, however, employers finally do lay off workers, bringing the level of employment back into line with output. With fewer workers relative to the level of output, productivity improves. Then, just as employers are slow to lay off workers at the beginning of a recession, there is a delay before they hire them back during a recovery. As a result, when the economy first starts to pick up speed, employers try to increase output for a while without adding new jobs. The result is a marked, though temporary, improvement in productivity.

The behavior of productivity assures that inflation will improve late in a recession and early in an economic recovery for reasons that have little to do with the supply of labor itself.

But by the mid-1970s, economists came to realize that quite apart from such cyclical fluctuations in productivity, the economy was going through a much more worrisome fundamental decline. Between 1948 and 1965, productivity had climbed at an average annual rate of 2.7 percent. But from 1965 through 1973, the growth averaged only 1.8 percent. And from 1973 through 1980, productivity rose on the average only 0.4 percent a year. As inflation subsided and the economy embarked on a period of sustained growth, productivity recovered marginally to 1.3 percent from 1981 through 1987. (See Table 2-3.)

Economists have offered a variety of explanations for the long-term decline, although they have found it difficult to quantify the importance of the various factors.

In part, most economists believe the decline reflects population trends in the United States. Some of the big productivity gains between 1948 and 1965 undoubtedly resulted from the shift of large numbers of workers out of agriculture into rapidly expanding manufacturing industries. In the 1970s and 1980s the fastest economic growth occurred not in manufacturing, but in the "services"—bank tellers and clerical workers, for instance—where it is much more difficult to achieve productivity gains because of the labor-intensive nature of services. And, economists complain, standard measures of output do not apply to many kinds of service jobs; McDonald's may count its hamburgers, but what do bank tellers produce?

Some economists also believe the large influx of the postwar "baby-boom" workers and women into the labor force in the 1960s and 1970s pulled down the productivity rate. Young and inexperienced workers normally are less productive than those who have been working longer. During the 1970s, the overall work force increased 27 percent, to 105 million from 82.8 million. But the number of workers between ages sixteen and nineteen grew 32 percent, to 8 million from 6.1 million. And the number of working women rose 39 percent, to 41.2 million from 29.7 million. (Those rates have changed somewhat since the 1970s. The number of younger workers, in fact, has fallen while youth unemployment has risen. The number of women in the workplace has risen by 2 percent since 1979, while the labor force has grown by slightly more than 14 percent.)

Economists believe that the population surge, which the Carter administration was to call a "demographic tidal wave," contributed significantly to inflation during the late 1960s and the 1970s by helping to slow productivity. There is also evidence that the dramatic growth of the labor force probably put continuous pressure on the government to adopt policies designed to reduce unemployment, rather than concentrate on fighting inflation.

Table 2-3 Productivity

Year	Output [a]	Hours of all workers	Output per hour	Payment per hour [b]	Unit labor cost
1948	5.6%	1.7%	3.8%	0.8%	4.6%
1949	−2.3	−3.9	1.7	4.0	1.3
1950	9.7	3.0	6.4	5.1	−0.3
1951	7.7	4.6	3.0	0.7	5.6
1952	3.2	1.0	2.2	3.3	3.3
1953	4.6	2.4	2.2	4.9	3.5
1954	−2.0	−3.4	1.5	2.8	1.8
1955	7.1	4.0	2.9	4.0	0.7
1956	3.1	2.5	0.6	4.6	5.5
1957	1.3	−0.6	1.9	2.2	3.8
1958	−2.0	−4.3	2.4	1.3	1.6
1959	7.7	4.3	3.2	3.3	0.9
1960	1.7	0.6	1.1	2.8	3.3
1961	2.0	−1.1	3.1	2.2	0.1
1962	5.5	2.1	3.3	2.9	0.8
1963	4.7	1.1	3.6	2.3	−0.1
1964	6.3	2.3	3.9	3.3	0.7
1965	6.4	3.8	2.5	1.7	0.8
1966	5.6	3.4	2.1	2.9	3.7
1967	2.5	0.3	2.3	2.6	3.2
1968	4.7	2.0	2.6	3.2	4.8
1969	2.7	3.2	−0.5	1.1	7.1
1970	−1.1	−1.3	0.3	0.9	6.7
1971	2.7	−0.3	3.0	2.1	3.4
1972	6.4	3.3	3.1	3.1	3.4
1973	6.2	4.3	1.8	1.5	6.0
1974	−1.8	0.4	−2.2	−1.3	12.0
1975	−2.3	−4.0	1.8	0.5	7.8
1976	6.0	3.4	2.6	2.5	5.7
1977	5.9	4.3	1.6	1.2	6.1
1978	6.0	5.1	0.8	0.9	7.7
1979	1.9	3.5	−1.6	−1.6	11.2
1980	−1.2	−0.7	−0.4	2.7	11.0
1981	1.7	0.7	1.0	−0.9	8.3
1982	−3.3	−2.7	−0.6	1.5	8.4
1983	5.0	1.6	3.3	1.1	1.0
1984	8.3	6.0	2.1	−0.3	1.8
1985	3.6	2.5	1.2	0.8	3.2
1986	3.2	1.6	1.6	1.9	2.2
1987 [c]	3.4	2.6	0.8	−0.8	2.0

Sources: Labor Department, Council of Economic Advisers.

Note: Percentage changes from previous year; nonfarm business.

[a] Gross domestic product, based on constant 1982 dollars.
[b] Adjusted for inflation.
[c] Preliminary.

Inadequate investment, too, had a perverse effect on productivity. By the mid-1970s economists began observing that the rate of investment in the United States was lagging behind that of most Western industrial nations. Ben Laden, an economist with T. Rowe Price Associates, estimated in 1981 that new capital investment per worker added to the labor force totaled only $21,600 during the 1970s (after adjustment for inflation). That was down from $25,400 in the 1960s.

In part, that low savings phenomenon probably reflected the effects of inflation, which discourages savings and encourages consumption thereby reducing money available for investment. It also reflected the economic instability of the 1970s, which reduced business profits and confidence. And the interaction between inflation and the tax system also tended to retard business investment during the 1970s.

Businesses have long been allowed to write off for tax purposes the cost of investment in plant and equipment. But during periods of inflation, the size of the write-offs tends to fall short of what is needed for businesses to make new capital investments. That was especially true during the inflationary 1960s and 1970s, when business depreciation allowances were based on the historical cost of equipment.

Knowing that, however, does not help explain why increased investment incentives adopted during the first Reagan years yielded so little productivity improvement.

The sudden rise in energy prices also played a role in the sharp slowdown in productivity after 1973. The abrupt rise in oil prices made it economically inefficient for industry to use much of the equipment that had been purchased when energy was fairly cheap. To save money, some businesses slowed down the rate at which such equipment was used, hurting productivity.

A simple example illustrates just how this can occur. To help save energy following the 1973 Arab oil embargo, Congress mandated that the speed limit on highways be reduced to fifty-five miles an hour. If a trucking company were to adhere to that slower speed limit, it would take longer for each truck to cover its route. As a result, it would require more time on the road to transport the same amount of goods the same distance. More time for the same output translates into lower productivity.

Finally, many analysts attribute some of the slowdown in productivity during the 1970s to the costs imposed on business by various federal regulations. Businesses were forced to spend more money on environmental quality, occupational safety, and health. Such regulation has a dual effect in retarding productivity. First, to the extent that businesses have to adapt existing equipment to new standards, it forces less efficient use of the equipment. With time, as new equipment is designed from the outset to meet the standards, that cost diminishes. Second, while regulations may enhance the quality of life, intangible forms of economic output such as clean air or better health are not measured in calculating productivity. Many regulations thus shifted some portion of the nation's economic output into "goods" that were not counted by traditional measurements of productivity.

Supply-Side Economics

The new supply-side theoreticians claimed they had a way out of the apparent economic impasse. While Keynesian policies cure inflation by reducing demand—which sounds like accepting a lower standard of living—the supply-siders said they could curb inflation by quickly increasing the supply of goods. The formulation came first from an early nineteenth century economist, Jean Baptiste Say, who contended that "supply creates its own demand." And, for twentieth-century supply-siders, the key, they said, was to reduce taxes and thus increase the incentives to produce.

The supply-siders disputed the Keynesian notion that once the government maintains an adequate level of demand, supply will be assured. The supply-siders said that people produce not merely in response to demand, but to increase their own income.

The fulcrum of economic activity, according to supply-siders, is the marginal rate of taxation—that is, the rate on the last dollar earned. Under a "progressive" income tax system like that in the United States, the rate of tax increases as income increases. Therefore, higher earnings result in higher tax rates.

People continually are deciding between work and leisure, and between saving and consumption. The higher the marginal tax rate, the less incentive a person has to work rather than be idle, or to save rather than consume, they contended. By reducing marginal tax rates, supply-siders concluded, the government can encourage more work and saving, in the process increasing income and economic well-being. It may have worked. During the Reagan years 1980-1987, inflation-adjusted per capita income increased almost 13 percent, whereas it grew only 7.5 percent in the preceding eight years. (See Table 2-4.)

Reagan's economists believed the effects of a cut in marginal tax rates would be felt by people at all levels of income, not just those at the top paying higher rates. But they also argued that the cut in marginal rates would be effective because the biggest benefits would go to people in the upper income brackets, who can afford to save and invest more.

Tax cuts that effectively redistribute income to poor people are more likely to increase consumption, they argued, because people in low tax brackets cannot afford to save.

Liberals said that "trickle-down" argument merely rationalized a program designed to benefit the well-to-do. But Reagan replied that the nation had grown tired of Democratic programs designed to redistribute income. "The taxing power of government must be used to provide revenues for legitimate government purposes," he said. "It must not be used to regulate the economy or bring about social change."

The 'Laffer Curve'

Modern-day supply-side thinking emerged basically in the thinking of two economists—Arthur Laffer of the University of Southern California and Robert Mundell of Columbia University. Their ideas captured the attention of Jude Wanniski, then an editorial writer at the *Wall Street Journal*. Wanniski, in turn, found an avid learner in Jack Kemp, who caught the ear of Reagan early in the 1980 presidential campaign.

Laffer's main contribution was the theoretical "Laffer curve." It was based on the proposition that the government would not take in any tax revenues if the tax rate is zero, and similarly, would not collect any taxes if the tax rate is 100 percent, since people would have no incentive to earn income.

From that thesis Laffer theorized that there must be a point at which tax rates get so high that they discourage work, in turn retarding the growth of supply, reducing income, and thus actually reducing the government's revenues. Laffer argued that U.S. taxes had become so high they were beginning to have this negative effect.

Laffer concluded that the government might never be able to balance the budget by raising taxes, but that a tax cut could actually spur so much economic growth that revenues would actually rise to balance the budget.

This new approach to budget matters had a politically liberating effect on Republicans, who traditionally had placed top priority on balancing the budget. Although Republican presidents Dwight D. Eisen-

Table 2-4   Personal Income

Year	Gross personal income (in billions) [a]	Per capita disposable income [b]	Personal savings rate [c]	Total population (in millions)
1929	$ 84.3	$ 4,091	3.2%	121.9
1933	46.3	2,950	−3.6	125.7
1939	72.1	3,812	2.6	131.0
1940	77.6	4,017	4.0	132.1
1941	95.2	4,528	10.9	133.4
1942	122.4	5,138	23.2	134.8
1943	150.7	5,276	24.6	136.7
1944	164.5	5,414	25.1	138.3
1945	170.0	5,285	19.2	139.9
1946	177.6	5,115	8.6	141.3
1947	190.2	4,820	3.1	144.1
1948	209.2	5,000	5.9	146.6
1949	206.4	4,915	3.9	149.1
1950	228.1	5,220	6.1	151.6
1951	256.5	5,308	7.3	154.2
1952	273.8	5,379	7.3	156.9
1953	290.5	5,515	7.2	159.5
1954	293.0	5,505	6.3	162.3
1955	314.2	5,714	5.8	165.2
1956	337.2	5,881	7.2	168.2
1957	356.3	5,909	7.2	171.2
1958	367.1	5,908	7.5	174.1
1959	390.7	6,027	6.3	177.0
1960	409.4	6,036	5.8	180.7
1961	426.0	6,113	6.6	183.7
1962	453.2	6,271	6.5	186.5
1963	476.3	6,378	5.9	189.3
1964	510.2	6,727	7.0	191.9
1965	552.0	7,027	7.0	194.3
1966	600.8	7,280	6.8	196.5
1967	644.5	7,513	8.0	198.7
1968	707.2	7,728	7.0	200.7
1969	772.9	7,891	6.4	202.7
1970	831.8	8,134	8.1	205.0
1971	894.0	8,322	8.5	207.6
1972	981.6	8,562	8.5	209.9
1973	1,101.7	9,042	9.4	211.9
1974	1,210.1	8,867	9.4	213.8
1975	1,313.4	8,944	9.2	215.9
1976	1,451.4	9,175	7.6	218.0
1977	1,607.5	9,381	6.6	220.2
1978	1,812.4	9,735	7.1	222.6
1979	2,034.0	9,829	6.8	225.1
1980	2,258.5	9,722	7.1	227.7
1981	2,520.9	9,769	7.5	230.1
1982	2,670.8	9,725	6.8	232.5
1983	2,838.6	9,930	5.4	234.8
1984	3,108.7	10,419	6.1	237.1

Table 2-4 *Continued*

Year	Gross personal income (in billions) [a]	Per capita disposable income [b]	Personal savings rate [c]	Total population (in millions)
1985	3,327.0	10,622	4.5	239.3
1986	3,534.3	10,947	4.3	241.6
1987 [d]	3,745.8	10,976	3.8	243.8

Sources: Commerce Department, Council of Economic Advisers.

[a] In current dollars.
[b] Constant 1982 dollars, less taxes.
[c] Percentage of disposable personal income.
[d] Preliminary.

hower, Richard Nixon, and Ford had acquiesced in deficit spending to stimulate the economy during recessions, they sought at other times to achieve surpluses. When inflation appeared to be the biggest threat, their belief in budget surpluses was even stronger. Laffer and his disciple Kemp argued that Republican devotion to balanced budgets had cost the party repeated electoral defeats. "As Republicans, we must rid ourselves of the perceived political idolatry of balanced budgets," Kemp said. "Republicans must not be bookkeepers for Democratic deficits."

The same idea was also advanced by Irving Kristol, another conservative thinker. "When in office, liberals ... will always spend generously, regardless of budgetary considerations, until the public permits the conservatives an interregnum in which to clean up the mess—but with liberals retaining their status as the activist party, the party of the 'natural majority,'" Kristol wrote. "The neo-conservatives have decided that two can play at this game—and must, since it is the only game in town. . . . They vigorously advocate increased defense spending and tax cuts, with [a balanced] budget remaining a secondary consideration."

Doubts

Not surprisingly, liberals scoffed at the economic reasoning behind supply-side eco-nomics. "Never have so many gambled so much on the basis of so little economic evidence," said Jeremy J. Stone in the liberal *Journal of the Federation of American Scientists.* Economist Lester Thurow warned that Reagan's desire to cut taxes while expanding the nation's military power would "wreck the economy."

Liberals argued that there was little evidence to support the supply-siders' claim that their tax cut would promptly increase economic output without boosting demand. "An across-the-board tax cut is a Keynesian remedy," declared Thurow. "The only thing President Reagan has done is rehabilitate it by calling it 'supply-side.' "

Still torn between fighting inflation and unemployment, liberals were deeply divided over the wisdom of tax cuts in the late 1970s. Those who remained unwilling to fight inflation by increasing unemployment supported instead a tax cut to bolster economic activity, although they doubted such a cut would cure inflation. Others, convinced that inflation had become the nation's biggest problem and that other approaches to curing it had failed, reluctantly resisted cutting taxes.

Criticism of the Reagan approach did not come only from liberals. George Bush, who ran against Reagan and later became his vice president, reflected mainstream Republican thinking during the 1980 campaign, dismissing Reagan's economic proposals as "voodoo economics." Bush eventually embraced much of Reagan's hard-line economic rhetoric, especially on the noxiousness of taxes, during his 1988 campaign to succeed Reagan. But he never did call himself a supply-sider.

Herbert Stein, who had served as Nixon's top economic adviser, was more sympathetic in 1981, but he nonetheless called the Reagan mix of policies "the sharpest change in economic policy since the time of Franklin Roosevelt."

By 1987, long after the 1981 tax cut had failed to generate any appreciable new revenue—at least none that was measurable given all the other changes in the economy—Stein was less charitable. Deriding the cause that many Reagan partisans carried to the White House as "punk supplysidism," Stein wrote that it was "the most spectacular example of an economic idea that rose like a rocket and then fizzled." The theory's fall, he said, "was due to its lack of intuitive credibility." Like many others, Stein noted that the theory made some fundamentally sound observations about the role of supply in the economy. But those ideas were not necessarily new.

Monetarist Economics

Reagan and his adherents adopted one other set of economic ideas that had been outside the mainstream of economic thinking for much of the postwar period—monetarism.

As developed by conservative economist Milton Friedman, monetarism holds that economic stability can be assured simply by holding the rate of growth in the supply of money to the growth rate of the actual economy. That view challenges the assumption of many economists that government can influence income—and thus economic activity—by changing the supply of money, just as it influences income via fiscal policy.

During much of the postwar period, most economists believed that the government could spur economic growth, and thus reduce unemployment, by increasing the money supply. That is because supply and demand theories about prices apply to money as well as goods. The larger the supply of money, the cheaper its cost—that is, the lower the rate of interest to borrow it. Lower interest rates would encourage investment, which in turn would lead to faster economic growth.

Similarly, a decrease in the supply of money is believed to slow the economy by driving interest rates up and discouraging investment. The resulting slowdown in economic activity would then ease inflation.

Monetarists concede that fluctuations in the money supply can affect income over the short run. But they contend that income is determined by actual economic output over the long run. When the supply of money rises faster than output, the value of each dollar has to decline because there is more money available to buy relatively fewer goods, they argue. "Inflation," according to Friedman, "is always and everywhere a monetary phenomenon."

Monetarists also concede that government surpluses can slow the economy—and deficits can accelerate it. But again, they maintain this is a short-run phenomenon. Over time, they say, neither surpluses nor deficits have any impact on growth or inflation. Instead, they merely influence the mix of public and private spending in the economy.

While generally considered a conservative doctrine, monetarism parts with many postwar theories in rejecting the claim that deficits are inflationary. Deficits cause inflation only if the government increases the supply of money to prevent government borrowing from driving up interest rates, monetarists contend. "Ongoing inflation is a monetary phenomenon and deficits stimulate inflation only when they are monetized consistently by the Federal Reserve," declared Beryl W. Sprinkel, Reagan's Treasury under secretary for monetary affairs, and later chairman of his Council of Economic Advisers.

By embracing monetarism, Reagan put most of the burden for controlling inflation on the Federal Reserve and managed to alleviate some fears within his own party that a large tax cut would be inflationary.

Nonmonetarists warned that Reagan's expansive approach to fiscal policy would collide with a monetary policy designed to wring inflation out of the economy. They predicted that the tax cut would require increased federal borrowing to finance the deficit at the same time that a tight money policy by the Fed would diminish the amount of money available for borrowing. The federal government would thus be a major competitor for a shrinking supply of lendable savings, with the result that interest rates would skyrocket and investment would be retarded, they said.

In 1980 and again in 1981, interest rates did reach the previously unimaginable level of 20 percent. But monetarists said that jump merely reflected fears among investors that the administration would not stick to its anti-inflation monetary policy. Once the public became convinced that the administration would not be swayed, interest rates would fall, they said.

The interest-rate phenomenon did provide a marriage of convenience between monetarists and supply-siders. The need to reduce federal competition for limited supplies of credit added to pressures to cut federal spending. And, although the Reagan administration was not happy about high interest rates, it did endorse such pressures.

But on other levels proponents of the two schools clashed, particularly Kemp and Friedman. Supply-side thinking was always a bit eclectic, embracing a range of conservative to libertarian views. And one of Kemp's favorite points was that to prevent

inflation the dollar needed to be stable, once again tied firmly to the price of gold in fact. For the author of the monetarist theory, whose support for flexible exchange rates was unshaken, views such as Kemp's were unhelpful and discredited by experience.

Economic Engines of the Government

During the 1930s, the government first took on responsibility for managing an economy that previous laissez-faire policy assumed to be self-regulating. A not-incidental sidelight of the New Deal was the host of programs it sparked to redistribute the nation's wealth from one group to another and from some regions to others.

"Over the next 40 years, this income redistribution function dramatically changed the structure of the federal budget and increased its share of the national wealth," according to Yale University School of Organization and Management associate dean Donald G. Ogilvie. "For the first time, federal officials and elected legislators began to influence the distribution of wealth significantly, initially through the tax system and then increasingly through direct spending programs of the federal government," he wrote in 1981.

Most New Deal initiatives were implemented as countercyclical programs to be phased out as economic conditions improved. Some were terminated within a few years. Others—such as the Social Security system and federal credit assistance for housing, small business, and farmers—remain major functions of the government. More significantly, the New Deal set precedents for federal government efforts to provide for the poor and assure economic security for all Americans when times were hard.

After the Depression ended, the federal government continued to expand in-

come transfer programs and take over more
and more functions that states, local governments, and individuals previously had performed. "In essence, almost without knowing it, we decided to tax ourselves at the
federal level and to commission the federal
government to provide goods and services
that we had historically provided for ourselves," Ogilvie noted.

Those programs, including many providing federal grants to state and local
governments to fund specific projects, grew
gradually over the years up to the 1960s.
Then starting in 1965, with a forceful President Lyndon B. Johnson prodding the
heavily Democratic Eighty-ninth Congress,
the government launched a stream of Great
Society programs extending its role in providing medical care, education aid, regional
development, nutrition, urban renewal, job
training, and other services for people and
localities. During the 1970s, Congress kept
enlarging most of these programs—and
adding a few new ones—despite the opposition of Republican presidents.

These new programs translated into
increased federal spending. During the
1930s, federal outlays rose from $3.5 billion
in fiscal 1931 to $9.5 billion in fiscal 1940.
From fiscal 1980 to 1981, the first belt-
tightening year under Reagan, outlays
climbed 14.8 percent to $678.2 billion. In
fiscal 1988, Reagan's final full year in
office, outlays were more than $1.06 tril-
lion, a 56 percent increase over seven years.

A government that spent 3.7 percent of
GNP in 1930 was spending 9.9 percent by
1940. The government's contribution to the
overall economy accelerated over the following two decades, reaching 16.0 percent
of GNP in 1950 and 18.2 percent in 1960.
Military buildups for World War II and the
Korean War brought sharp temporary
spending increases, but the budget resumed
steady growth after defense outlays slacked
off. The federal share of GNP grew more
slowly in the 1960s, 1970s, and 1980s but

still climbed above 23 percent in the early
Reagan years, where it leveled off. (See
Figure 2-1.)

Hand in hand with increases in spending went higher taxes. And, when taxes fell
short of spending, deficits and ultimately
the total national debt grew. And just as
federal spending drives GNP, so do taxes
and the debt affect the economy, especially
when they rise—the former by limiting
private consumption and savings, the latter
by limiting borrowing. Moreover, the government also strongly affects the economy
through monetary policy, but with the independent Federal Reserve Board moving
those levers outside the direct control of
politicians.

Spending Money: The Budget

During the 1930s, Keynes repeatedly
urged Roosevelt to spend the economy out
of the Depression. "The notion that, if the
government would retire altogether from
the economic field, business, left to itself,
would soon work out its own salvation, is, to
my mind, foolish," he said in 1934. "I
conclude, therefore, that for six months at
least, and probably a year, the measure of
recovery to be achieved will mainly depend
on the degree of the direct stimulus to
production deliberately applied by the administration."

Roosevelt never fully embraced
Keynes's ideas, but he did increase government spending to help offset the economic
hardship caused by the Depression. Federal
outlays had edged up to $4.7 billion in 1932
from $3.1 billion in 1929. But due to unem-
ployment relief and a variety of other public
works projects, they jumped up to $6.5
billion in 1934, and to $8.2 billion in 1936.

Still, although the economy did climb
out of its Depression lows by the end of the
1930s, it failed to approach anything like
full employment, however that term is defined, except during World War II, the

Figure 2-1 Growth in Revenues, Outlays, and Debt (as percentage of GNP)

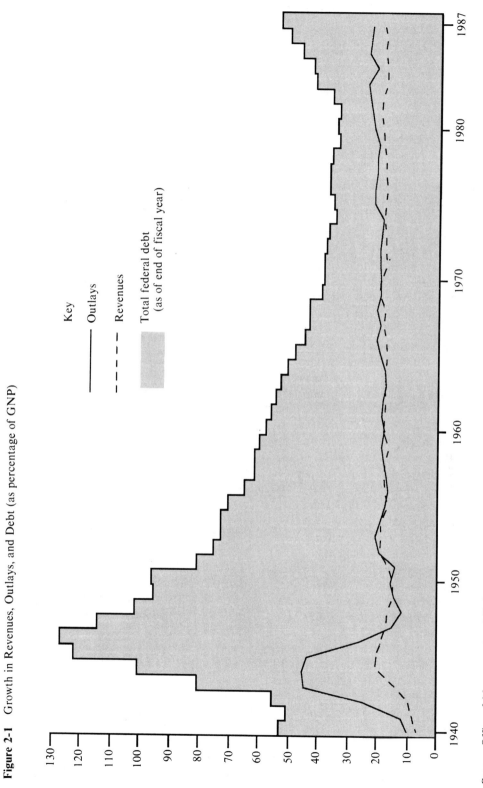

Key

—— Outlays

- - - - Revenues

Total federal debt
(as of end of fiscal year)

Source: Office of Management and Budget.

Note: GNP = gross national product.

Korean War, and possibly Vietnam. (Some economists have revised upward their estimates of the level of natural unemployment to argue that the economy was experiencing full employment in 1988.)

During Roosevelt's administration, some believed that the failure to eliminate joblessness was because the president was never willing to apply the full dose of deficit spending needed to restore consumer demand. At least through the middle years of his tenure, FDR remained hopeful that he could balance the federal budget.

Conservative analysts argued that the economy did not recover fully because business investment was stifled by the growth of government during the New Deal. Left to its own devices, these conservatives contended, business investment eventually would have recovered. But, they said, New Deal intrusion of the government into the private sector had the ironic consequence of holding back business and thus preventing the private economy from getting back on its feet.

The same debate would recur throughout the postwar period. In any event, in 1939, after more than a decade of depression and stagnation, 9.5 million Americans (more than 17 percent of the labor force) were still unemployed. And since that time the definition of full employment has been adjusted to fit political and economic circumstances. Until the mid-1970s, 3 percent unemployment was widely regarded as a reasonable goal for the economy. To try to reach below that level would risk imbalance and inflation.

In the late 1980s more and more women entered the work force, teenage unemployment swelled, and families relied upon multiple wage-earners. As a result, many economists—but by no means all—have altered their views of what constitutes "structural" or "frictional" unemployment, the rate that occurs more or less naturally in an otherwise well-performing economy. In-

stead of 3 percent, the full employment goal of the 1990s, some contend, might in fact be 6 percent or even 7 percent. (See Table 2-5.)

Impact of War

In no period of U.S. history has government spending been as great, or its impact as significant on the economy, as in wartime.

The New Deal notwithstanding, it was World War II that abruptly pulled the economy out of its Depression doldrums. Federal expenditures skyrocketed, from $9.5 billion in 1940 to $92.7 billion in 1945. Between 1940 and 1944, when government expenditures accounted for almost half of total output, gross national product more than doubled. And by 1944 unemployment had dropped to a mere 670,000, or about 1.2 percent of the work force.

The sharp contrast between prewar stagnation and wartime prosperity had a profound effect on public perceptions of the role of government in the economy. Full employment—jobs for everyone able and willing to work—became the "flag around which everyone could rally," according to economist Stein.

"One important lesson of the war was that the benefits of full employment were not confined to those persons who had previously been unemployed. . . . Everyone, or almost everyone, was better off than he had ever been before," Stein wrote. "It was not only incomes that full employment provided; it was also opportunity and mobility and freedom of many kinds. Therefore the idea spread that full employment was the important and essential means to deliver what every group wanted for itself and had been seeking by other more limited means."

During the Korean War, federal outlays as a percentage of GNP jumped to levels not seen since 1946—peaking at 20.8 percent in fiscal 1953. Spending then fell off just as rapidly. Unemployment, which tripled from 1945 to 1949, was cut in half to 2.9 percent in 1953. It has never been as low since.

And then came Vietnam, which undoubtedly helped prolong an economic expansion that began in February 1961 and extended through December 1969, the longest sustained period of U.S. growth since records have been kept. Unemployment, which had pushed back into the 4 percent to 5 percent range after Korea, again fell into the upper end of the 3 percent scale from 1966 through 1969. That was the last time for those numbers.

At the same time as the 1965 Vietnam buildup Johnson began pushing for his Great Society programs. "We have the opportunity to move not only toward the rich society and the powerful society, but upward to the Great Society," he said on May 22, 1964. Coupled with the war in Southeast Asia, Johnson's War on Poverty put considerable strain on an economy that already was operating near its full capacity as a result of tax cuts in 1964 and 1965.

Strong government demand quickly bid up prices for goods and services, setting off renewed inflation. As early as the first months of 1966 many economists, including some who had advocated a tax cut in 1964, were calling for an increase in taxes or a cut in federal spending to cool the overheating economy. They would not get their wish until a 10 percent income tax surcharge was enacted in 1968 to finance the war. By then, however, inflation was at 4.2 percent, and though small by 1980s' standards, that was four times the level it had been in 1961 and the highest since 1951. The tax increase came too late to cool off the economy, and unbridled growth came to a crashing halt after 106 continuous months.

Deficits during Recessions

If Roosevelt provided the first significant swing toward government influence on the economy, and World War II was the second, the aftermath of that wartime mobilization on the economy was the third.

"If there was a 'fiscal revolution' in the first postwar decade, it was in the willingness to allow the government budget to move into deficit during recessions, thus allowing the automatic stabilizers to work, in contrast to the destructive tax increases engineered by Herbert Hoover in 1932 under the budget-balancing rulebook of the pre-Keynesian fiscal policy," noted Northwestern University economist Robert Gordon.

The economy had slipped into recession in 1953, largely as a result of the drop in federal spending at the end of the Korean War. Eisenhower said the recession was merely a "minor readjustment," and he opposed congressional proposals to stimulate the economy. "Economic conditions do not call for an emergency program that would justify larger federal deficits and further inflation through large additional tax reductions at this time," he said in 1954. Eisenhower's position was strengthened by the fact that about $6 billion in tax cuts already had taken effect with the automatic expiration of the Korean War tax increase and the enactment in 1952 of a cut in excise taxes.

The Eisenhower administration's conservative fiscal policies were attacked by Democrats as a return to Hoover economics. But even some liberals conceded that criticism was not fully deserved. In his first economic report to Congress, issued in early 1954, Eisenhower pledged to use the full "arsenal of stabilizing weapons boldly, but not more frequently than is required to help maintain reasonable stability." The new president noted that "minor variations in [economic] activity are bound to occur in a free economy." But he said flexible policies aimed at minimizing economic fluctuations should not interfere "any more than is necessary" with the goal of reducing federal expenditures and taxes, and balancing the budget.

Table 2-5   Employment and Unemployment of Civilian Labor Force

Year	Total labor force (in thousands) [a]	Labor force participation rate [b]	Unemployment rate
1929	49,180	—	3.2%
1933	51,590	—	24.9
1939	55,230	—	17.2
1940	55,640	55.7%	14.6
1941	55,910	56.0	9.9
1942	56,410	57.2	4.7
1943	55,540	58.7	1.9
1944	54,630	58.6	1.2
1945	53,860	57.2	1.9
1946	57,520	55.8	3.9
1947	59,350	58.3	3.9
1948	60,621	58.8	3.8
1949	61,286	58.9	5.9
1950	62,208	59.2	5.3
1951	62,017	59.2	3.3
1952	62,138	59.0	3.0
1953	63,015	58.9	2.9
1954	63,643	58.8	5.5
1955	65,023	59.3	4.4
1956	66,552	60.0	4.1
1957	66,929	59.6	4.3
1958	67,639	59.5	6.8
1959	68,369	59.3	5.5
1960	69,628	59.4	5.5
1961	70,459	59.3	6.7
1962	70,614	58.8	5.5
1963	71,833	58.7	5.7
1964	73,091	58.7	5.2
1965	74,455	58.9	4.5
1966	75,770	59.2	3.8
1967	77,347	59.6	3.8
1968	78,737	59.6	3.6
1969	80,737	60.1	3.5
1970	82,771	60.4	4.9
1971	84,382	60.2	5.9
1972	87,034	60.4	5.6
1973	89,429	60.8	4.9
1974	91,949	61.3	5.6
1975	93,775	61.2	8.5
1976	96,158	61.6	7.7
1977	99,009	62.3	7.1
1978	102,251	63.2	6.1
1979	104,962	63.7	5.8
1980	106,840	63.8	7.1
1981	108,670	63.9	7.6
1982	110,204	64.0	9.7
1983	111,550	64.0	9.6
1984	113,544	64.4	7.5

Table 2-5 *Continued*

Year	Total labor force (in thousands) [a]	Labor force participation rate [b]	Unemployment rate
1985	115,461	64.8	7.2
1986	117,834	65.3	7.0
1987	119,865	65.6	6.2

Sources: Labor Department, Council of Economic Advisers.

[a] Civilian labor force included persons fourteen and older prior to 1947, and persons sixteen and older since. Because of periodic census adjustments and other changes in calculations, data are not strictly comparable over time.
[b] Percentage of civilian noninstitutional population.

Reviewing the administration's economic policies, liberal economist John Kenneth Galbraith concluded in 1955 that the new president had shown "considerable grace and ease in getting away from the cliches of a balanced budget and the unspeakable evils of deficit spending."

Looking back, economists believe that the willingness of the government to tolerate deficits significantly muted the impact of the 1953-1954 recession. When the economy slumped, tax receipts dropped and spending for programs such as unemployment compensation increased. Both had the effect of softening the effect of the economic slowdown. For that reason, economists referred to them as "automatic stabilizers."

But Eisenhower fought to minimize countercyclical swings in government fiscal policy because he was eager to demonstrate that private business could provide a prosperous economy on its own—as long, that is, as government did not interfere and distort private sector decisions. And when the economy slumped again in 1957, again Eisenhower denounced calls by Democrats and some Republicans for tax cuts or spending increases as a "sudden upsurge in pump-priming schemes."

The 1957-1958 recession proved to be sharp, though fairly short. However, the ensuing recovery abruptly halted in 1959. A national steel strike helped cause the recession by idling thousands of workers that depended upon the steel industry's output. But federal fiscal policy also played a role. The president was determined to balance the budget following the 1957-1958 downturn. By cutting back on spending sharply, the government managed to eke out a $269 million surplus in fiscal 1960 following a $12.9 billion deficit the preceding year.

Critics said that the administration had swung budget policy too sharply and that the sudden contraction of the deficit had pulled spending power out of the economy too quickly. Eisenhower replied that ominous underlying economic trends forced his dramatic tightening of fiscal policy. During the 1957-1958 recession, he noted, wages and prices had defied traditional patterns and continued to increase. He warned that trend could lead to "real inflationary trouble in a time of prosperity."

By the time Eisenhower left office in January 1961, he could claim that his policies had achieved some demonstrable success. The Consumer Price Index rose only 11.1 percent from 1953 through 1960, an enviable pace compared with the rates that occurred later. But that success had been achieved at a considerable price. At the end of Eisenhower's term, the nation had suffered its longest, most severe bout of unemployment since World War II. The jobless rate had not been below 4 percent in any year since 1953. In 1960 it stood at 5.5 percent, and a year later it was 6.7 percent.

One vigorous dissenter from the administration's restrictive fiscal policy was Eisenhower's vice president, Richard Nixon, who in 1960 was running for president himself. Nixon had argued for a more stimulative policy. Later he was to say that he lost the election to John F. Kennedy partly because of Eisenhower's failure to shift to a policy geared at bringing unemployment down.

Collecting Money: Taxes

Nothing in postwar fiscal policy making has led to more fights between Democrats and Republicans than taxes. That is because revenue is viewed not only as fuel for government spending but also as an economic stimulus all its own.

The late 1940s, for instance, saw a protracted battle between President Harry S Truman and congressional Republicans over cutting taxes. The Republicans, who by 1946 had been in the minority for sixteen years, depicted Democrats as the party of high spending and high taxes. They clamored for a tax cut. Truman, in turn, described the Republicans as the party of inflation. He argued it would be a mistake for the government to cut taxes until wartime spending could be reduced, especially since employment already was full. He called for a balanced budget, proclaiming the "pay-as-you-go idea" as the "soundest principle of financing that I know."

In June and July of 1947, Truman vetoed congressionally approved tax cuts, calling them "the wrong kind of tax reduction at the wrong time." He vetoed a tax cut for the third time in April 1948, but this time Congress overrode him.

That proved to be fortuitous; six months later the economy slipped into its first postwar recession. The 1948-1949 recession turned out to be relatively mild. Its impact was cushioned both by the tax cut and by the government's willingness to see budget surpluses of fiscal 1947, 1948, and

1949 give way to a deficit in fiscal 1950. As late as January 1949, Truman had sought a tax increase to balance the budget, but he finally dropped the idea in July because of the recession. By 1950 he was able to boast, "We have met and reversed the most significant downturn in economic activity since the war."

For the most part Eisenhower's relations with Congress over taxes were similarly stalemated—he wanted to balance the budget and therefore eschewed tax cuts. He did pressure Congress in 1954 for a business tax cut to stimulate investment, but Congress rejected it as only a benefit to the well-to-do. Congress preferred a tax cut aimed at low-income persons, but neither side prevailed.

A Tax Cut to Stimulate the Economy

Seeking an explanation for weakness in business activity, administration economists in the 1960s concluded that the tax system was imposing a serious "fiscal drag" on the economy. As the economy expanded and personal income grew, taxes tended to rise faster, they noted. That was because U.S. income taxes are "progressive," with higher rates being imposed on higher levels of income. With government taxing an increasing share of people's income, it was feared that the economy would come to a halt well before it reached full employment levels.

In June 1962 Kennedy decided to advocate a large cut in individual income tax rates. It marked the first time the government had decided to stimulate the economy even though there was no recession. The decision was a difficult one, and it came only after the administration concluded that the private economy, if left alone, would not propel the nation to full employment.

"The decision taken in June 1962 to cut taxes was not a prompt response to a minor change and uncertain forecasts of further changes in the economy," Stein wrote later. "It was a delayed response to a chronic condition after hopes of a spontaneous recovery were dimmed."

The tax cuts could not have been approved if the deadlock over tax policy that had occurred during the previous administration had continued unbroken. Democrats, facing a protracted battle with Republicans in Congress over spending, worried that spending increases might be too little too late to strengthen the economy. So they set aside long-term spending plans in favor of a tax cut that would stimulate the economy.

Republicans, for their part, could not resist the opportunity to vote for a tax cut. However, to protect themselves from sharing any possible political backlash against deficits, they did try, unsuccessfully, to make the tax cuts contingent on spending cuts.

Kennedy, still sensitive to potential criticism, argued that there actually was no conflict between the tax cut and the goal of balancing the budget. Without the cut, he said, the economy could not grow rapidly enough to produce the revenues needed to balance the budget.

"Our present choice is not between a tax cut and a balanced budget," Kennedy said. "The choice, rather, is between chronic deficits arising out of a slow rate of economic growth, and temporary deficits stemming from a tax program designed to promote fuller use of our resources and more rapid economic growth. . . . Unless we release the tax brake which is holding back our economy, it is likely to continue to operate below its potential, federal receipts are likely to remain disappointingly low, and budget deficits are likely to persist."

But Would It Work?

Despite the apparent consensus on the tax cut, lawmakers of different persuasions had varying opinions on what the economic impact of the cuts would be. Liberals believed the cuts would increase personal income, thus boost demand. But conservatives argued that the main impact would be to increase the incentives of individuals to work, save, and invest. By boosting the amount of income a person could keep after taxes, the conservatives argued, the tax cuts would make work and savings more rewarding.

The conservative argument later became the theme of the supply-side economists ushered into government under Reagan. Kennedy's own view was somewhat ambiguous. In the effort to sell the tax cuts, he made both arguments, emphasizing the incentive aspect before conservative audiences.

Enacted in 1964 after the president's death, the tax cut was a success for a time. The amount of stimulus was substantial. When it was fully effective in 1965 the tax cut added more than $11 billion to private purchasing power. Government officials called it the largest stimulative action ever undertaken in peacetime.

The tax cuts initially appeared to be an outstanding success. The unemployment rate, which seemed stuck at 5.7 percent in 1963, dropped to 5.2 percent in 1964 and 4.5 percent in 1965—close to the 4 percent "interim full employment" goal Kennedy's advisers had set at the beginning of his term in office. And, at the outset at least, the inflationary costs of the tax cuts seemed acceptable. Consumer prices rose modestly, and barely at all by 1980s standards: 1.2 percent in 1963, 1.3 percent in 1964, and 1.7 percent in 1965.

Most economists viewed 1965 as a year of triumph. Harvard economist Otto Eckstein, who served on Johnson's Council of Economic Advisers, was later to look back on the early 1960s as "a golden age for economic policy." Full employment seemed to have been achieved at a fairly modest cost in terms of inflation. Analysts declared that the business cycle had been tamed, and the government had found the way to keep the economy on a long-term growth path.

On the theoretical level, economists proclaimed the emergence of a "neo-Keynesian synthesis," which they said united the Keynesian and classical traditions of economic analysis. Under the synthesis, economists basically accepted the classical theory that prices and wages are determined primarily by the interplay of supply and demand. But they added one Keynesian caveat—that government intervention was needed to assure steady consumer demand.

Unfortunately, the "synthesis" came unraveled almost as soon as it was "achieved." Economic historians attribute its demise to one of the biggest mistakes in postwar economic policy making—the huge increase in Johnson's Great Society domestic spending at the time of the Vietnam buildup. With not enough revenue to pay for the government's largess, deficits mounted, and so did inflation.

According to Johnson, in 1966 he had discussed the possibility of a tax increase with members of Congress and was convinced that it could not be enacted. Finally, on January 10, 1967, he asked for a 6 percent income tax surcharge. On August 3, 1967, with inflation still mounting, he raised the request to 10 percent. But Congress acted slowly on the president's request. The surcharge was not enacted until June 28, 1968, almost eighteen months after it had been first requested and almost three years after many economists believed it was needed. By then, the nation was experiencing its worst sustained inflation since World War II.

A Replay in 1981

The huge tax cut that was the centerpiece of Ronald Reagan's economic platform in 1981 drew upon Kennedy-era conservative arguments in favor of a boost for private savings and investment. In the end, however, to the degree that the tax cut provided stimulus to the economy, it may have been as much due to Kennedy-era liberal beliefs about boosting private spending. That Keynesian view is bolstered by the decline in private savings registered after 1982 and the growth in consumption—fed by the $35.6 billion first year tax cut, which ballooned in later years.

Supply-side theorists had used Kennedy's words about the tax code being a brake on the economy; some, as Kennedy had, argued that releasing that brake would even cause revenues to grow as the unfettered economy took off.

But Walter W. Heller, Kennedy's chief economist, denounced their 1980s claim to his legacy. When Kennedy proposed his tax cut the economy's capacity was severely underutilized and inflation was almost nonexistent, Heller said. By the late 1970s, he argued, inflation was a severe problem and tax cuts were no longer so desirable.

And a major change since the Kennedy years has been the federal deficit. During the 1950s and 1960s, except for 1959 and the peak Vietnam year of 1968, there were no years with double-digit deficits. But from a budget surplus of $3.2 billion in 1969, the deficit grew to $78.9 billion in 1981. In the wake of that year's tax cut, it swelled to $127.9 the next year and $207.8 billion in 1983.

Perhaps the 1981 tax cut was fortuitous, as was the case with the Truman tax cut of 1948. By the time the 1981 cut was enacted, the economy had slid into the deepest recession since the 1930s. The stimulus provided by increased private consumption and the federal deficit helped to pull it out. Moreover, the Federal Reserve's monetary policy, which had brought on the recession, had also eliminated the high inflation that had troubled Heller.

The only remaining problem was the deficit. Spending cuts of sufficient size to reduce the deficit could not be enacted after 1981—there was no stomach for them on Capitol Hill. That left only tax increases.

And despite Reagan's stated opposition to them, he signed four large increases into law between 1982 and 1987, one in 1983 to finance the nearly bankrupt Social Security system.

The tax law of 1986 was an anomaly. In it, Congress and the president agreed neither to raise revenue nor to reduce it. The entire design was to make the tax code more fair by eliminating tax breaks that favored the few, in return for rate increases that favored everyone. In theory, it would provide a stimulus, following the supply-side argument that high tax rates discourage increased earnings, because more of every dollar earned goes to the government. It remained to be seen, however, if the decline in savings and investment in the 1980s would turn around once the law was fully in effect after five years.

Creating Money: The Fed

If fiscal policy is set largely in the open, by a Congress and president weighing political and economic options, monetary policy is set largely in private by the Federal Reserve, the nation's central bank. The Fed can influence the money supply through a variety of methods, but its key device is "open market operations," the buying and selling of government securities.

If the Fed wants to increase the money supply, it buys government securities from banks, in essence by printing money. That puts new dollars in the hands of the banks, which they in turn can then lend out—multiple times. Conversely, if the Fed wants to cut the money supply back, it sells government securities to banks, thus draining cash out of the banking system. The Fed can also influence the money supply by directly changing the amount of cash reserves banks are required hold in their vaults against their deposits. Increasing the level of mandatory reserves reduces the amount of money banks can lend and put into circulation; decreasing

the amount of reserves adds to the sums available in the economy.

The Fed also has the power to move interest rates by varying the two over which it has control: the discount rate, which is charged to bank borrowing from the Fed, and the federal funds rate, which banks charge each other on overnight loans. The Fed can change the discount rate directly. It moves the federal funds rate by selling or buying securities, and thereby increasing or decreasing bank cash reserves. Banks that have larger reserves than required can lend the excess to those that need it to meet reserve requirements. The more the Fed increases the supply of reserves, the less will be the interbank lending rate. The more reserves are tightened, the higher the rate goes.

It has been widely accepted during the postwar period that monetary policy should be set separately from fiscal policy. Otherwise, the government could simply decide to create more money to pay for its deficits—a practice that obviously would undermine the value of the currency.

"To oversimplify only slightly, the question is whether the principal office in charge of paying the government's bills should be entrusted also with the power to create the money to pay them," explained William McChesney Martin, Jr., chairman of the Federal Reserve Board in 1964. To be effective, Martin said, monetary management "should be insulated so far as possible from private pressures just as much as political pressures."

Freeing Monetary Policy

Perhaps the most important economic development of the Korean War period involved the freeing of monetary policy to act as a force for economic stabilization. A 1951 "accord" between the Treasury and the Federal Reserve established the basis for independent policy decisions.

At the insistence of the Treasury, the Federal Reserve after World War II had continued a policy of "pegging" interest rates on government bonds. It did that by agreeing to purchase at face value all bonds offered on the open market. The policy served to keep the prevailing interest rate on all Treasury bonds at or below 2.5 percent, which helped minimize the cost of servicing the national debt. But it prevented the Federal Reserve from using monetary policy to offset inflation or recession.

During the period immediately after World War II, when inflation was the nation's main economic problem, the board's stable interest rate policy tended to increase the money supply and aggravate inflation. That was because, as demand mounted, the natural tendency was for interest rates to rise as well. In that climate, investors had little incentive to continue holding the low-price government bonds. As a result, they sold their bonds to the Federal Reserve, obtaining cash that they could invest elsewhere.

The perverse effect of that monetary policy worked in the opposite direction during the 1948-1949 recession. The economic slowdown led to a fall in the demand for money and to a decline in interest rates. When market rates dropped below the pegged level on government bonds, investors had an obvious incentive to trade in their cash for the higher-price bonds. The result was that the supply of money shrank further, exacerbating the effects of the recession.

The Treasury conceded that the policy of pegged interest rates did not make sense during the recession and, thus, allowed the Fed to move away from its inflexible wartime policy. But when inflation pressures renewed in 1950 and 1951, Treasury resisted allowing the Fed to be as flexible against inflation as it had been in fighting recession.

A lengthy battle between the administration and the Fed followed. In the end, the administration and the Fed announced that they had reached "full accord." It took some time to determine exactly what the agreement was, but it eventually became clear that the Fed had achieved a greater measure of independence. Subsequently, interest rates became more variable, and monetary policy was conducted in ways designed to stabilize the economy.

Political Pressures

Consultation between the Fed and Treasury and even between the Fed and Congress is not uncommon, nor is it necessarily visible. Congress, which created the central bank in 1913, has gone out of its way to reinforce the view that the Fed should not bow to presidential pressures to stimulate the economy by relaxing the money supply. The fear of such stimulus—with its parallel threat of rising inflation—comes principally in election years, when job creation is typically a more pressing concern than high prices.

But Congress itself occasionally tries to pressure the Fed to behave one way or another. After the Fed had switched courses twice in the mid-1970s, first promoting money growth in late 1974, and then turning to a restrictive stance against inflation in 1975, it came under congressional pressure to accelerate money supply expansion to accommodate a faster recovery. But the House backed away from proposals by Rep. Henry S. Reuss, D-Wis. (1955-1983), for Congress to dictate money supply goals. Reuss could not persuade the Banking Committee that setting strict goals was a good idea.

Nevertheless, Fed chairman Arthur F. Burns did agree to disclose monetary growth target ranges in periodic House and Senate testimony, and that requirement was eventually written into law in 1978.

Following the Fed-induced recession of 1981-1982, congressional and other cries against the central bank grew loud again. First the Fed had decided in October 1979 to switch from an emphasis on regulating short-term interest rates (by controlling the federal funds rate) to watching the money supply. In fact, according to Columbia University economist Frederic S. Mishkin, the evidence suggests that the Fed did not overly concern itself with the money supply but instead allowed interest rates to rise significantly (short-term rates reached 15 percent in March 1980) to drive out inflation. A six-month recession ensued, ending in July 1980, and the Fed backed off.

But inflation was not gone—hovering around 10 percent in 1981—so the Fed tightened the money supply and ran short-term interest rates back up above 15 percent, sparking a second, much deeper recession. Inflation fell to 6.1 percent in 1982 and 3.2 percent in 1983. "With the inflationary psychology apparently broken, interest rates were now allowed to fall," Mishkin wrote in 1987. (See Table 2-6.)

Mishkin and other admirers, notably Sen. William Proxmire, D-Wis. (1957-1989), who was chairman or ranking minority member of the Banking Committee during the period, praised Fed chairman Volcker for the political courage he exhibited in taking on inflation.

But some leading Democrats in 1982 tried unsuccessfully to force Congress to act on bills to require interest rate reductions, and to relax the money supply. Others—Republicans and Democrats—vilified Volcker for the recession. "Never before has a president's economic policy had to succeed without help from the Federal Reserve," complained supply-side guru and Georgetown University professor Paul Craig Roberts in 1987.

Sen. John Melcher, D-Mont. (House 1969-1977; Senate 1977-1989), was so disturbed that he went to federal court. There he unsuccessfully challenged the existence of the Fed's Open Market Committee—the seven members of the Fed's board of governors, plus five of the twelve presidents of the regional Fed system banks—which sets monetary policy.

Supply-sider Jack Kemp joined with Volcker's Democratic congressional critics. And monetarist Milton Friedman complained that the Fed's ostensible interest in controlling money growth was a sham. "The key fact of monetarism is a steady and predictable monetary policy. Recent Fed policy has been, if anything, unsteady and unpredictable," Friedman said in 1987.

But Volcker's success earned him a second, four-year term as chairman in 1983. And he was roundly praised when he stepped down in favor of economist Alan Greenspan in 1987. Greenspan's political past (he was an informal Nixon adviser and chief economist in the Ford White House) worried some at first, though he assured the Senate Banking Committee that he would be as independent as Volcker. "It's conceivable my advice will turn out to be wrong. My actions may turn out to be wrong. But it certainly would not be on the basis of politics rather than economics," he testified at his confirmation hearing in July 1987.

By January 1988, confronted by criticism from the president's Council of Economic Advisers and some Treasury Department officials, Greenspan was lashing out and proving his independence—so much so that Treasury secretary James A. Baker III had to defend the Treasury and pronounce that he was in "fundamental agreement" with Fed policy, whether it was true or not.

Legislating to Tune the Economy

Much of what Congress and the president have done with the economy in the postwar era has been in the nature of short-term macroeconomic stimulus—spending and tax increases and reductions. There have been, on occasion, direct efforts at

Table 2-6 Consumer Price Index

Year	All items	Food	Medical care	Energy
1929	0.0%	1.3%	—	—
1933	−5.1	−2.9	—	—
1939	−1.4	−2.8	0.3%	—
1940	1.0	1.7	0.0	—
1941	5.0	9.1	0.6	—
1942	10.7	17.4	3.1	—
1943	6.1	11.5	5.0	—
1944	1.7	−1.4	4.2	—
1945	2.3	2.2	2.7	—
1946	8.5	14.6	5.8	—
1947	14.4	21.5	8.5	—
1948	7.8	8.5	6.7	—
1949	−1.0	−4.0	3.7	—
1950	1.0	1.4	2.3	—
1951	7.9	11.1	5.1	—
1952	2.2	1.8	6.4	—
1953	0.8	−1.5	3.6	—
1954	0.5	−0.2	3.0	—
1955	−0.4	−1.4	2.9	—
1956	1.5	0.7	4.0	—
1957	3.6	3.3	4.3	—
1958	2.7	4.2	4.9	0.2%
1959	0.8	−1.6	4.8	1.7
1960	1.6	1.0	4.0	2.6
1961	1.0	1.3	3.7	0.2
1962	1.1	0.9	3.2	0.3
1963	1.2	1.4	3.0	0.3
1964	1.3	1.3	2.4	−0.4
1965	1.7	2.2	3.2	1.8
1966	2.9	5.0	5.4	1.6
1967	2.9	0.9	8.7	2.2
1968	4.2	3.6	7.3	1.5
1969	5.4	5.1	8.1	2.7
1970	5.9	5.5	7.1	2.7
1971	4.3	3.0	7.3	3.9
1972	3.3	4.3	3.7	2.8
1973	6.2	14.5	4.4	8.0
1974	11.0	14.4	10.3	29.3
1975	9.1	8.5	12.6	10.6
1976	5.8	3.1	10.1	7.2
1977	6.5	6.3	9.9	9.5
1978	7.7	10.0	8.6	6.3
1979	11.3	10.9	9.7	25.2
1980	13.5	8.6	11.3	30.9
1981	10.4	7.9	10.7	13.5
1982	6.1	4.0	11.9	1.5
1983	3.2	2.1	8.7	0.8
1984	4.3	3.8	6.0	1.0
1985	3.6	2.3	6.0	0.7
1986	1.9	3.2	7.7	−13.2
1987	3.7	4.2	6.6	0.4

Sources: Labor Department, Council of Economic Advisers.

Note: Percentage change year to year.

resolving over a longer period the two most difficult problems—nagging unemployment and persistent inflation.

One such effort, the Employment Act of 1946, did establish a framework for setting fiscal policy. But like its successor, the Humphrey-Hawkins full employment act of 1978, the 1946 law has had little to do ultimately with whether the economy reaches full employment. And the most conspicuous effort to adjust inflation, the Nixon administration's wage and price controls, had the opposite effect. When the inflation dam was finally removed, prices surged out of control.

Not all of these efforts failed because the policy was wrong. Sometimes they failed because of politics; the policy was never really tested. Both employment acts, for example, were relatively toothless tigers by the time they were enacted, defanged by conservative fears of managed economies. And the price controls were filled with exceptions.

Conservative views have always tempered the labors of liberals to use government to adjust economic performance. The U.S. economic system, Reagan said shortly after his election, "has never failed us." But, he added, the country has failed the economy "through a lack of confidence and sometimes through a belief that we could fine-tune [it] and get a tune to our liking."

Full Employment

The massive conversion of the economy to the war effort in the 1940s created an enormous backlog of demand for business and consumer goods. In addition, extensive federal borrowing to finance the war, combined with the limited supply of consumer goods, left consumers holding large amounts of savings in the form of government securities and bank deposits. That guaranteed consumers would have the means to pay for such goods.

Those forces produced a postwar economic boom, helped by the fact that some 4.3 million workers withdrew from the labor force, leaving room for newly discharged GIs. But before the end of the war, that outcome was far from taken for granted. Instead, many analysts feared that demobilization would result in a rise in unemployment and a return to the stagnant conditions of the 1930s.

Policy makers were committed to prevent that economic nightmare from occurring. As early as 1942, the National Resources Planning Board had called "imperative" the development of a "positive program of postwar economic expansion and full employment, boldly conceived and vigorously pursued." In 1944 Roosevelt endorsed that goal, declaring that every American had "the right to a useful and remunerative job."

Employment Act of 1946

Congress took up the question of how to assure that right in 1946. At the outset, advocates of an aggressive federal program to guarantee everyone a job proposed that Congress enact a "full employment" law committing the federal government to "stimulate and encourage the highest feasible levels" of private investment and spending. To the extent that the private sector failed to provide full employment, they said the government should be required to "provide such volume of federal investment and expenditure as would be needed to assure continuing full employment."

The policy was to be carried out through a "national production and employment budget," which would estimate private investment and propose federal spending to fill any gap between private investment and "full employment."

Conservative critics of the bill complained that "full employment" was impossible to define. And even if it could be defined, they said, it would be impossible to achieve without causing inflation, or at least leading the government to impose wage and price controls. Many critics feared that the bill would be used to authorize continual deficit spending. Others complained that it placed too much power in the hands of the president.

After considerable debate, Congress approved a bill that was much less ambitious than its original sponsors had intended. Gone was the commitment to provide "full employment." The law was renamed simply the Employment Act of 1946. Instead of committing the government to policies to achieve full employment, the law merely gave it the responsibility "to use all practicable means consistent with its needs and obligations and other essential considerations of national policy" to promote "maximum employment, production and purchasing power." The final version of the act also dropped the notion that the federal budget was to be the prime tool for accomplishing "maximum" employment.

Instead, the law simply directed the president to submit an annual economic report—separate from the budget recommendations—on how the goals of the act would be achieved. The report was to be prepared by a Council of Economic Advisers, whose three members were to be confirmed by the Senate. And the congressional Joint Economic Committee was created to receive the report. Both the economic report and the committee, however, have survived, providing a consistent forum for economic debate between the two branches of government. That debate has not always been effective in altering the course of policy, however. The Joint Economic Committee has no legislative authority, and presidents have been known to ingore their economic advisers.

Some conservatives had attempted during the debate on the employment act to include the achievement of "price stability" among the economic responsibilities of the federal government. They were unsuccessful. By inference, the final version of the act assigned greater importance to achieving a low unemployment rate than to maintaining price stability, although it did acknowledge "other essential considerations of national policy."

When he signed the employment act on February 20, 1946, Truman described it as "not the end of the road, but rather the beginning." The law, he said, represented a "commitment" by the government "to take any and all of the measures necessary for a healthy economy."

Humphrey-Hawkins Full Employment Act

Years after the 1946 law was enacted, in the midst of the 1973-1975 recession, Democrats in Congress clamored for a more stimulative fiscal policy than President Ford would give them.

Supported by organized labor and many black leaders, liberals pushed for adoption of the Humphrey-Hawkins "full employment" bill, which would commit the government to holding the jobless rate for adult men to 3 percent. Echoing anti-Eisenhower rhetoric of twenty years earlier, Sen. Hubert H. Humphrey, D-Minn. (1949-1964; 1971-1978), said in 1976 that adoption of the bill would "reject the discredited economic doctrine of the present administration and replace it with a new economics that puts all of America's resources back to work."

Ford's resistance kept the bill from reaching his Oval Office desk. And, despite the fact that the measure became a political litmus test for liberals in the mid-1970s, it was even difficult to persuade Democratic presidential candidate Jimmy Carter to endorse it. He finally reluctantly endorsed the bill late in the primary season—perhaps to appease liberals he had offended by speaking favorably about "ethnic purity" in urban neighborhoods. But as president he objected to setting the 3 percent unemployment rate as a goal of government policy.

The Humphrey-Hawkins bill that finally passed was effectively toothless. It increased the Joint Economic Committee's responsibilities, first established in 1946, to review the president's economic report, and it gave the Budget committees the option to write economic goals into budget resolutions. It required the president to set unemployment goals of 3 percent for adults and 4 percent for all workers over age sixteen. But it also set a seemingly conflicting inflation goal of 3 percent by 1981 and zero by 1988. At the time unemployment was about 6.1 percent and inflation 6.3 percent; policies designed to bring down one quickly would probably drive up the other.

Most importantly, key provisions to establish broad national economic planning and to require the government to serve as employer of last resort, through a commitment to public service jobs, were stricken.

In the same legislative session, however, Congress extended for four years the Comprehensive Employment and Training Act (CETA), first adopted in 1973. A major component of CETA was a public service jobs program. However, CETA was racked by complaints that it created no permanent jobs, was too costly, and was mismanaged. The program was allowed to expire in 1982—taking with it the last of the government's commitment to hire workers to boost employment, an idea that was formed in the New Deal and applied repeatedly over fifty years. Only the job training program was preserved, in the Job Training Partnership Act.

Wage and Price Controls

Congress and the president have found it somewhat easier to act affirmatively to reduce inflation than to reduce unemployment. But the results in the long run have been no better.

Price controls are a routine device in times of wartime shortages. During World War II controls had prevented prices from rising in tandem with the supply of money. As a result, after the war there was more money relative to the available goods than there had been before the war. That meant that the "real," or inflation-adjusted, value of money had declined. And when all remaining price and wage controls except for ceilings on rents, sugar, and rice were eliminated on November 9, 1949, prices jumped to correct the imbalance.

The same problem occurred twenty-five years later, after Nixon had tried to stem rising inflation at the tail end of the Vietnam period.

By 1971, some Nixon administration economists—among them assistant Treasury secretary Murray L. Weidenbaum, who in 1981 became chairman of Reagan's Council of Economic Advisers—were warning that the traditional relationship between unemployment and inflation was coming unhinged.

They were joined by Burns, who said in May 1970: "The excess demand that bedeviled our economy during the past four or five years has been eliminated." But fiscal and monetary restraint was not succeeding in reducing inflation. The reason, according to Burns, was that inflation no longer resulted from "demand-pull" pressures caused by an overheated economy, but instead from "cost-push" pressures in the form of excessive wage increases that were driving up business costs.

Burns warned that using fiscal restraint to suppress wages would lead to a recession, which in turn would create irresistible pressures for further demand stimulus. As a result, he warned, "our hopes of getting the inflationary problem under control would . . . be shattered."

Weidenbaum and Burns concluded that the administration would have to add some form of "incomes policy" to its economic arsenal. That term, which soon came into fashionable use, referred to a broad range of activities designed to influence incomes through wages and prices instead of through fiscal and monetary policy.

During the Kennedy-Johnson years, the government had issued wage and price "guideposts," indicating roughly what wage and price increases it considered economically appropriate. Begun in 1962, the guideposts were intended partly to defray criticism that the expansive fiscal policy Kennedy planned would be inflationary.

The idea of an incomes policy was anathema to the laissez-faire economic philosophy of Republicans. "I will not take this nation down the road of wage and price controls, however politically expedient that may seem," Nixon promised in June 1970. He explained that controls "only postpone a day of reckoning, and in so doing they rob every American of an important part of his freedom."

Using the Jawbone

During this period, Nixon had been fighting a protracted battle with the Democratic-controlled Congress over reducing federal spending. Partly to shift responsibility for inflation back to the president, Congress in August 1970 added to a Defense Production Act extension an amendment empowering the president to freeze salaries, rents, and prices. The president opposed the amendment and vowed he would never use the authority, though he did sign the bill.

Nixon did try to jawbone prices down by issuing two "inflation alerts" to publicize excessive wage and price increases. In December he announced measures to offset oil price increases and plans to intervene in wage negotiations in the construction industry if strikes and rising costs were not abated. "Unless the industry wants government to intervene in wage negotiations on federal projects to protect the public interest, the moment is here for labor and man-

agement to make their own reforms in that industry," Nixon warned.

Burns noted ominously a few days later, "We are dealing, practically speaking, with a new problem—namely, persistent inflation in the face of substantial unemployment." The Fed chairman cautioned that "classical remedies may not work well enough or fast enough in this case."

Nixon was unwilling, however, to risk a severe recession to stabilize wages and prices. The Republican party had suffered a net loss in the 1970 congressional and gubernatorial elections. Many politicians interpreted that as a rejection of Nixon's policy of gradualism, which apparently had failed to prevent a recession. By 1971 Nixon also might have been haunted by Eisenhower's prediction three years earlier.

"I think Dick's going to be elected president, but I think he's going to be a one-term president," Eisenhower had said. "I think he's really going to fight inflation, and that will kill him politically."

Perhaps with that prediction in mind, Nixon abandoned his orthodox conservative fight on inflation in favor of fiscal stimulus in early 1971. That shift in policy all but assured large federal deficits, but Nixon justified them in much the same terms as Kennedy had nine years earlier. "I am now a Keynesian in economics," he told an interviewer in January 1971.

Nixon announced that his new fiscal policy was designed to ensure a "full employment budget," meaning that the deficits he projected for 1971 and 1972 would not have occurred if the economy had been operating at full employment and output. The actual deficits, he said, represented the loss of federal revenues caused by economic performance that was below potential.

The Nixon Controls

Fiscal stimulus may have helped solve the unemployment problem, but it only added to concerns about inflation. Unable to solve both problems simultaneously, Nixon, in a dramatic reversal, announced in August 1971 that he would accompany his stimulative policies with a wage and price freeze.

The Nixon controls, which went through four "phases" before Congress allowed them to lapse in 1974, initially were well received by the public. Even Milton Friedman conceded that Nixon, having failed to convince the public there was any other way to end inflation, had acted "the only way a responsible leader in a democracy could."

With controls in place, the economy appeared for a while to have finally accomplished the coveted goal of price stability and full employment. Consumer prices rose only 4.3 percent in 1971 and 3.3 percent in 1972, while unemployment averaged 5.9 percent in 1971 and dropped to 5.6 percent in 1972 on its way to a 4.9 percent average in 1973.

Imposition of controls probably helped Nixon win reelection in 1972. Economic policy was not even an issue during the presidential campaign that year. But the controls failed to provide a lasting solution to the nation's economic woes. Instead, Nixon's stimulative fiscal policy the year before the election led to a further buildup of inflationary pressures, which the controls only temporarily capped. That became evident soon after the election.

By 1974 the system of controls was riddled with holes. By preventing prices from mediating between supply and demand, the controls led to serious disruptions in economic activity. As world prices rose above controlled domestic prices, exports surged and domestic shortages appeared for many metals crucial to the nation's defense. Paper products were also in short supply. As paper exports from the United States increased, the U.S. publishing industry found itself short of newsprint.

The Nixon controls provided many examples of the inability of the government to manage the economy efficiently. For example, coal production weakened because controls made it unprofitable to produce mine roof bolts. Similarly, meat prices were frozen while feed grain prices were allowed to rise uncontrolled, with the result that production of livestock and poultry became unprofitable. That led farmers to slaughter large numbers of their stock, eventually creating meat shortages that in turn caused sharp price increases in 1978 and 1979.

As pressures and distortions built up, the Nixon administration was forced to grant an increasing number of exemptions from its controls program. By 1974 the list of industries excluded from the controls program included fertilizer, cement, zinc, aluminum, automobiles, mobile homes, rubber tires and tubes, all retail trade, furniture, paper, coal, shoes and other footwear, canned fruit and vegetables, petrochemicals, prepared feeds, and semiconductors.

Some economists believe that controls did manage to reduce the inflation rate in late 1971 and early 1972 by about 1 percentage point below its previous level. But the rate steadily rose from the second half of 1972 onward, as more and more exemptions were allowed. And when controls were removed entirely, pent-up inflation reasserted itself with a vengeance. Inflation shot to 6.2 percent in 1973 and 11.0 in 1974.

The nation's unhappy experience with controls in the early 1970s reaffirmed the free market philosophy of most economists. Later, in 1980, when oppressive inflation again led to pressures for controls, Carter led the resistance. Charles Schultze said controls suffered at least two "fatal defects": First, "they cannot be maintained long enough to do the job; and second, they are likely to cause major harm to the economy."

Supply Shocks in the 1970s

Contributing to the explosion of pent-up inflation in the mid-1970s were a series of unexpected and severe shocks from the outside that presented a new set of problems to policy makers.

Poor harvests in many countries in 1972, along with a continued rise in international demand, led to a 20 percent jump in U.S. consumer food prices. Worse, energy shortages culminating in the October 1973 oil embargo by the Organization of Petroleum Exporting Countries (OPEC) sent oil prices skyrocketing. The average price of a barrel of oil imported into the United States rose from $3.33 in 1973 to $11.01 in 1974. The total U.S. oil import bill tripled in one year, leaping from $8.4 billion in 1973 to $26.6 billion in 1974.

Following a brief respite in 1976, consumer prices shot back up to 6.5 percent in 1977 and 7.7 percent in 1978. And to make matters worse, OPEC started pushing oil prices up again. The average price of a barrel of imported oil surged from $13.29 in 1978 to $30.46 in 1980. The total cost of oil imports into the United States jumped from $42.3 billion in 1978 to $78.9 billion in 1980. Price controls on domestically produced oil softened the impact on consumers, but prices still soared 11.3 percent in 1979 and 13.5 percent in 1980.

Traditional economic policies, already unable to deal with the growing rigidity of the U.S. wage and price structure, were also ill-equipped to respond to the problem posed by the 1970s supply shocks. Because it is difficult for consumers, at least in the short run, to reduce their demand in response to a rise in prices for necessities such as oil, the dramatic increase in food and energy costs made inevitable a decline in "real" income—the purchasing power of the dollar.

Strategies designed to deal with demand-induced inflation or unemployment proved unsuited to cure inflation that originated on the supply side of the economic equation—at least at a politically acceptable cost. Restraining the economy would have driven up unemployment; increasing incomes without increasing the supply of oil would have pushed prices even higher.

Eventually the Carter administration concluded that the only long-term solution to the nation's energy problems was to let prices rise and discourage consumption. To prevent the rise in prices from translating into a new general round of inflation, the administration tried to use adverse publicity to keep wages from rising to offset the higher oil prices.

Many economists agreed that the government should bolster income to prevent a drop in economic activity rather than stand by and allow the increase in oil prices to touch off a severe recession. The result would be more inflation, they conceded, but that would be much better than a rise in unemployment.

"There's no sense in shooting ourselves in the foot to show how much we care about inflation," Arthur Okun said in 1979. "Inflation is a terribly serious problem, but it's not going to be cured by deep recession. Or if it is, the cost may not be worth it."

3

Shaping Budget Policy

Presidents and presidential candidates long have railed at big-spending Congresses and, lately, blamed the size of the budget deficit on the legislative branch. Members of Congress, too, flay themselves for lack of political courage and failure to force the government to live within its means. Some, however, blame a weakness in the procedures Congress has adopted instead of a weakness of will.

But rhetoric notwithstanding, Congress does hold the power of the purse, and the government's revenue cannot be spent until Congress has approved. Through action on the president's annual requests to appropriate money, Congress determines what federal agencies can spend during the upcoming fiscal year, and often for years thereafter. Moreover, by committing the government to meet certain needs of its citizens, Congress has obligated itself to come up with money year after year, no matter what the state of the Treasury. As a result, three-quarters of total annual federal outlays are beyond easy command of either Congress or the president.

"We have a hemorrhaging budget," Rep. Robert N. Giaimo, D-Conn. (1959-1981), observed as he retired from Congress. Giaimo, who had served as chairman of the House Budget Committee, was among the first in Congress to struggle under procedures in effect since 1975 designed to bring sense and a measure of control to the process of shaping budget policy.

His complaint would seem to be understated, coming as it did before $100 billion deficits were dreamed of, much less the record $221.2 billion deficit of 1986. He spoke before the total federal debt reached $1 trillion—and long before that debt exceeded $2.3 trillion, as it did in 1987.

Because Congress has responsibility for passing laws that set budget policy, it may deserve blame for spending and deficit excesses. But that blame must be shared with the president; the federal government is an enormous enterprise that cannot easily be harnessed by the legislative branch, the executive, or both. It is still a simple truth, as political scientist and federal budget expert Aaron Wildavsky observed in 1964, that "the largest determining factor of the size of this year's budget is last year's budget."

President Ronald Reagan's budget request for fiscal 1988 ran more than two thousand pages, comprising four volumes plus multiple supporting documents. It laid out in fine print what the government does and where the administration hoped to take the country. It anticipated a budget deficit in 1988 of $107.8 billion. It did not propose a balanced budget, one where revenues would equal outlays and where the national debt would not grow—except in the dim, optimistic reaches beyond 1992.

Even the president acknowledged the difficulty of bringing spending in line with income. "There is no firm guarantee that progress toward a steadily smaller deficit and eventual budget balance will continue," Reagan said in his 1987 budget message to Congress. "This decline is gradual and vulnerable to potential fiscally irresponsible congressional action on a multitude of spending programs. It is also threatened by the possibility of a less robust economic performance than is projected."

By February 1988, in the fifth month of the 1988 fiscal year, the deficit looked to Reagan more like $146.7 billion than $107.8 billion. That month he proposed a fiscal 1989 budget with a $129.5 billion deficit, almost $37 billion more than he had expected twelve months earlier. And the elusive goal of a balanced budget had retreated to beyond 1993.

Political realities make federal spending decisions rest heavily on the executive as well as the legislative branch.

The president commands the veto and the power to move public opinion. It was public opinion—or the 1980 election's manifestation of it—that led Congress during Reagan's first months in office to cede much of its power to determine the shape of the nation's budget.

That was not the first time Congress had allowed a president considerable latitude to make fiscal policy; Congress first conferred budget-making authority on the president just after World War I. Since 1921 it had left to the executive branch the task of drawing up a yearly federal budget proposing fiscal policy and setting forth revenue, outlay, and deficit or surplus targets.

Much as it has wanted to control the government's purse strings, Congress rarely bothered with overall fiscal policy until 1974. That year, Congress passed and the president signed the Congressional Budget and Impoundment Control Act in an effort to tie separate legislative actions to overall tax and spending totals. That law was the first comprehensive effort by Congress to take hold of the government's budget and its own procedures. In response to some of the perceived shortcomings of the 1974 budget act, and the shortcomings of congressional will to reduce the deficit, the law was amended by the Balanced Budget and Emergency Deficit Control Act of 1985. Commonly called the Gramm-Rudman antideficit act, the 1985 law set statutory limits on the size of the budget deficit and made other procedural changes. Portions of Gramm-Rudman were declared unconstitutional by the Supreme Court in 1986, and the law was amended in 1987 by Gramm-Rudman II—the optimistically named Balanced Budget and Emergency Deficit Control Reaffirmation Act.

The Constitution, while granting the government impressive financial powers, does not specifically require it to keep an annual budget. But over time both Congress and presidents have seen the need for budgets as tools for planning and political control. Over the last seven decades, presidents have used budget-making powers that Congress conferred to tighten the White House grip on the far-flung departments and agencies of government.

Today, although the president can propose a budget, more often than not his blueprint is changed by events and congressional decisions. However, usually such changes are at the margins.

Sometimes a president has seized the upper hand, as did Richard Nixon, who repeatedly chose simply to ignore congressional intent and refused outright to spend billions of dollars in appropriated money. Congress eventually rebelled, enacting constraints on executive branch authority to "impound" appropriations and creating for itself new procedures and obligations for writing a budget. Reagan also took the initiative. But after yielding at first to him, Republicans and Democrats in Congress became concerned that they were losing their dominant role. And bipartisan worries about the efficacy of the administration's tax and spending plans put an end to blind acquiescence in executive branch budget demands.

Yet, throughout Reagan's two terms, Congress's efforts to retain superiority have been tempered by a strong measure of executive will—primarily against tax increases. It may be Congress's right to make spending and taxing decisions, but the executive still plays a guiding role.

The Power of the Purse

The congressional power of the purse is firmly rooted in the Constitution adopted in 1789. Article I, which spells out the powers of the legislative branch, grants Congress authority to raise revenues through taxes, tariffs, and other levies; to direct the spending of the funds raised; and to borrow money on the nation's credit:

• Section 8, Paragraph 1 grants Congress the power "to lay and collect taxes, duties, imposts and excises, to pay the debts and provide for the common defense and general welfare of the United States. . . ."

• Section 8, Paragraph 2 grants Congress the power "to borrow money on the credit of the United States."

• Section 9, Paragraph 7 declares that "no money shall be drawn from the Treasury, but in consequence of appropriations made by law. . . ."

The taxing power is specific, and it was vastly enlarged in 1913 by the Sixteenth Amendment authorizing a federal tax on incomes. Over the years, Congress devised a tax system that in 1988 raised $909 billion, not quite half from individual income taxes. (For a fuller discussion of the tax power, see Chapter 4.)

The spending power was described by congressional historian George B. Galloway in 1955 as "the constitutional birthright of Congress." The spending power is more vague, but it has been enlarged by expansive interpretation of the other authorities that the Constitution grants to Congress. For fiscal 1988, total federal outlays swelled beyond $1.06 trillion.

The borrowing power carries no constitutional restrictions at all, allowing Congress to borrow any amount of money for any purpose. With the budget in deficit for fifty of the fifty-seven fiscal years from 1931 through 1987, Congress ran up a national debt that was expected to exceed $2.8 trillion by midyear 1989.

Those enormous sums may be beyond the grasp of most Americans, including presidents and members of Congress. Indeed, Reagan probably had no idea how understated was the forecast in his first economic policy address to Congress in February 1981. In it he said: "Before we reach the day when we can reduce the debt ceiling we may in spite of our best efforts see a national debt in excess of a trillion dollars. Now this is a figure literally beyond our comprehension."

The Power to Spend

The Constitution sets few specific limits on the spending power. The paragraph that gives Congress the authority to vote appropriations goes on to require that "a regular statement and account of the receipts and expenditures of all public money shall be published from time to time." Elsewhere, Article I, Section 8, Paragraph 12 prohibits appropriating money "to raise and support armies" for longer than two years.

Besides those explicit powers, the Constitution implies much more authority to spend government revenues. It directs the government to perform various functions—establish post offices, roads, armed forces, and courts and take a decennial census—that could be done only by spending money. And by authorizing Congress to collect taxes "to pay the debts and provide for the common defense and general welfare of the United States," the Constitution opened the way for expansive interpretation of the congressional power to spend money to address a growing nation's changing problems and challenges.

When the Republic was founded, political leaders differed over what spending for the general welfare meant. One strict interpretation, voiced by James Madison in *The Federalist*, insisted that such outlays were limited to the purposes connected with the powers specifically mentioned by the Constitution. A looser construction, advocated by Alexander Hamilton, contended that the general welfare clause conferred upon the government powers separate and different from those specifically enumerated in the Constitution. Under the latter interpretation the federal government was potentially far more powerful than the strict constructionists intended; in fact, it was something more than a government of delegated powers.

Deep disagreement about the extent of congressional spending powers continued well into the twentieth century. The broad interpretation came to be the generally accepted view, but it was not until 1936 that the Supreme Court had an opportunity to give its opinion on the meaning of the controversial wording.

In a decision that year (*United States v. Butler*) the court invalidated the Agricultural Adjustment Act of 1933, which had provided federal payments to farmers who participated in a program of production control for the purposes of price stabiliza-

tion. Although this law was held unconstitutional, the court construed the general welfare clause to mean that the congressional power to spend was not limited by the direct grants of legislative power found in the Constitution. Instead, an expenditure was constitutional "so long as the welfare at which it is aimed can be plausibly represented as national rather than local."

The 1933 law was overturned on other grounds but was later reenacted on a different constitutional basis and was sustained by the court. Further decisions in the years immediately following *Butler* upheld the tax provisions of the new Social Security Act, thus confirming the broad scope of the general welfare clause.

History of Appropriations

Before World War I, neither the expenditures nor the revenues of the federal government exceeded $800 million a year. No comprehensive system of budgeting had been developed, although the methods of handling money had undergone various shifts within Congress. During the pre-Civil War period, both taxing and spending bills were handled in the House by the Ways and Means Committee. That eventually proved too difficult a task for a single committee, and in 1865 the House Appropriations Committee was created. A similar situation existed in the Senate, where an Appropriations Committee was created in 1867.

In later years, however, both the House and Senate dispersed appropriations power to other committees as well. Between 1877 and 1885 the House took jurisdiction over eight of fourteen annual appropriations bills from the Appropriations Committee and placed those measures under the purview of other panels. The Senate eventually followed the House lead in reducing the authority of what members considered excessively independent appropriations panels. The division of labor gave committees most familiar with government programs the power over appropriations for them. But that divided responsibility also frustrated any unified control over government financial policy.

After World War I, Congress again consolidated appropriations powers while giving the executive branch stronger budgeting capabilities. The House in 1920 restored to the Appropriations Committee exclusive appropriations authority, and the Senate in 1922 gave similar power over spending measures to its Appropriations panel. What evolved from those steps was a two-stage process by which legislative committees now draft bills authorizing federal programs and the Appropriations panels draft bills specifying exactly how much will be spent to carry them out.

Through the budget procedures it began using in 1975, Congress has set overall spending goals to guide its appropriations deliberations. But Congress never votes on a government agency's planned expenditures as such. What Congress acts on are requests for new spending or budget authority, the legal permission for agencies to enter into contractural obligations to make immediate or future payments of money from the Treasury.

Most agency budget authority is provided through appropriations bills. Most, though not all, of that authority is used by agencies to spend money during the fiscal year. Some budget authority results in outlays only during later years—often on major construction projects, such as aircraft carriers, that require long lead time. Additional spending during the fiscal year comes from unused budget authority approved by Congress and the president in previous years—or from permanent appropriations and various other "backdoor spending" devices that legislators have used to circumvent the annual appropriations process. (See Figure 3-1.)

Authorization Bills First

By its own rules, Congress cannot consider appropriations for a federal program until the president has signed a bill into law authorizing its functions during the fiscal year. The House has had a rule since 1837 that provides that "no appropriation shall be reported in any general appropriations bill, or be in order as an amendment thereto, for any expenditure not previously authorized by law." There are some exceptions, such as a portion of the annual military spending that is authorized by the Constitution, and in recent times the rule has been waived often, but generally appropriations must await authorizations.

This requirement has led to conflict in Congress on numerous occasions. In the 1950-1970 period, Congress required to be authorized annually more and more programs that previously had permanent or multiyear authorizations. The trend to annual authorizations represented a victory for the legislative committees—in particular the Education and Labor Committee in the House—which believed they had lost effective control over programs ostensibly under their jurisdiction to the Appropriations panels, which could make year-to-year changes in spending levels. By the same token, the Appropriations committees, particularly in the House, took a dim view of annual authorizations, in part because they tended in some degree to diminish their power.

In more recent years, multiyear authorizations have regained their popularity. This is especially true for major social programs, such as those for elementary and secondary education or farm price supports. But the entire defense budget, nearly a third of the government's spending, is subject to annual authorizations and appropriations, as is foreign aid and spending for dozens of agencies.

Conflicts over annual authorizations continue. In the case of defense, for example, as the Reagan administration sought to increase the size of the military, the authorization-appropriation dance occasionally led

Figure 3-1   Sources of Spending

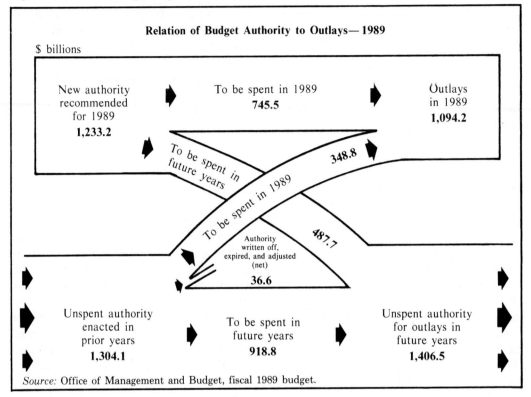

One difficulty of understanding the federal government's budget is that it carries appropriated money on its books for years without spending it.

Less than two-thirds of the new budget authority requested for fiscal 1989 was planned to be spent in that year. The rest was to be carried forward for future years. In fact, for fiscal 1989 the amount of retained, unspent budget authority from prior years slightly exceeded requested new budget authority (see figure above). And that pool of money available for future spending was to grow by almost 8 percent during the year, even though a portion was to be siphoned off for fiscal 1989. There are several reasons for the disparity between appropriations (new budget authority) and outlays (actual spending):

• Construction. Money for most federal contracts for procurement and construction—for everything from submarines and missiles to office buildings—is appropriated at the beginning of a project. As a construction project is completed, payments are made on the contract from the original appropriation.

• Loans and Insurance. Direct loans, guaranteed loans, and federal insurance funds (such as those protecting farmers' crops) are often financed in advance for several years or have money appropriated in addition to expected outlays to cover contingencies.

• Trust Funds. Probably the largest single contributor to the disparity between appropriations and outlays is the money held in trust by the government for specific purposes. The largest of these trust funds are set up to pay for the Social Security retirement and disability programs and the Medicare health program for the elderly. Since 1983, when Congress enacted major increases in Social Security taxes, these trust funds have been developing very large surpluses for the early years in the twenty-first century when the "baby boom" generation retires. Spending for the Social Security and Medicare trust funds is permanently appropriated and matches the taxes collected for those funds and their annual earnings. Other trust funds that are financed by special taxes pay for federal highway and local airport construction. These trust funds are also for the most part permanently appropriated.

In virtually all cases, budget authority carried forward is earmarked for specific, identified future uses and cannot be easily diverted for other programs.

to multiple fights in a single year on such contentious issues as the president's proposed strategic defense initiative—a space-based antiballistic missile system, popularly called "star wars."

And the difficulty of enacting authorizations and appropriations for foreign aid led Congress to dodge those authorizations through most of the Reagan administration. Congress managed to enact a two-year authorization for foreign aid programs in 1981. But it failed in successive years until 1985, when another two-year measure was enacted. Congress failed again in 1987. In that instance, and in other cases where authorizations have expired but Congress wanted the programs to continue, it merely put the money in a continuing appropriations resolution, which has also become the main vehicle for making appropriations. A continuing resolution is not considered a "general" appropriations bill subject to the rule prohibiting authorizing language on a spending bill.

The Appropriations Process

The Constitution requires that the House originate tax bills, but it contains no specific langauge to that effect concerning appropriations. However, the House traditionally has assumed the responsibility for initiating all appropriations and has jealously guarded this self-assumed prerogative whenever the Senate has attempted (as it has from time to time) to encroach upon it.

In the mid- and late-1980s, as protracted budget battles have pushed enactment of appropriations later and later into the year, the Senate Appropriations Committee has taken to acting on some spending bills before its House counterpart. However, the Senate has not taken them up on the floor before the House acted. In 1987, for instance, the Department of Agriculture appropriations bill was approved by the Senate panel October 16—more than two weeks into the start of the fiscal year it was

to cover, and four days before the House committee acted. And in 1984 the Senate committee approved the foreign aid appropriations measure almost three months before the House committee acted; in the two prior years the Senate panel approved foreign aid spending bills and the House panel never did.

Though somewhat less true than in earlier years, the bulk of basic appropriations decisions are made in the House committee. The general shape of any appropriations bill is derived from House consideration of the measure; what the Senate does in effect is to review the House action and make changes in the allotments accorded government agencies by the House. The Senate is free to make alterations as it deems necessary, but important changes usually are limited to revisions in the financing for a relatively small number of significant or controversial government programs.

House procedure on appropriations bills permits amendments from the floor, unlike other legislative measures, for which floor debate and amendments are often closely controlled. However, the power and prestige of the House Appropriations Committee is such that few major changes are ever made.

By and large, the amounts endorsed by the Appropriations Committee during the post-World War II period have been accepted by the House. Administration efforts to restore spending that the House committee cut have been concentrated on the Senate; during the Reagan years, however, the Senate often was no more amenable to administration requests. Nevertheless, most appropriations bills carry larger total amounts when they pass the Senate than when they passed the House, probably as a result of the Senate's more open procedure for floor amendments. The differences are resolved in conference, generally by splitting the difference between the two chambers.

Appropriations Committees' Power

The 1974 budget act gave Congress a process for debating the president's budget as a whole. But the House and Senate still act on budget details in piecemeal fashion, through multiple individual appropriations bills and often one or two midyear "supplemental" measures. The Gramm-Rudman amendments and other procedural changes have attempted to clamp down on the appropriations process. But true power to shape actual spending remains fragmented among the House and Senate Appropriations subcommittees.

Since 1968 there have been thirteen regular appropriations bills and thirteen parallel subcommittees in each chamber to handle them. In the House, Appropriations Committee members sit on that panel alone, as do those on the Rules and Ways and Means committees (except for the few designated to represent their panels on the Budget Committee). House Appropriations members therefore generally are better able to develop expertise than are senators, who are spread more thinly among committees. Few in Congress have an opportunity to become expert at appropriations work. Consequently, the subcommittees, and particularly their chairmen, wield substantial power over spending.

Before 1970, House Appropriations subcommittee hearings were traditionally closed, with testimony almost always restricted to that given by agency officials. A voluminous record of the hearings, along with the parent committee's report, usually was not made public until shortly before House floor action on an appropriation bill. As a result, few if any members not on the subcommittee were prepared to challenge the bill.

The Legislative Reorganization Act of 1970 required that all House committee and subcommittee hearings be open, except if a majority explicitly determines other-

wise. In 1974 the Appropriations Committee opened 90 percent of its hearings but closed almost half of its markup sessions—meetings where legislative decisions are made. Nine of the House panel's thirteen subcommittees opened all of their markups in 1974, compared with only two in 1973.

By the 1980s, only the rarest of hearings—usually involving national security—were closed, but perhaps half of all House subcommittee sessions at which appropriations bills were written or marked up were still behind locked doors. Those markup sessions that were not formally closed—including those of the full committee—were often in rooms so small that few spectators could attend. Moreover, there frequently was no background material so that those reporters or lobbyists who could get in could not easily follow along.

In 1987 House Appropriations Committee chairman Jamie L. Whitten, D-Miss. (1941-   ), a crusty Southerner whose often incomprehensible drawl contributed to spectator difficulties, defended his committee's procedures. Closed meetings are better, he said, because "people will give you their opinion more honestly." And, he said, briefing papers must be withheld because often "something unexpected needs to be corrected."

In the Senate, other than for discussions on matters of national security, appropriations subcommittees rarely close their doors to the public.

At the start of the Ninety-fourth Congress (1975-1977), House Democrats approved steps to weaken the independent power of conservative Appropriations Committee chairman George Mahon, D-Texas (1935-1979), and other senior Democrats who chaired Appropriations subcommittees. After 1975 the caucus of all House Democrats had to approve all subcommittee chairmen. (Although they controlled the Senate from 1981 to 1987, Republicans had not held a majority of the House since 1954, and thus had no say in committee or subcommittee chairmanships.)

The caucus also voted to limit senior Democrats to serving on only two subcommittees of the same committee. Aimed mainly at the Appropriations Committee, that rule was intended to keep senior, and often more conservative, members from continuing to dominate key subcommittees that handle defense, agriculture, and health, education, and labor spending.

The Growth of Continuing Resolutions

In part because Congress must reauthorize some programs during each session, and in part because spending decisions involve a fair amount of political brinkmanship, since 1948 Congress has finished work on all appropriations before the start of the fiscal year only two times, in 1976 and 1988. But even in those two years the bills did not reach the president's desk in time to signed into law before the start of the fiscal year. Often only one or two of the dozen or more regular appropriations bills (the number is currently thirteen, but it changes periodically) were enacted on time.

In the 1974 budget act, Congress pushed the start of the fiscal year back by three months from July 1 to October 1 and set deadlines of May 15 for legislative committees to report authorization bills and mid-September for Congress to complete action on all appropriations. Even with more time, however, Congress has continued to slip badly behind schedule in considering spending bills. Gramm-Rudman struck the authorization bill deadline and set June 30 as the deadline for the House to finish work on appropriations. Although Gramm-Rudman technically prohibited the House from adjourning for more than three consecutive days in July until it had completed action on all appropriations bills, the rule was not enforced before 1989.

As a result, the government has frequently begun the fiscal year without most spending measures in place. Congress has gotten around the problem by adopting so-called continuing resolutions—or CRs, for short. These measures, named because they are introduced as joint resolutions (which have the same legislative status as House or Senate bills), allow agencies to keep spending money for some specified period—often only for a few days—usually at the level that Congress provided for the previous fiscal year.

If appropriations, short- or long-term, are not enacted on time, the government presumably must shut down. For years, the executive branch occasionally shifted resources to cover gaps when all appropriations were not in place for a few days. But in 1980 Attorney General Benjamin R. Civiletti ruled that nonessential costs could not be incurred in the absence of enacted appropriations, and one agency, the Federal Trade Commission, was shut down for a few hours. In 1981, after Reagan vetoed a full-year continuing resolution for virtually the entire government, federal workers were sent home, the Statue of Liberty and Washington Monument were closed to visitors, and the Constitution was lowered into its protective vault at the National Archives. A short-term continuing resolution expired in 1984, and Reagan again sent federal workers home.

In September 1981, with none of its thirteen regular appropriations bills cleared in time for fiscal 1982 to begin October 1, Congress first extended spending authority for government agencies with a short-term CR for fifty days into the new fiscal year. Failing to finish by mid-November, Congress then extended most spending with a second stop-gap bill until mid-December. In 1987, it took four temporary measures to carry the government until December 22, when a full-year CR was finally signed into law. In every year from 1954 through 1987, Congress had to enact at least one special or omnibus CR, and frequently there were as many as five in one year; no CR was required in 1988.

Expanded Role of CRs

The process of buying time with continuing resolutions so that Congress can finish its appropriations work dates at least to 1876, according to the Congressional Research Service. But since 1975, continuing resolutions have acquired a much more important and broadening role. They have been used to pay for certain agencies for a full year, not merely a few days, weeks, or months.

More significantly, because full-year appropriations must eventually be enacted into law, these measures have begun serving as legislative vehicles for bills that might otherwise have been subject to veto, filibuster, or other jeopardizing tactics.

A full-year continuing resolution for fiscal 1985, for example, carried with it a sweeping modification of federal criminal law that had been on the drafting boards since 1973. The same bill contained a provision—the Boland amendment—cutting off U.S. government aid to the contra rebels fighting the Marxist government of Nicaragua; it was that provision that became a focus of heated congressional inquiries in 1986 and 1987 into contra assistance that possibly violated the law and into related arms sales to Iran.

Putting aside the use of continuing resolutions as engines to pull other legislative trains, the expanded role of CRs peaked when the measures were used to finance all appropriations. Before 1987, continuing resolutions often bundled a half-dozen or more uncompleted appropriations bills into one, huge package. For fiscal 1987 and again for fiscal 1988, all thirteen regular appropriations bills were swept into single continuing resolutions that appropriated $576 billion for 1987 and $604 billion for 1988. (Though huge, and by far the largest spending measures in the nation's history,

they did not account for all federal spending. Some sizable programs, Social Security and interest payments on the federal debt, for example, are not subject to annual appropriations.)

Good Policy or Bad?

Critics from Reagan to congressional leaders—Democrats and Republicans—have objected to the use of continuing resolutions to finance full-year government spending.

The criticisms range from the specific—for fiscal 1988, an $8 million appropriation for a school for North African Jews in Paris went unnoticed until the measure was law—to the general: "There is no question in my mind that this is a lousy way to do business," complained Rep. Leon E. Panetta, Jr., D-Calif. (1977-), in 1986. "You just can't put that much spending in one bill with one up-or-down vote and do your work responsibly."

In signing the 1988 measure and a companion deficit-cutting bill on December 22, 1987, Reagan echoed Panetta. "Wrapping up the entire legislative business of our country into two, 1,000-page bills on the eve of Christmas is not the way to do business." And in his State of the Union address the following month, Reagan drew loud, bipartisan applause when he dropped the two thirty-pound documents on the Speaker's rostrum in the House chamber with a loud thud and professed never again would he sign such a bill.

In Congress, embarrassment over the money for the Paris school led to quick enactment of a bill repealing that appropriation. And Democrats and Republicans alike—for varied reasons, political and practical—said they, too, would fight in the future against the legislative logrolling embodied in huge continuing resolutions. Some heard a death knell in the announcement by the House Democratic leadership in February 1988 of its intent to move all thirteen appropriations bills early and separately.

But similar promises had been made before, and some observed that the protests may have been more for political gain than heartfelt. The intentional combining of all thirteen regular appropriations bills for 1987 and 1988 served the aim of providing a clear picture of the magnitude of total appropriations—and a way to measure progress in holding down spending—something that is much more difficult when thirteen bills move independently.

A single omnibus appropriations measure is not a new idea, and some budget process critics even suggest that it makes sense. "In some respects it makes it easier to see the dollars, to look at the goals under Gramm-Rudman and see how we're doing," observed Susan Joy of the nonpartisan Committee for a Responsible Federal Budget in 1986.

In 1950, during an earlier congressional effort at spending restraint, a new appropriations process was established requiring one omnibus bill. A single bill was enacted for fiscal 1951, the first time the entire government had been financed with one measure since 1793. But the process, and a fight over water projects, nearly brought the House and Senate Appropriations chairmen to blows. Rep. Clarence Andrew Cannon, D-Mo. (1923-1964), who was seventy-one at the time, and Sen. Kenneth Douglas McKellar, D-Tenn. (House 1911-1917; Senate 1917-1953), who was eighty-one, had to be separated by their colleagues. The process, however, was abandoned the following year. "So far as I know, it was the most terrible experience I have had in my whole life," McKellar said.

Whether intended or not, the act of financing fiscal 1987 through one omnibus bill might have helped stem the deficit's growth. In 1987 total federal government outlays grew by only 1.1 percent, after averaging 9.9 percent from 1960 to 1986 and 9.0 percent through Reagan's first six years.

The political and practical pressure to meet the fiscal 1987 Gramm-Rudman deficit target was certainly significant, but some congressional observers suggested that the single appropriations measure was an important factor in a year of rising prices. (By one measure inflation was 3.7 percent in calendar 1987, and only 1.9 percent in 1986.)

Beyond providing a tally against which spending and deficit targets can be compared, a single spending bill also is a useful political tool—for wedging in favors and forcing compromises; the threat that a veto could cause the government to shut down is real to the president and Congress.

In the 1988 measure, both Reagan and congressional Democrats won victories. Reagan, for instance, won an additional $14 million for the contra rebels in Nicaragua. He also forced Congress to drop a provision that would have written into law a thirty-eight-year-old Federal Communications Commission (FCC) rule requiring broadcasters to air all sides of contentious issues. The FCC had decided to drop the so-called fairness doctrine, and Reagan had vetoed a bill earlier in the year to restore the rule.

Democrats, on the other hand, won limits on the contra aid, preventing it from being used to buy "lethal" arms. And spending for education was higher and defense lower than Reagan would have preferred. In short, both Reagan and Congress found advantages in a single appropriations bill.

Backdoor Spending

Although appropriations would, by their nature, seem to be controllable by a Congress and a president, in fact less than half of all appropriations can be altered without also changing the authorization laws that created them.

The costs of Medicaid, the health program for the poor, and Aid to Families with

Dependent Children, the chief federal-state welfare program, are not easily controlled. The same goes for farm price supports and Guaranteed Student Loans. All are big chunks of the budget and all are appropriated, but Congress is obliged to pay these programs' bills and appropriate more if money runs out midyear.

All are "relatively uncontrollable" expenditures in the parlance of federal budget aficionados. So, too, are Social Security and Medicare, two programs that aid the elderly. But these are not even subject to annual appropriations; their appropriations are permanent. The Treasury is obliged to pay the bills as long as there is money in the coffers.

Congress deliberately authorized some uncontrollable or "backdoor" spending simply because it believed that the government must shield certain obligations from yearly political controversy. An example of that kind of spending is the permanent appropriation, enacted in 1847, to pay interest as it comes due on the national debt. The government must meet that obligation to retain its borrowing credibility.

For other programs, Congress set up backdoor financing requirements to shield their spending from annual scrutiny from conservative Appropriations committees, which for years were dominated by rural southerners. Other congressional committees, particularly those that authorized social programs providing benefits primarily to urban areas, often bypassed the normal appropriations procedures by writing spending obligations into the original authorizing bills.

Backdoor spending obligations take several forms. For some programs, Congress authorized agencies to enter contracts, borrow money, or guarantee loans that eventually obligate the government to make payments. And Congress excluded some quasi-government agencies—such as the Postal Service—from the annual federal budget, effectively exempting them from overall fiscal controls. (The Gramm-Rudman antideficit law brought the Postal Service and other off-budget spending back under the budget process umbrella. Social Security, however, was taken off budget, except that its revenues and spending are taken into account in deficit calculations. Despite the program's enormous expenditures, Social Security revenues after 1983 were much larger, leading to the appearance overall of a smaller budget deficit.)

Backdoor spending devices in effect in 1987 had removed more than 75 percent of federal spending from real control by annual appropriations measures. Much is not even subject to appropriations, since Social Security payments and interest on the debt are the second and third largest items in the budget, behind defense. The fiscal 1988 continuing appropriations resolution was expected to yield outlays of $593.2 billion; total outlays for the year were more than at $1.06 trillion.

About 17 percent of the money the government spends each year fulfills contracts and obligations that agencies entered into in previous years. And a growing proportion of outlays—almost 50 percent in the late 1980s—now is set aside to meet entitlement and other open-ended commitments the government has made through fixed provisions that Congress previously wrote into law.

Entitlements Surge

By far the largest backdoor outlays resulted from the tremendous growth of federal entitlement programs—so-called because Congress by law entitled their recipients to the benefits the government programs provide.

Federal entitlement programs range from massive ones such as Social Security, Medicare, and interest on the national debt to relatively tiny ones such as an indemnity program for dairy farmers whose milk is contaminated by chemicals or other toxic substances. Federal programs are entitlements if they provide benefits for which the recipients—individuals or, in some cases, government agencies—have a legally enforceable right.

Each entitlement is a benefit that some past Congress deemed so important that it bound the federal government to pay it, with the threat of judicial action, if necessary, to force Uncle Sam to write the check. Entitlements are not totally uncontrollable; Congress can change the basic laws that set them up. However, such changes are politically difficult. The reconciliation process created by the 1974 budget act is a tool to accomplish just that aim—trimming entitlements. Some such programs, however, Social Security in particular, have remained effectively immune.

Moreover, many cash entitlements, from Social Security to federal government workers' pensions, are indexed to inflation; their benefits increase annually as the Consumer Price Index or some other measure of the cost of living rises. Other federal spending, particularly the two main health care programs—Medicare and Medicaid—essentially are in-kind payments to citizens. Their costs are reimbursed through formulas that are not indexed but must nevertheless be adjusted upward as costs to those who provide the services rise.

Though indexing is designed to protect beneficiaries from inflation, it runs counter to federal efforts to restrain inflationary pressures. Indexing increases federal spending at precisely the time that traditional fiscal policy calls for budgetary restraint to curtail demand for goods and services and encourage lower prices. That can cause prices to rise. But indexing also makes it easier for Congress to avoid the pressure of annual votes to increase benefits—pressure that might lead to enactment of higher benefits than the inflation index would require.

Contracts and Borrowing

Entitlements are not the only form of government spending that is relatively uncontrollable by Congress. While entitlements constitute by far the largest portion of uncontrollable outlays, other forms of backdoor spending still take up about one-sixth of the total.

The 1974 budget act limited some types of backdoor spending, but there are still a great number of existing or potential federal obligations that the government at some point may have to pay off.

Before the 1974 budget act, a favorite form of backdoor spending was the use of contract authority, which allows agencies to enter into contracts without immediately providing money to pay the debts incurred. When the bills do come due, Congress has no choice but to provide the money.

The budget act required that new contract authority be subject to the appropriations process. But this new authority did not affect existing authority, which agencies could continue to use to enter into contracts. According to a 1976 study, more than $200 billion in existing contract authority could be used in the future. Moreover, the budget act exempted some new contract authority from appropriations.

Likewise, some agencies have long had unbridled authority to borrow, from the Treasury or the public; Congress must approve spending to pay off the debts incurred.

Like contract authority, new borrowing authority was sharply limited by the budget act. But there is a large volume of past authority that can still be used. In 1982 Federal agencies had about $90 billion in specific unused borrowing authority, which could be used without congressional action. In addition, agencies such as the Farmers Home Administration and Federal Housing Administration can borrow unlimited amounts from the Treasury.

Federal Credit

The federal government is not only a big spender in its own right, it is also the nation's largest supplier of credit. The government was owed $252 billion in direct loans at the end of 1986, and another $450 billion in outstanding, privately originated loans were backed by government guarantees. Moreover, government-sponsored enterprises had lent another $453 billion.

Over time, the makeup of the direct and guaranteed loan program has varied dramatically. Direct loans to business have shrunk to less than 40 percent of the total; they were almost twice that in the early 1960s. But loans to farmers—the bulk of price-support payments are loans—topped $26.6 billion in 1986 and are almost 60 percent of all direct loans.

Students and businesses hold slightly less than 20 percent of guaranteed loans; housing—mostly mortgages backed by the Veterans Administration and the Federal Housing Administration—makes up the balance.

Federal credit activity rose dramatically in the 1970s, as the volume of direct loans by the government and federal guarantees of private loans increased. During the decade, Congress also authorized use of the government's credit to finance a growing number of projects, such as synthetic fuels, nuclear fuel, and Earth-orbiting satellite development, and to bail out financially troubled New York City, Lockheed Corp., and Chrysler Corp.

The government provides credit in four forms:

- Direct loans of government cash, secured by land or promises to repay the government.
- Loan guarantees made when a federal agency pledges to use government money to repay a private lender if a borrower defaults.
- Loan insurance through which a federal agency protects lenders against default by pooling risks and charging premiums.
- Tax-exempt status for interest paid by state and local governments on bonds. The use of such bonds to raise capital for private industrial, housing, hospital, and pollution control investments has been sharply curtailed in recent years, particularly by the Tax Reform Act of 1986.

Guaranteed loans have appeal over direct loans because they allow Congress to encourage the flow of capital to a desirable enterprise without using federal dollars and, therefore, without any initial cost. But loan guarantees are particularly uncontrollable, because spending is dependent on the financial health of millions of borrowers, large and small. Each default on a loan creates an unavoidable obligation on the government.

Not all federal credit results in government outlays, since many loans are repaid with interest. In some cases, however, borrowers are so likely to default that the awarding of credit amounts to direct federal grants. Education loans have been subject to particularly high default rates, and defaults by farmers on their crop loans are an accepted way of life; it is merely the way the government keeps a price floor under those crops.

Under many loan programs, the government provides subsidies through below-market interest rates or easy repayment terms that also are the equivalent of outlays.

The Power to Borrow

As rapidly as federal revenues have grown, they have not kept up with the increase in spending. As a result, the government since the 1930s has broken away from a longstanding practice of keeping the federal budget in balance except in times of war. In the process, Congress has expanded use of its power to borrow money on the nation's credit.

The borrowing power is extensive. In their *Introduction to American Government,* Frederic A. Ogg and P. Orman Ray noted that the "power to borrow not only is expressly conferred in the Constitution, but is one of the very few federal powers entirely unencumbered by restrictions—with the result that Congress may borrow from any lenders, for any purposes, in any amounts, on any terms, and with or without provision for the repayment of loans, with or without interest."

Ogg and Ray noted also that the United States has no constitutional debt limit, whereas many state constitutions and state charters for local governments impose debt ceilings. The United States has had a statutory debt ceiling for many decades, but the ceiling can be easily altered by Congress and, in fact, has been raised repeatedly—although seldom without an intense political fight in Congress.

Through much of the nation's history, a surplus resulting from an excess of revenues over expenditures has been used, at least in part, to reduce outstanding debt. Since the long string of federal budget deficits began in fiscal 1931, there have been budget surpluses in only seven years, the last in 1969.

Philosophy Prior to the 1930s

Throughout most of the nation's history, the principal concern of government in regard to budget policy was to assure that revenues were sufficient to meet expenditure requirements. This practice of an approximate balance between receipts and outlays was generally accepted from the beginning until the early 1930s.

Lewis H. Kimmel described the philosophy in *Federal Budget and Fiscal Policy, 1789-1958:* "At the outset, acceptance of the balanced budget philosophy was facilitated by the adverse financial experience during the Revolutionary War and under the Articles of Confederation. There was an awareness that the public credit is a valuable resource, especially in an emergency."

Moreover, according to Kimmel, federal officials and economists alike during the period leading up to the Civil War generally believed that a low level of public expenditures was desirable, that the federal budget should be balanced in time of peace, and that the federal debt should be reduced and eventually extinguished. "These ideas," he observed, "were a reflection of views that were deeply rooted in the social fabric."

This pay-as-you-go philosophy held until the Civil War, which, like major wars of modern times, resulted in a much enlarged national debt. The reported debt in 1866 amounted to almost $2.8 billion in contrast to less than $90.6 million in 1861. The debt was gradually reduced after the war to a low of $961 million in 1893. However, after the Civil War, there was less concern about eliminating the outstanding debt; increasingly, the emphasis was on servicing the debt in an orderly manner. Proposals to liquidate it became fewer and fewer.

From the post-Civil War low point in 1893, the debt increased very slowly for half a dozen years and then hovered between $1.1 billion and $1.2 billion until 1917, when the United States entered World War I. The debt jumped from just under $3 billion in fiscal 1917 to a peak of $25.5 billion at the end of fiscal 1919. In the 1920s the debt receded steadily, year by year, down to $16.2 billion at the end of fiscal 1930.

Rise of the Debt

British economist John Maynard Keynes justified peacetime deficits—which he said were needed to ensure stable economic growth—just as the government saw a need for economic stimulus during the Great Depression. As a result, the government abandoned the former insistence on balancing revenues and outlays.

Of the early years of the Depression,

Kimmel noted that a concerted effort was made by the president and the leadership of both parties in Congress to adhere to the balanced-budget philosophy. "Yet a balanced federal budget was almost impossible to attain," he said. "The annually balanced-budget dogma in effect gave way to necessity."

The practice of using the federal budget to help solve national economic problems was found increasingly acceptable. Budget deficits and a rapidly growing national debt were the result. The debt rose to nearly $50 billion—almost twice the World War I peak—at the end of fiscal 1941. Then came Pearl Harbor.

The debt passed the $100 billion mark in fiscal 1943 and exceeded $269 billion in fiscal 1946. No steady reduction followed World War II. The debt total fluctuated for a few years but then began a new rise that took it past the World War II peak in fiscal 1954, past $300 billion in fiscal 1963, and all the way to $475 billion at the end of fiscal 1974—when Congress finally acted to get a rein on spending.

Since then, the debt has increased fivefold. It surpassed the $2 trillion level in 1987 and would hit $2.8 trillion in 1989—as the government ran unprecedented peacetime deficits. The debt would clearly grow well into the future.

Federal Debt Limit

Although it holds the power to borrow, Congress generally has sidestepped responsibility for a mounting federal debt. By permanently appropriating payments for interest owed by the government, Congress has spared members the pain of voting each year to set money aside for that purpose. And only since 1975 have the House and Senate gone on record on the level of deficit for each fiscal year projected by congressional budget resolutions.

The debt itself consists of various types of obligations, "public debt" issued by the Treasury and "agency debt" issued directly by agencies (or since 1973 by the Federal Financing Bank on their behalf). Treasury and agency securities are sold in a variety of denominations and maturities, mostly to the public. But an increasingly large share of the federal debt is "sold" to government trust funds, which by law must be invested in government securities.

About 18 percent of the total federal debt was "owned" by federal government trust funds at the end of 1986. Most of the rest was owned by U.S. and foreign citizens, except for about 9 percent, which was held in the vaults of the Federal Reserve System and used by the Fed to adjust the money supply. Interest earned on the Fed's holdings is virtually all returned to the Treasury.

Some, but not all, public securities are "marketable"; that is, they can be resold to other investors. Some, like savings bonds, may not be sold but are redeemable for cash or other securities.

Prior to World War I, Congress had to vote separately on every issue of bonds, notes, or other securities issued to finance government activities. Since then, however, there has evolved a statutory limit on the total amount of government borrowing, and the Treasury has been able to sell securities so long as the total debt outstanding did not exceed that ceiling. And as the federal debt continued to rise, the House and Senate have had no choice but to raise the ceiling while members lamented deficit spending.

Congress established the first overall debt ceiling in 1917, when the Second Liberty Bond Act fixed a limit at $11.5 billion. By 1945 Congress had amended that act sixteen times, lifting the ceiling to $300 billion to accommodate World War II borrowing. In 1946 Congress reduced the limit to a "permanent" $275 billion level but soon thereafter added temporary and permanent extensions above that amount.

By 1971 the permanent ceiling had risen to $400 billion, and in 1982 the temporary increase above the permanent ceiling reached $890.2 billion. Congress ended the distinction between permanent and temporary in May 1983, setting a permanent ceiling of $1.389 trillion. In May 1987 the ceiling was raised to $2.8 trillion. With that extension came a congressional repair to certain constitutional problems with the Gramm-Rudman antideficit law and hopes for further downward pressure on the deficit.

Although virtually all government borrowing is covered by the debt limit, a small percentage is not. Borrowing by the Federal Financing Bank, the Tennessee Valley Authority, and a few other agencies is exempt, although most of those agencies have their own statutory borrowing limits. That flexibility became important in late 1985, when the original version of Gramm-Rudman was added as an amendment to a bill increasing the debt limit. The protracted debate over the amendment in a House-Senate conference committee prevented the timely enactment of the debt-ceiling increase, and the Treasury had to engage in some quick tricks to keep the government in business for about a month. One maneuver was to borrow $14.2 billion from the Federal Financing Bank.

A Political Foil

Although Congress actually has had little choice but to increase the statutory debt limit, the heated debates—primarily in the House—suggested that the events were milestones in public financial affairs. The controversy over rising debt ceilings flowed essentially from the broader issue of government spending. Proponents of a statutory debt ceiling saw the ceiling as a form of expenditure control. They believed that a firm commitment by Congress not to increase the debt limit would force a halt in spending, especial-

ly spending that exceeded tax revenues.

Officials in the executive branch responsible for paying the government's bills, as well as many members—indeed, a majority—of Congress, were convinced that a ceiling on the debt could not control expenditures. Throughout the postwar period, secretaries of the Treasury expressed their opposition to use of the debt ceiling for that purpose.

When it came down to actual voting, Congress always has raised the debt limit enough to allow the government to keep borrowing money to finance daily operations (except for the Gramm-Rudman episode in 1985).

Congressional conservatives used the debt-limit debates to throw a spotlight on the deficit and take token stances against rising spending. From time to time, Congress has used debt-limit extensions to carry controversial amendments to the president's desk—most notably the Gramm-Rudman law in 1985 and its successor in 1987. Presidents have been reluctant to veto debt-ceiling increases because the government would be unable to meet its financial obligations and roll over expiring debt if the ceiling were breached.

Since 1979, the House has managed to avoid several votes on raising the debt ceiling. Under a House rule crafted by Rep. Richard A. Gephardt, D-Mo. (1977-   ), when the House has voted to adopt the conference report on a budget resolution, it in effect has also voted on a debt-limit extension sufficient to cover the deficit presumed by the budget resolution.

A joint resolution to raise the debt ceiling is then forwarded to the Senate, which still must vote on it separately. Once the Senate takes action on the debt-limit increase, presuming it has changed it in some way, the measure must go back to the House for its concurrence in the amendment. House leaders still have not found a way to dodge that vote.

Getting a Rein on Spending

The government operated for 132 years without a formal budget. After the Constitution was ratified, Congress in September 1789 established the Treasury Department and directed the secretary to "prepare and report estimates of the public revenues, and the public expenditures." But efforts by Alexander Hamilton, the first Treasury secretary, to set up an executive budget for the government were frustrated, Lewis Kimmel noted, by "congressional jealousy and existing party divisions."

Kimmel contended that "the budget idea ... was clearly in the minds of leading political and financial leaders as early as the Revolutionary and formative periods." But because the government relied on abundant customs receipts for most of its money throughout the nineteenth century, officials felt no need to weigh expenditures against revenues. Such decisions tended, therefore, to be haphazard and uncoordinated; federal agencies for the most part submitted budget requests directly to Congress, seeking whatever sums the agency heads wanted. And budget-making efforts deteriorated until after the turn of the century.

The President's Prerogative

Things changed after World War I. In 1910 President William H. Taft had appointed a Commission on Economy and Efficiency to study the need for a federal budget. The commission concluded that the government's loose system for determining its financial needs and providing money for them should be restructured. But Congress at first resisted the commission's proposal; its report was not even considered by the House Appropriations Committee to which it was referred.

The war had dramatically boosted federal revenue collections and spending. Congress appropriated $6.5 billion for fiscal 1920, the first year after World War I. The amount was nearly ten times the $713 million spent in 1916, the last year before the war. As a result, Congress decided to reorganize the federal financial machinery both to retrench on spending and to tighten control over the execution of fiscal policy.

In the following two years, the House and Senate both gave their respective Appropriations committees exclusive power over federal spending bills. And, in the Budget and Accounting Act of 1921, Congress gave the executive branch new budget-making structures.

The 1921 law required the president to prepare and submit to Congress an annual budget covering actual revenues and expenditures in the most recently completed fiscal year, estimates for the current year, and the administration's proposals for the forthcoming year. The law also created a Bureau of the Budget to strengthen presidential control over fiscal management. Operating under the president's direction, the bureau served as a clearinghouse for budget requests by federal agencies. In that way, Congress denied the agencies the right to go directly to Capitol Hill with their requests.

Budget Circular 49, approved by President Warren G. Harding on December 19, 1921, required that all agency proposals for appropriations be submitted to the president. Agency proposals were to be studied for their relationship to "the president's financial program" and were to be sent on to Capitol Hill only if approved by the president. The bureau, though placed in the Treasury, was kept under the supervision of the president.

Under President Franklin D. Roosevelt and his successors, the bureau became the president's most potent agent in directing the affairs of the executive branch. In 1935 Roosevelt broadened the clearance function to include all substantive policy proposals, as well as appropriations requests. According to presidential scholar Richard E. Neustadt, Roosevelt's new clearance system was not a mere extension of the budget process. "On the contrary ... this was Roosevelt's creation, intended to protect not just his budget, but his prerogatives, his freedom of action, and his choice of policies in an era of fast-growing government and of determined presidential leadership."

Congress in 1939 approved Roosevelt's Reorganization Plan No. 1 creating an executive office of the president. The plan transferred the Budget Bureau from the Treasury to the new White House structure. By presidential directive, Roosevelt also broadened the bureau's clearance function by giving it responsibility for coordinating executive branch views on all measures, not just appropriations bills, that Congress passed and sent to the president to be signed or vetoed. Roosevelt required that any recommendation to veto a bill be accompanied by a draft veto message or memorandum of disapproval in the case of a pocket veto.

From Budget Bureau to OMB

Before World War II, the president's administrative budget largely accounted for the full extent of federal finances. But in the following decades Congress excluded an increasing proportion of federal outlays by separating them from the president's budget. Congress drew a line between revenues that the government owned and those it collected in a fiduciary capacity for the trust funds set up to finance Social Security, civil service retirement, veterans' and other benefits.

It also set apart the earnings and expenditures by government-backed enterprises such as the Post Office Department (much later the quasi-independent Postal Service), Commodity Credit Corporation, Export-Import Bank, Federal National Mortgage Association, Small Business Ad-

ministration, Tennessee Valley Authority, and other ventures established to carry out federal objectives. In addition, the government's role in making direct loans, or guaranteeing or insuring others, was only partially reflected in the budget.

President Lyndon B. Johnson in 1968 expanded his budget to take account of such activities. For decades, observers had contended that the budget documents were too complex and too easily distorted by the party in power to hide information. Johnson, following recommendations made in 1967 by a study commission he had appointed, adopted what became known as the unified budget incorporating trust fund receipts and outlays in computing the federal deficit.

Roosevelt's successors had strengthened White House budget-making procedures. Then, in 1970, President Nixon tightened control over the budgetary process when he set up the Office of Management and Budget (OMB). Nixon's reorganization plan, accepted by Congress that year, built the new office around the nucleus of Budget Bureau experts and transferred to the president all statutory authority previously assigned to the bureau. It also gave OMB sweeping authority to coordinate the way federal agencies carried out White House policies.

By creating OMB, Nixon rearranged the president's relationship with cabinet officers and budget officials for the first time in thirty years. The reorganization plan was suggested by a presidential advisory commission chaired by Litton Industries president Roy L. Ash. In 1972, Ash became the second director of OMB, succeeding George P. Shultz, who had been secretary of labor until his appointment to OMB in 1970 and was leaving to be Treasury secretary.

OMB's responsibilities were extended and greater use made of organization and management systems, development of executive talent and a broader career staff, better dissemination of information, and appropriate use of modern techniques and equipment. The rationale for these changes was to provide greater executive capability for analyzing, coordinating, evaluating, and improving the efficiency of government programs. The new office was to coordinate the complex system of federal grants, which often involved not only more than one federal agency but also state and local agencies and government entities at the state and local levels. But one of its most significant jobs was to evaluate the cost effectiveness of particular programs and the relative priority of needs they were designed to meet.

OMB Draws Fire

The House Government Operations Committee tried unsuccessfully to block the reorganization plan, protesting that transferring the Budget Bureau authority to the president would give him "almost unlimited power to restructure the administration of those functions ... without any action or review by Congress." In 1974, after Nixon used OMB to attempt large-scale cutbacks in federal programs, Congress enacted a law making future directors and deputy directors subject to Senate confirmation.

The Paperwork Reduction Act of 1980 created in OMB an Office of Information and Regulatory Affairs, which almost immediately became the target of new congressional criticism that it was improperly overturning agency regulatory decisions.

The agency's authority was bolstered by two presidential directives. Less than a month after taking office, on February 17, 1981, Reagan issued Executive Order 12291 prohibiting agencies from proposing or issuing rules until OMB had reviewed them and determined that their benefits would exceed their costs. Executive Order 12498, issued in January 1985, extended OMB's reach to "pre-rulemaking activity"—defined as almost any action that

could lead to consideration of the need for a rule. Agencies were required to submit an annual regulatory program for OMB approval and could not take any action not part of that program.

Complaints from members of Congress that significant environmental protection regulations were being delayed or killed by OMB lead to a series of lawsuits, some of them successful, and even efforts to terminate the appropriation or authorization for the regulatory affairs office.

Annual Budget Requests

The president's budget proposal serves as a comprehensive statement of the administration's plans for defending the nation, conducting foreign affairs, and meeting domestic needs. Computing the budget's projected deficit—or, more rarely, its hoped-for surplus—requires the administration to make judgments about the economic state of the country and the need for measures to stimulate growth or retard inflationary pressures.

The complex budget process usually gets under way a year and a half before the fiscal year begins. During the spring before the budget is sent to Congress, the president, OMB, and department officials evaluate proposed and ongoing programs and project economic conditions before setting general budget guidelines. The White House then gives policy directions and planning ceilings to federal agencies to govern preparation of their budget requests.

Through fall and early winter, OMB brings together agency estimates of the money they need to carry out government programs. OMB coordinates those requests with presidential policies and expected revenues. Officials also draw up three-year projections of revenues and outlays to accompany the budget, and they prepare a "current services" budget to indicate what the government would spend if ongoing federal programs remained in place and no new initiatives were undertaken. (Under the 1974 budget act, the current services budget was to be submitted to Congress November 10, and the annual budget request was to be filed in late January. That requirement was changed by Gramm-Rudman to require submission of the current services budget and budget request simultaneously in early January.)

But, like any other budget, that for the federal government is primarily a schedule of estimated receipts and expenditures. It attempts to show, as nearly as can be reliably estimated, what the government will take in and spend during the fiscal year due to commence the following October 1. By the time that fiscal year ends, twenty months after the budget was proposed, actual revenues and outlays may have varied widely from the president's initial projections.

For one thing, the economy's performance can dramatically change budget parameters. If the gross national product rises faster than expected, revenues climb and outlays fall off for countercyclical programs such as unemployment insurance. On the other hand, lagging economic output will undercut revenue estimates while boosting outlays for welfare programs and other government assistance to jobless workers or troubled industries.

For another, Congress holds final authority to alter the president's appropriations requests or to change tax laws to raise or lower revenues. Most often, the administration budget sets the terms for debate and offers starting points for congressional action on agencies' spending requests. Except for the first year of Reagan's presidency, since the early 1970s spending battles with Nixon, Congress has been more determined than ever to dictate federal spending priorities.

Congress's First Budgets

As a deliberative body representing different regions and economic interests,

Congress has always been ambivalent about budget control. In the few instances that the House and Senate voted for overall budget restraints, they were unable or unwilling to cut enough from individual programs to meet those goals. Throughout the postwar years, the momentum of those separate spending decisions sooner or later overwhelmed whatever devices Congress has used to try to keep the budget in check.

Immediately after World War II, Congress attempted to use legislative budget procedures to relate appropriations to overall fiscal objectives. In three years of trying, the House and Senate never fully implemented a legislative budget created by the Legislative Reorganization Act of 1946. After unsuccessful attempts in 1947, 1948, and 1949, Congress abandoned the experiment as an unqualified failure.

Similar in some respects to the reform procedures later adopted by Congress in 1974, the 1946 act required that Congress approve a concurrent resolution setting a maximum amount to be appropriated for each fiscal year. That appropriations ceiling was part of a legislative budget based on revenue and spending estimates prepared by a massive Joint Budget Committee composed of all members of the House and Senate Appropriations committees and of the tax-writing House Ways and Means and Senate Finance committees.

In 1947 House-Senate conferees deadlocked over Senate amendments to the budget resolution providing for use of an expected federal surplus for tax reductions and debt retirement. In 1948 Congress appropriated $6 billion more than its own legislative budget ceiling, and in 1949 the legislative budget never was produced as the process broke down completely.

One of the principal reasons the legislative budget failed was the inability of the Joint Budget Committee to make accurate estimates of spending so early in the session and before individual agency requests had been considered in detail. In addition, the committee was said to be inadequately staffed and, with more than one hundred members, much too unwieldy for effective operation.

Controlling Appropriations

Failure of the legislative budget prompted a serious effort in Congress in 1950 to combine the numerous separate appropriations bills into one omnibus measure. The traditional practice of acting on the separate bills one by one made it difficult to hold total outlays in check.

In 1950 the House Appropriations Committee agreed to give the omnibus-bill plan a trial. The overall bill was passed by Congress about two months earlier than the last of the separate bills had been passed in 1949. The appropriations totaled about $2.3 billion less than the president's budget request. The omnibus approach was praised by many observers and was particularly well received by those seeking reductions in federal spending.

But members were not as pleased about the process, and in January 1951 the House Appropriations Committee voted 31-18 to go back to the traditional method of handling appropriations bills separately. Two years later, in 1953, the Senate proposed a return to the omnibus plan, but the House did not respond. The plan was dead. Opponents said the omnibus bill required more time and effort than separate bills. Equally important was the opposition of the House Appropriations subcommittee chairmen, who feared that their power would be eroded under the omnibus-bill plan.

With the failure of those efforts, Congress's only means of budget restraint was to write into appropriations bills specific restrictions on how funds could be spent. Those provisions provided little overall spending restraint, and during the postwar years Congress discussed but did not try several other plans for restraining outlays.

Seven times between 1952 and 1965 the Senate approved creation of a Joint Budget Committee, but the House never acted on the Senate measures. Other spending control measures proposed during that time included a mandatory balanced budget, statutory spending ceilings, and a separate congressional budget session to handle only appropriations bills.

Spending Ceilings

In the late 1960s and early 1970s, spending for President Johnson's Great Society programs combined with military outlays in Vietnam to push the budget into deficit. Four times between 1967 and 1970, Congress wrote federal spending limits into law. But those limits proved ineffective.

Distressed by ever-increasing levels of federal spending growth, House Republicans launched an economy drive in 1966. Their first efforts—to cut several annual appropriations bills by 5 percent—were unsuccessful.

Fiscal conservatives were more successful in 1967. In an amendment tacked on to a routine continuing appropriations measure after months of controversy, Congress in December directed federal agencies to cut fiscal 1968 spending on controllable programs by $4 billion. Nonetheless outlays for uncontrollable programs rose about $5 billion, leaving a net spending increase of $1 billion.

A better handle for insisting on spending curbs developed when Johnson in 1967 proposed a 10 percent tax surcharge. The Ways and Means Committee refused to act on the proposal, however, as Chairman Wilbur D. Mills, D-Ark. (1939-1977), held out for expenditure control commitments from the administration before action on raising taxes.

That stalemate finally was broken in June 1968, when the Senate added the surcharge and a $108.1 billion spending ceiling to a House-passed excise tax bill.

After lengthy conference deliberations, the House gave in, and the measure was enacted into law.

Congress again enacted spending limits in 1969 and 1970, after Republican Nixon succeeded Democrat Johnson. But Congress simply raised both ceilings when they proved too low to accommodate spending required by existing programs. Congress in 1969 tacked a $191.9 billion fiscal 1970 ceiling onto a supplemental appropriations bill, with provisions adjusting the ceiling to accommodate any congressional action increasing or decreasing spending and allowing the president to raise the limit by up to $2 billion to accommodate uncontrollable expenditures.

That cushion proved insufficient, so Congress in 1970 raised the fiscal 1970 ceiling to $197.9 billion, again with allowance for another $2 billion in uncontrollable outlays. In the same bill, Congress set a $200.8 billion fiscal 1971 limit with a cushion for uncontrollables and unlimited additions for spending increases by congressional action.

Nixon Spending Limits

No spending ceiling was enacted for fiscal 1972, but Nixon's request for a $250 billion limit on fiscal 1973 spending provoked a dispute with Congress that was thrashed out amid the 1972 presidential election campaign.

In what Democrats conceded was a masterful political stroke, Nixon in July 1972 asked Congress for authority to trim federal spending as he saw fit to meet a $250 billion ceiling on fiscal 1973 outlays. If such power were denied, Nixon warned, Congress would be responsible for tax increases in 1973.

The House complied by writing the ceiling into a bill increasing the limit on the federal debt. But the Senate balked at giving the president unlimited discretion to cut federal outlays, adding strict guidelines

on the size and nature of spending reductions. The ceiling was dropped altogether after the Senate turned down a White House-backed compromise limiting presidential authority to dictate where reductions could be made.

The following year, the House and Senate approved different ceilings on fiscal 1974 outlays as part of bills limiting the president's impoundment authority. Those measures died in conference after Congress decided to include the impoundment limits in the bill that eventually became the 1974 budget act. Twice in 1974, the Senate rejected amendments by Sen. William Proxmire, D-Wis., to set a $295 billion ceiling on fiscal 1975 spending. Late in 1974, after Nixon resigned the presidency and was replaced by his vice president, Gerald R. Ford, the House in an inflation-fighting gesture approved a $300 billion target for fiscal 1975 outlays. But the Senate never acted on the House resolution, which set no binding outlay ceiling.

Nixon, Ford Vetoes

With Congress unwilling to observe spending limitations, both Nixon and Ford resorted to the president's veto power to hold down outlays. Nixon vetoed five bills in 1970, three measures in 1971, sixteen in 1972, and five more in 1973, primarily on budgetary grounds. Congress overrode two 1970 vetoes, but the others were sustained. In some cases, threatened vetoes prompted Congress to tailor appropriations measures to fit the president's budget plans.

Ford and Congress fought repeatedly in 1975 and 1976 as the president vetoed measures that the House and Senate approved to step up spending to help climb out of a steep recession. Ford in 1975 vetoed seven measures on budgetary grounds, including four appropriations and three authorization bills Democrats designed to stimulate the economy through increased spending; Congress overrode four of those vetoes. In 1976 Congress overturned Ford's vetoes of bills authorizing costly public works and countercyclical grants to state and local governments and a separate bill appropriating $4 billion more than the administration requested for the Departments of Labor and Health, Education and Welfare.

The GAO: Congress's Auditor

As it strengthened presidential control over federal budget decisions, Congress in 1921 also tried to improve its own capability to monitor the way federal revenues are spent. In the Budget and Accounting Act of 1921, Congress set up the General Accounting Office (GAO) to give it that additional capability.

The GAO is headed by the comptroller general and assistant comptroller general, appointed by the president with the advice and consent of the Senate, for fifteen years. They can be removed only by joint resolution of Congress, thus making the agency responsible to Congress instead of the administration. (It was this factor that led to a Supreme Court decision in 1986 that threw out as unconstitutional the original Gramm-Rudman process for making automatic spending cuts when deficit targets are exceeded. The law gave final authority to the GAO to direct the president in specifying those cuts. That, the court said, violated the Constitution's doctrine of separation of powers.)

The comptroller general was granted wide powers to investigate all matters relating to the use of public money and was required to report annually to Congress, including in his report recommendations for greater economy and efficiency. Many of the auditing powers and duties of the comptroller general had already been established by the Dockery Act of 1894, which assigned them to the new office of the comptroller of the Treasury. But under that law the comp-

troller and his staff remained executive branch officers, and Congress lacked its own agency for independent review of executive expenditures.

Routine audits are conducted of agency operations and presidential decisions to "defer," or withhold spending, appropriated money. The GAO also conducts specialized reviews and audits, when requested by Congress, and continues to have a role in reviewing the execution of a "sequester," the automatic spending cuts ordered by Gramm-Rudman.

The results of GAO audits are transmitted to Congress by the comptroller general, usually to the individual member or committee that has requested an investigation. It also reports annually to the House Government Operations and Senate Governmental Affairs committees.

During the 1970s controversy was generated by congressional proposals to order GAO audits of the semi-autonomous Federal Reserve System. Because the Federal Reserve financed its own operations through assessments on member banks, the GAO had no authority to monitor the bank regulatory agency's operations. But House Banking and Currency Committee chairman Wright Patman, D-Texas (1929-1976), a longtime critic of Federal Reserve monetary policies that he contended drove interest rates too high, for years advocated GAO audits as a way to force congressional review of the system's operations.

Federal Reserve Board officials, led by Chairman Arthur F. Burns, objected that GAO investigations might intrude on the board's secretive decisions on sensitive monetary policy. Shortly after Burns resigned from the Fed in 1978, Congress ordered the audits, limited to the Federal Reserve's function as supervisor of the nation's banking system. The law barred auditors from examining the board's monetary policy decisions and international financial transactions.

The 1974 Budget Act: A Major Step

Two issues came to a head in 1974—spending that was perceived to be out of control and congressional impotence to counter presidential power over spending. The result was enactment of the Congressional Budget and Impoundment Control Act, an achievement that held out much more promise than it could deliver in the face of constituent pressures, committee power, and partisan politics.

Nevertheless, the new law changed the rules of the game significantly. Congress gave itself new procedures and upset institutional inertia a bit through creation of new Budget committees. However, the committees, in fact, had little authority. Such power as they exercise often varies with the leadership of the committees and the politics of the moment.

The legislative branch did acquire new power to counter the administration by creating a Congressional Budget Office (CBO) to provide independent analysis of administration budget requests and economic conditions. And it vastly circumscribed presidential power to refuse to spend money appropriated by Congress.

But Congress still makes actual decisions on revenues and spending through separate bills, written by different House and Senate committees. And the budget process still leaves congressional tax, authorizing, and appropriations panels considerable power to shape particular programs and make room for them within budget totals.

At the end of the 1970s, newly formed House and Senate Budget committees began asserting an indirect role in congressional tax and spending deliberations. Budget panel chairmen more and more took the floor to urge members to keep budget goals

in mind while acting on separate measures. For the first time in 1980 and then again in 1981—under pressure from the White House—the Budget committees enforced spending cuts by winning House and Senate support to direct other panels to recommend reconciliation savings in entitlement and other previously untouchable programs.

And in the 1980s the Budget panels—through their chairmen in the Senate and rank and file members in the House—forced closer adherence to spending targets in appropriations bills by insisting on floor votes to overturn points of order. Under rules of both chambers, as amended by the 1974 budget act and Gramm-Rudman, authorizing and appropriations bills must conform to existing budget resolutions. If they do not they are out of order for consideration. In the Senate, many of those points of order must be overturned by three-fifths majorities, which can be very difficult to achieve.

But the budget panels have no automatic authority to force Congress to adhere to tax and spending limits. "The president and his budget office are not merely the equals of the agencies they seek to control," federal budget expert Allen Schick has noted. "In Congress, the Budget committees stand on level ground with the committees subject to budgetary constraint." And those long-established panels, particularly the House and Senate tax and Appropriations committees, still wield impressive clout over congressional budget decisions.

Control over the President

President Nixon's campaign to curb federal spending brought to a head long-simmering differences over whether the government must spend all the money that Congress appropriates.

Enlarging on a practice that most previous presidents had followed, Nixon in the early 1970s impounded—simply refused to spend—billions of dollars Congress had provided for government programs over the administration's objections. By withholding the appropriations, Nixon set off a legal and political struggle over whether the executive or the legislature held final authority over how the government spent its money.

"The Nixon administration treated the president's budget as a ceiling on Congress," according to Louis Fisher, a Congressional Research Service specialist. "Any funds that Congress added to the president's budget could be set aside and left unobligated." In addition, Nixon administration officials seized on the permissive language that Congress wrote into some authorization and appropriations bills, contending that the provisions gave the president authority to suspend or cancel programs.

House and Senate Democratic leaders contended that Nixon used impoundments to impose his own priorities in defiance of laws passed by Congress. The Nixon impoundments suggested, Fisher said, that "whatever Congress did during the appropriations phase to fix budget priorities was easily undone by officials during the budget execution phase." The dispute embittered Nixon's relations with Congress and probably contributed to congressional support for 1974 impeachment proceedings that forced the president to resign in the wake of the Watergate scandal.

A 1975 Supreme Court decision subsequently backed the congressional position. Congress in the meantime moved to restrict use of impoundments as part of its landmark 1974 budget law. And in the following years Congress monitored more closely executive branch agencies and policies to make sure that legislative mandates were observed.

Constitutional Ambiguity

The Constitution did not spell out whether the president was required to promptly spend money appropriated by Congress or whether he could make independent judgments on the timing and even the necessity of putting appropriated money to use. Under the umbrella of that constitutional ambiguity, presidents had impounded appropriations almost from the beginning of the Republic.

Congress even gave the executive some authority for impoundments when it passed the Anti-Deficiency Act of 1950. That measure, to improve the management of federal finances, required the executive branch to subdivide appropriations among accounts to ensure that government agencies did not make commitments in excess of amounts appropriated. A 1950 omnibus appropriations act provided additional authority for the executive branch to create reserves for contingencies or to take advantage of savings made possible by developments after appropriations had been voted.

In the post-World War II period, presidents more and more began to use impoundment as a fiscal policy tool. Presidents Harry S Truman, Dwight D. Eisenhower, and John F. Kennedy all got into scrapes with Congress by withholding appropriated money for defense projects.

And in 1966 President Johnson cut back federal spending by $5.3 billion to curb the inflationary impact of the Vietnam War escalation. Major impoundments included $1.1 billion in highway money, $760 million for housing and urban development, and large amounts for education, agriculture, health, and welfare.

Nixon Impoundments

Nixon's extensive use of the power to withhold appropriations intensified the conflict between a Republican administration pledged to hold down domestic spending and a Democratic Congress determined to preserve the health, welfare, environmental, public works, and other programs it had put in place during the preceding decade.

Nixon argued that he was withholding money only as a financial management technique, primarily to slow inflation through temporary reductions in federal spending. Congressional Democrats saw Nixon's impoundments as attempts to emasculate the social programs they wanted to continue.

The conflict took on new urgency in early 1973. The Senate in October 1972 had killed Nixon's request for a $250 billion fiscal 1973 spending ceiling; but the president set out to meet that goal anyway through liberal use of vetoes and broadly interpreted impoundment authority. In mid-January Rep. Joe L. Evins, D-Tenn. (1947-1977), chairman of the House Appropriations Subcommittee on Public Works, released estimates that the administration had impounded $12 billion in appropriations, including $6 billion of $11 billion in sewage treatment money that Congress had authorized over Nixon's veto in 1972.

Congress responded by seeking to limit the president's impoundment authority. Government Operations Committee chairman Sam J. Ervin, Jr., D-N.C. (House 1946-1947; Senate 1954-1974), characterized Nixon's use of impoundments as "an item or line veto"—a power he said was prohibited by the Constitution—allowing the president to disapprove spending levels for particular programs without vetoing the entire appropriations bill that provided the money.

Nixon January 31 told a news conference that his constitutional power to impound money "when the spending of money would mean either increasing prices or increasing taxes . . . is absolutely clear." And Deputy Attorney General Joseph T. Sneed told Ervin's committee February 6 that the president had "an implied constitutional right" to impound money.

The Senate ultimately passed a bill that would have forced the president to release impounded money after sixty days unless both chambers approved his action by concurrent resolution. Congress could have forced release of the money before the end of sixty days by adopting a concurrent resolution disapproving the impoundment.

In the House, the Rules Committee voted to empower either chamber to overrule a presidential impoundment. The Rules Committee bill also would have set a $267.1 billion fiscal 1974 spending limit. On the floor, Republicans failed by one vote to require both the House and Senate to approve resolutions forcing the release of impounded money; eventually the bill passed.

But with Nixon's veto a certainty, and the close votes on several Republican amendments underscoring House divisions on the measure, Congress temporarily abandoned the effort. As momentum for reform of the congressional budget process took hold, and Nixon's clout waned under the continuing Watergate revelations, Congress again took up the cause of restricting impoundments. Late in 1973, the House overwhelmingly passed its version of what became the budget act, with its impoundment controls attached. The Senate followed suit the following year. A significantly different compromise version survived in the final bill.

New Impoundment Procedures

The 1974 budget act set up two procedures for presidents to follow to delay or cancel spending—rescissions for permanent cancellation of appropriations and deferrals for temporary postponements. Both were subject to congressional review, and only one stood the test of time and the Constitution.

Under the budget act, a deferral could last until the end of the fiscal year for which it was proposed, and until either the House or Senate adopted a simple resolution directing that the money be spent. Congress could act on a deferral at any time. The procedure proved to be a popular one for presidents and resulted in a battle with Reagan reminiscent of those with Nixon.

Eventually, in the 1980s, the courts, in two steps, struck that provision from the law, at least as it applied to deferrals based on policy instead of management decisions. Deferrals for management reasons—holding up spending on a housing construction contract for weather considerations, for instance—which were clearly allowed before the budget act, are still allowed.

The rescission provisions have survived. If a president believes appropriated money should not be spent at all, he must propose that Congress rescind it. But both the House and Senate must approve a rescission within forty-five days for it to take effect, and if either or both do not act, the president must release the money at the end of the forty-five days. There is no procedure for Congress to force early release of appropriations proposed to be rescinded.

The General Accounting Office is authorized by the budget act to review deferral and rescission requests for accuracy, and the comptroller general, who heads that agency, may report to Congress any executive branch action that impounds money without proper prior notice. Such a report from the comptroller general triggers rescission or deferral proceedings as though the president had requested them.

The comptroller general also may reclassify deferrals as rescissions, or vice versa, and may go to federal court to enforce the law's impoundment requirements.

Use of Procedures

From the beginning, there were concerns that the wording and legislative history of the impoundment provisions, and therefore congressional intent, were vague. Some members complained about the forty-five-day rescission period, during which Congress could do nothing to force the president to spend the money. And there were early disagreements between House and Senate over the use of deferral authority to make policy changes.

Criticisms aside, the measure's authors predicted that rescissions and deferrals for policy reasons would amount to only a few dozen each year. But after the law went into effect, Fisher noted, President Ford requested 330 deferrals and 150 rescissions in less than three years. Fisher said 120 of Ford's deferrals and 133 rescissions were on policy grounds, not routine cost-saving steps. "The large number of policy rescission proposals shows that Ford attempted to continue the presidential custom of reshaping budget priorities enacted by Congress," Fisher contended. "Ford used the rescission-deferral mechanism to frustrate congressional adjustments to his budget."

During Ford's presidency, Congress adopted sixteen resolutions disapproving deferrals in fiscal 1975, twenty-six in fiscal 1976, and three in fiscal 1977, Fisher reported. President Jimmy Carter, a Democrat, proposed far fewer policy deferrals, and Congress took exception less often. But defense-minded members protested in 1977 when Carter took steps to terminate contracts for the B-1 bomber and Minuteman III missile programs, then requested rescissions two weeks later.

And in 1981 Reagan drew congressional ire over his use of deferrals. Under pressure from Reagan to make 12 percent cuts in all federal programs but defense, Congress failed to enact any appropriations bill before the start of the fiscal year. A resulting continuing appropriations resolution was enacted to carry the government until November 20. During those fifty days, OMB instructed agencies to spend only at the level envisioned by Reagan's 12 percent cuts. Only after Congress learned of the notices were five deferral messages totaling $2.76 billion sent to Capitol Hill. "We felt we could have ordered the lower rates anyway, but we sent up deferrals just to be sure," said Ed Dale, OMB spokesman. Congress took no action on the five deferrals, which expired November 20; neither did

Congress comply in full with Reagan's call for 12 percent cuts.

Conflict Renewed over Deferrals

That small altercation was nothing compared with deferral battles with Reagan later on. In June 1983, in an unrelated case (*Immigration and Naturalization Service vs. Chadha*), the Supreme Court struck down the budget act procedure for overruling deferrals. The one-house legislative veto by which either chamber could reject an executive branch action was declared unconstitutional; it had been made part of more than two hundred laws for more than fifty years.

Immediately, the distinction between deferrals and rescissions was muddied. Since Congress could only overturn a deferral by passing a bill that the president signed into law—a dubious proposition in the case of a deferral a president wanted very badly—the president could in effect rescind appropriations merely by proposing the same deferral year after year.

That is just what Reagan did. For fiscal 1985 and again for 1986, Reagan deferred spending for housing and other low-income assistance programs. For 1986, the money amounted to $5.1 billion. Both years, Congress managed to reject the deferrals and the money was spent. But in 1986 the National League of Cities and four House members sued the administration over its action.

A resulting federal District Court decision, upheld in January 1987 by the Court of Appeals for the District of Columbia Circuit, threw out the concept of deferrals for policy reasons. The courts noted that the one-house veto was inseparable from the deferral authority granted the president by the budget act. When the legislative veto was struck down, so was the deferral authority. The Gramm-Rudman amendments of 1987 clarified the original budget act language to limit deferrals to those for management efficiency and to eliminate the legislative veto.

Taking Control of Congress

Frustrated by the impoundment battle and acknowledging that it had forfeited control of the budget through the arbitrary way it dealt with presidential spending requests, Congress in 1974 significantly changed the way it handled the federal budget.

Under the new budget act, Congress decided to vote each year to set specific spending, tax, and deficit limits. Perhaps more importantly for the long-run course of the U.S. economy, Congress also gave itself the machinery necessary to shape the federal budget to the government's fiscal policy objectives.

The budget law steered a careful course through the crosscurrents of congressional politics. It left the jurisdictions of previously existing tax and Appropriations committees intact, and it left legislative committees free to push new and additional spending proposals. The 1974 measure did not require a balanced budget or impose specific spending ceilings but instead superimposed an annual budget review process on top of the yearly congressional procedure for appropriating money for government agencies.

Genesis of the Process

In revising its budgetary procedures, Congress once again undertook a task that had been tried and abandoned in the legislative budget experiments nearly twenty-five years earlier. But in the early 1970s, congressional leaders finally concluded that the House and Senate had to put their own fiscal procedures in order to hold their own in budget policy struggles.

After a lively political sparring match completed in the month before the 1972 presidential election, Congress denied Nixon's request to set a $250 billion ceiling on fiscal 1973 spending and to give him authority to enforce it. But it did enact a little-noticed provision setting up a joint House-Senate study committee to review the way Congress acted on the budget.

The thirty-two-member panel, composed almost entirely of members from the House and Senate tax-writing and Appropriations committees, proposed major changes in congressional procedures in April 1973. Their recommendations included creation of House and Senate Budget committees, to be dominated by members from the tax and Appropriations panels. The study committee urged adoption of a concurrent resolution—which would not require the president's signature—early in each session to set binding limits on spending and appropriations for the fiscal year, followed by a second resolution later in the session to adjust ceilings as necessary to meet unanticipated budget requirements.

The plan called for floor procedures requiring that amendments to budget resolutions raising outlays for one program category be accompanied by equivalent cuts from another category or by tax increases to provide the additional money. They also proposed that all future backdoor spending programs, including entitlements, be subject to limits set through the annual appropriations process. Other proposals included binding limits on outlays written into appropriations measures and wrap-up appropriations bills to reconcile spending totals at the end of each congressional session.

Congressional Deliberations

What followed during the rest of 1973 and first six months of 1974 turned into a landmark exercise in congressional power brokering. Powerful committee chairmen jockeyed backstage to preserve their panels' existing authority to shape tax and spending decisions. Conservatives sought restrictive

budget procedures, while liberals resisted proposals that they felt would squeeze domestic programs. Through the give-and-take of House and Senate deliberations, the process that emerged "was an accommodation to the most salient interests of the affected parties," budget expert Schick has said.

In the House serious resistance among liberals both inside and outside of Congress forced the Rules Committee to reduce the number of Ways and Means and Appropriations committee members assigned to the new Budget Committee. In general, the liberals suspected that fiscally conservative southern Democrats and Republicans from those panels "would lock the congressional budgetary process into a conservative mold for generations to come," according to a report of the liberal-leaning Democratic Study Group.

In a significant departure from the joint panel's proposals, the House bill made the initial budget resolution a flexible guideline that would set targets but not bind subsequent decisions on separate appropriations and spending measures. The Rules Committee report argued that the change would "preserve and enhance the appropriations process which has consistently demonstrated its effectiveness."

The initial Senate version of the budget control bill was more rigid than the House version. But tight budget ceilings, along with provisions making backdoor spending programs subject to the regular appropriations process, aroused concern among the powerful high-ranking members of the existing legislative committees. If committees were subject to a firm initial ceiling that would be difficult to adjust, their power to initiate new programs or step up existing federal efforts would be severely limited. The upshot was a final version with procedures and timetables less stringent than the House bill.

The House passed its version of the bill by a 386-23 vote December 5, 1973. The

Senate passed its compromise version without dissent March 22, 1974. Conferees negotiated some further refinements, particularly on impoundment controls, and the conference report won easy approval. The House adopted it by a 401-6 vote on June 18; two Republicans and four Democrats opposed the measure. The Senate gave its approval by a 75-0 roll call on June 21.

Nixon signed the final measure into law on July 12, 1974, less than a month before the threat of impeachment forced him to resign the presidency.

Creating the Budget Committees

New Budget panels, with somewhat different mandates and political constraints, were created in both chambers to report budget resolutions, to keep track of congressional actions to spend and raise money—the so-called scorekeeping function—and to oversee the newly created Congressional Budget Office.

In the Senate, the committee began with sixteen members, permanently appointed, with no special regard for their other committee assignments. Its membership has been allowed to grow first to twenty in 1979, then twenty-two in 1981, and back to twenty in 1987.

In the House, the committee was established at twenty-three members, with twelve of them specially designated: five each from the Appropriations and tax-writing Ways and Means committees, and one each from the Democratic and Republican leadership. No House Budget committee member was allowed to serve for more than four out of ten years (or two Congresses out of five).

By rotating members off the House panel, and stacking the deck with designated representatives, its power was seen to be somewhat diminished. But over time its membership has grown: first to twenty-five in 1975, then to thirty in 1981, thirty-one in 1984, thirty-three in 1985, and thirty-four in 1988. During that time there was no increase

in designees from Appropriations or Ways and Means, greatly diluting their strength.

Beginning in 1979, House members were allowed to serve six years out of ten, and the chairman an additional two, if his tenure as chairman had previously been for only two years. That further relaxed leadership control over the panel's work. Conversely, the leadership's hand was strengthened because the leadership's designee to the panel was not required to rotate off.

The rotating nature of House appointees to the Budget panel makes it likely that more House members than senators will be exposed to the intricacies and trade-offs of budget making. But the long tenure and accumulated knowledge and stature of Senate Budget members has in recent years made them more effective advocates of budget restraint on the floor. Both Pete V. Domenici, R-N.M., and Lawton Chiles, D-Fla. (1971-1989), who have served either as chairman or ranking minority member of the Senate panel since 1981, have been on it from its creation. Together they particularly have been effective at keeping Appropriations members from exceeding spending targets for their bills since 1985.

Getting Information: The CBO

Congress saw its need for information, distilled yet as unbiased as possible, as most critical. It had required the administration to submit a unified budget since 1921; it had required the administration to detail its economic views since 1946, through the Economic Report of the President. But the communication was mostly one-way.

Administration cost estimates were difficult, if not impossible, to contradict, because there was no alternative source of information other than outside interest groups, whose reliability could easily be doubted. With the creation of the Congressional Budget Office Congress saw it would finally be able to rebut administration views on something other than a political basis.

The budget act was simple in its requirements. CBO was to report to Congress annually by April 1 a list of expiring program authorizations, and its analysis of the government's fiscal outlook and of spending and revenue alternatives. And CBO was to project five-year costs of every authorizing bill to help the Budget committees with their scorekeeping responsibilities.

The annual reports have evolved into a set of three documents: an analysis of the president's budget request, a study of budget alternatives, and an economic and fiscal outlook, which are now due in February. The economic outlook is also updated in August. Charged with the task of analyzing policy options, CBO in response to committee and member requests, and on its own, produces scores of reports each year on specialized topics.

With a staff of 226 in 1988 in separate fiscal, economic, and policy analysis branches, and a budget of $17.9 million, it is a formidable counterpart to OMB. Much of the agency's credibility is tied up in its ability to duplicate the administration's sophisticated review of the budget, which in turn is a credit to CBO's computer capability. More than $5 million a year now goes for computers alone.

"I don't think [computer capability] has made much difference in Congress in a political sense. But it has made them more competent adversaries," said presidential budget director David A. Stockman in 1985, just before leaving OMB.

"We're all equal now. Before, we were at the mercy of OMB," agreed Sen. Ted Stevens, R-Alaska (1968-   ).

Part of CBO's clout has come from its top. The first two directors were credited with bringing the agency up to speed and giving it credibility and stability. Alice M. Rivlin, who came to head CBO in February 1985 from the Brookings Institution, a liberal-leaning Washington, D.C., think tank, was the first.

Highly visible, Rivlin caused some early sparks in Congress, an ego-driven political institution, where staff is to be seen—but not on television. Her Democratic credentials and the newly created agency's early studies on spending and tax matters drew attention and criticism, even when their nature was purely advisory and not advocating a specific policy step. But the agency soon settled into a more anonymous niche, and despite a rocky beginning, after more than a decade the agency's reputation for nonpartisanship was virtually unsullied.

Rivlin served two full, four-year terms and stayed on an extra seven months when a replacement was not immediately found at the end of January 1983. She returned to Brookings in September, and Rudolph G. Penner, a Republican with credentials similar to Rivlin's, came aboard from the American Enterprise Institute for Public Policy Research, Brookings's conservative counterpart.

Where Rivlin was credited with getting the organization on its feet, Penner was seen as a stabilizing influence, more in tune with the agency's technical needs. "Alice built the institution," said Carol G. Cox of the Committee for a Responsible Federal Budget. "Rudy helped it mature."

Penner stayed one term before leaving for the Urban Institute in Washington, and after his departure in March 1987, the agency faced a new political crisis. As of October 1988, no permanent successor had been named. The budget act prescribed four-year terms for the director and gave the Speaker of the House and president pro tempore of the Senate appointment authority. They could not agree, however, with Speaker Jim Wright, D-Texas (1955-   ), insisting on his choice and the Senate united with House Republicans in opposition, arguing that Wright was out to undo years of proving CBO's impartiality and nonpartisanship.

There was no sign of resolution, but Penner, among others, was concerned that the delay in filling the job, as well as the apparent partisan debate over a successor, would tarnish the agency's image. "There's no way it can't," Penner lamented.

Establishing a Procedure

The 1974 budget act set up a permissive, in many ways ambiguous, process for Congress to set priorities and to force adherence to those priorities. Deadlines for action were not enforceable and not enforced; spending limits that were supposed to be binding could be waived. Some of those loopholes have since been closed, and Gramm-Rudman added a new club—its automatic cuts—in a threatening effort to make the process more likely to succeed. (For a review of the post-Gramm-Rudman budget process, see Appendix A.)

To give Congress more time to consider the budget during annual sessions starting in January, the law pushed the start of the fiscal year, formerly July 1, back to October 1, effective with fiscal 1977.

To give Congress a quicker start in shaping the budget, the act required the executive branch to submit a "current services" budget by November 10 for the fiscal year that would start the following October 1. Building on the programs and spending levels in effect for the ongoing fiscal year, the current services budget was to project the spending required to maintain those programs at existing commitment levels without policy changes through the following year.

The president was to submit a revised federal budget to Congress within fifteen days after Congress reconvened. Customary budget totals and breakdowns were to be projected over five years, and the budget was to include a list of existing and proposed tax expenditures—revenue lost to the Treasury through preferential tax treatment of certain activities and income.

After reviewing the president's request, and considering the advice of CBO and other committees, the House and Senate Budget committees were to draw up a first concurrent resolution—which does not require a president's signature—outlining a tentative alternative congressional budget. Committees were to report their recommendations to the Budget panels by March 15.

By April 15 the Budget committees were to report resolutions to the House and Senate floors, and one was to be finally adopted by May 15.

The initial budget was to set target totals for spending, revenues, the budget surplus or deficit, and the federal debt. Those targets then were to be allocated among authorizing and Appropriations committees, and were to be followed as the panels acted during the year. But, importantly, the budget resolution was not binding.

There were rules adopted to prevent floor action on bills appropriating money, changing taxes or the public debt limit, or creating new entitlement programs before adoption of the first budget resolution, but those rules could be avoided. Authorization bills were to be reported by May 15, the deadline for adoption of the budget resolution, after which the traditional appropriations process was to begin, with a deadline of seven days after Labor Day for enactment of all thirteen.

The budget act authorized holding up appropriations, and entitlement bills may be kept from the president's desk after final action, to allow Congress to take another look at the budget. A second budget resolution affirming or revising the first, but with binding targets, was to be adopted by September 15, and it could require reconciliation of its budget targets with the separate spending measures. If those measures do not fit the second budget resolution totals, the resolution may dictate changes in appropriations, entitlements, revenues, and the debt limit.

The resolution would direct the committees that had jurisdiction over those matters to report reconciliation recommendations making the required changes. If all the required changes fall within the jurisdiction of one committee in each house—appropriations changes that the Appropriations committees would consider, for example—those committees then would report a reconciliation bill to the floor.

If the changes involve two committees they would submit recommendations to the Budget committees, which then would combine the recommendations without substantial change and report them to the floor as a reconciliation bill. Such bills were to be considered under expedited procedures.

The law attempted to bring most forms of new backdoor spending programs under the appropriations process, but existing backdoor programs remained outside that process. The bill required annual appropriations for new contract authority or borrowing authority programs. And bills creating new entitlement programs that exceeded budget resolution totals were to be reported to the Appropriations committees for fifteen days, after which they would go on to the floor.

Exempted from the act's backdoor spending procedures were all Social Security trust funds, all trust funds that received 90 percent or more of their financing from designated taxes instead of from general revenues, general revenue sharing, insured and guaranteed loans, federal government and independent corporations, and gifts to the government.

4

Shaping Tax Policy

There would be no government if it could not spend. And there would be no spending without revenue. That may seem obvious, but it was important to the founders when they chose to give the government constitutional authority to raise revenues. The failure in the 1780s of the national government under the Articles of Confederation was caused, in part, by its inability to tax.

Nowadays, disputes over how much—and by what fashion—revenue is to be raised dominates Congress's time almost as much as disputes over how that revenue is spent. The willingness and ability of Congress to raise revenues, and the particularly difficult issue of taxes, bear significantly on that political and economic conundrum—the deficit.

George Washington identified the problem explicity in his farewell address to Congress in 1796: "It is essential that you should practically bear in mind that toward the payment of debts there must be revenue; that to have revenue there must be taxes; that no taxes can be devised which are not more or less inconvenient and unpleasant."

In two hundred years, nothing has changed.

The Constitution, along with the Sixteenth Amendment ratified in 1913,

granted Congress the right to enact virtually any tax or tariff. In Article I, Section 8, the Constitution specified that Congress may "lay and collect taxes, duties, imposts and excises." That was authority broad enough to encompass nearly all known forms of taxation, including tariffs on imported goods and excise taxes on the manufacture, sale, use, or transfer of property within the United States. And, in general, both Congress and the courts have construed the taxing power liberally to generate additional sources of federal revenue.

Constitutional historian C. H. Pritchett, in his book *The American Constitution,* noted that adequate sources of revenues and broad authority to use them were "essential conditions for carrying on an effective government.... Consequently, the first rule for judicial review of tax statutes is that a heavy burden of proof lies on anyone who would challenge any congressional exercise of fiscal power. In almost every decision touching the constitutionality of federal taxation, the Supreme Court has stressed the breadth of congressional power and the limits of its own reviewing powers."

The Constitution did set some limits. Article I, Section 8, Paragraph 1 directed that "all duties, imposts and excises" be imposed uniformly throughout the nation.

Section 9, Paragraph 5 forbade export duties. And Section 9, Paragraph 4 prohibited "direct" taxes unless each state paid a share in proportion to its population. Although it is not clear what the framers intended by this clause, it was eventually used to stop income taxes and was superseded by the Sixteenth Amendment.

Implied limitations, as interpreted by the Supreme Court in *McCulloch v. Maryland* (1819), exempted state and local governments—and by extension income from state and local bonds—from federal taxes. However, in recent years Congress has moved closer to taxing municipal bond interest, with the Supreme Court's permission. In 1982, state and local bond-issuing authorities were required for the first time to register their bonds. And for the first time federal limits were established for industrial development bonds, those issued tax-free by municipalities for the benefit of privately owned businesses—not public purposes such as roads or parks.

In 1988 the Supreme Court in *South Carolina v. Baker* upheld the 1982 law and said there was no constitutional prohibition on Congress taxing the earnings from industrial development bonds.

And in a major rewrite of the tax code in 1986, interest on industrial development bonds was made subject to the individual and corporate minimum income tax, though it effectively remained tax-exempt for all but high-income taxpayers. The 1986 tax law made no change in the tax-free treatment of public purpose municipal bonds or those issued on behalf of charitable institutions, such as private colleges and universities.

Early Reliance on Tariffs

The first congressional measure to raise revenue was a tariff act, approved July 4, 1789. Until the demands of the Civil War made Congress look to taxes, customs duties produced sufficient revenue to meet most of the government's needs, accounting for more than 90 percent of total federal receipts. (See Table 4-1.)

Because of the need for revenue, tariffs were applied to virtually all imports in the nation's early years. During the 1800s the cost of all tariffs ranged from one-fourth to one-half of the value of all imports—including those that were duty-free. But in addition to supplying money for government operations, tariffs protected the nation's fledgling industries against foreign competition. By the early 1900s, tariffs were applied to fewer and fewer goods, but at very high, protectionist rates.

Through most of the nation's history, until the early years of the Great Depression in the 1930s, regions and economic interests often fought over tariff policy. During the first half of the nineteenth century, the tariff laws offered protection mainly to manufactured goods. Western and Northern farmers supported a protectionist policy for manufacturers on the assumption that industrial development, aided by high tariffs, would create a profitable home market for their products.

The Republican party, founded in the West in 1854, lined up behind the protectionist principle on the eve of the Civil War, thereby availing itself of a policy that was to ensure it the enduring adherence of Northern and Eastern industrial elements after settlement of the slavery issue. Meanwhile, the Democratic party generally favored a moderate- or low-tariff policy that helped it to retain the solid support of the agricultural South for years.

After the Civil War, tariff policy was the major issue in many presidential and congressional elections, and a change in administrations often led to passage of new tariff laws. Congress devoted an inordinate amount of time to tariff making, not only because the customs duties were made and remade so frequently but also because tar-

Table 4-1 Sources of Revenue, 1860-1988 (in millions)

Fiscal year	Customs	Taxes [a]	Other [b]	Total
1860	$ 53	—	$ 3	$ 56
1870	195	$ 185	32	411
1880	187	124	23	334
1890	230	143	31	403
1900	233	295	39	567
1910	334	290	52	676
1920	323	5,405	921	6,649
1930	587	3,039	132	4,058
1940	331	6,204	14	6,548
1950	407	38,790	247	39,443
1960	1,105	90,174	1,212	92,492
1970	2,430	186,952	3,424	192,807
1980	7,174	497,190	12,748	517,112
1988 [c]	16,399	873,384	19,380	909,163

Sources: Office of Management and Budget, Treasury Department.

Note: Totals may not add due to rounding.

[a] Includes individual and corporate income, social insurance, excise and estate and gift taxes.
[b] Includes earnings on deposits of the Federal Reserve System.
[c] Estimate.

iffs potentially affected the interests of many segments of American commercial life.

Two things changed that: the growth of the income tax and the Smoot-Hawley Tariff Act of 1930. Revenue demands of World War I stimulated higher and higher tax collections, but it was the Smoot-Hawley tariff that put an end to starkly protectionist duties.

Enacted as the country was sliding into the Great Depression, Smoot-Hawley was designed as a modest, but immediate, aid to farmers faced with competition from cheap, imported foodstuffs. Congress, however, engaged in a protectionist frenzy, putting tariffs as high as 60 percent on tens of thousands of items. The action drew like retaliation from the nation's chief trading partners, the U.S. gross national product was cut in half from 1929 to 1932, and exports fell from $5.2 billion to $1.6 billion in the same period. U.S. imports recorded a similar drop and world trade tumbled from

$60 billion in 1928 to $25 billion ten years later.

With protectionism judged to be a clear contributor to international economic decline, high tariffs became much less attractive, and the stage was set for greatly reduced trade limits—and, correspondingly, limits on tariffs as a source of government revenue.

In the Reciprocal Trade Agreements Act of 1934, Congress delegated to the president significant authority to reduce tariffs. By then, individual and corporate income taxes had far outpaced customs receipts as sources of revenue. In 1910 customs duties still brought in more than 49 percent of federal revenues; by the 1970s they contributed about 1 percent, even though customs receipts had passed the $2 billion mark. And in the late 1980s, as consumer demand for high-priced imports surged, tariff collections climbed as well but still remained under 2 percent of all revenues.

A Shift to Taxes

The Sixteenth Amendment removed an obstacle to income taxes posed by the constitutional prohibition on so-called direct taxes. Such taxes had not been allowed, unless apportioned among the states according to population, which by definition an income tax could not be. That constitutional barrier was only erected in 1895, however, by a decision of the Supreme Court. Prior to that time, an income tax had been viewed as essential to governmental purposes only sporadically and was judged not to be a prohibited direct tax.

Congress in 1862 levied a tax on individual incomes to help finance the Civil War. That tax brought in a total of $376 million, accounting for 25 percent of internal revenue collections in 1866, before expiring in 1872. The Supreme Court ruled in 1881 that the income levy was not a direct tax subject to the Constitution's apportionment requirement.

During the 1870s and 1880s, little interest was shown in reenactment of the tax. But growth of the country and accumulation of large fortunes began in the 1890s to generate pressure for a return to income taxation. After the depression of 1893 had reduced federal revenues, Congress yielded and in 1894 levied a tax of 2 percent on personal incomes in excess of $3,000. Before the new tax law became operative, it was challenged, and this time the Supreme Court held that an income tax was a direct tax and unless apportioned was unconstitutional (*Pollock v. Farmers' Loan & Trust Co.,* 1895).

Although the court had blocked the road to this attempted expansion of the tax system, a solution was afforded by the power of Congress and the states to revise the Constitution. A campaign to do so was begun immediately, and on February 23, 1913, the Sixteenth Amendment was officially declared ratified. The one-sentence amendment says tersely: "The Congress shall have power to lay and collect taxes on incomes from whatever source derived, without apportionment among the several states, and without regard to any census or enumeration."

Thus the problem of apportioning income taxes was swept away, and Congress was left free to do what it had tried to do two decades earlier. The new grant of power came at a providential time, for the great expansion of federal revenue soon required by World War I would have been difficult, if not impossible, to achieve by any other means.

Congress imposed a federal income tax the same year the amendment was ratified, applying the tax to wages, salaries, interest, dividends, rents, entrepreneurial income, and capital gains from the sale of assets. It set the initial rate at 1 percent, plus a surtax of 1 to 6 percent on larger incomes.

The 1913 law exempted income up to $3,000 ($4,000 for a married couple). It allowed deductions for personal interest, tax payments, and business expenses. Almost immediately, however, Congress began to craft exemptions and special rules to encourage specific activities. Since then, Congress has greatly complicated the federal income tax code and frequently changed tax rates and the level of exempted income. Maximum effective rates reached as high as 90 percent during World War II, although the marginal rate—that leveled on the last dollar of income earned—was technically even higher. Congress has frequently made major changes in the tax code, most recently in 1981 and again in 1986, both times enacting sharp cuts in maximum tax rates. With the cuts enacted in 1981 and 1986, the maximum rate was reduced almost to the low rates that prevailed from 1913 until 1932 (except for the years during and just after World War I).

Corporate Income Taxes

Congress did not encounter with a corporation income tax the constitutional difficulty that it had experienced with the tax on individual income. A corporation income tax was levied in 1909 in the guise of "a special excise tax" at a rate of 1 percent of net income in excess of $5,000. That tax, like the 1894 individual income tax, was challenged in the courts, but the Supreme Court let it stand as an excise on the privilege of doing business as a corporation.

Following ratification of the Sixteenth Amendment, an outright corporation income tax at the same rate was made a part of the Revenue Act of 1913 alongside the individual income tax.

In most years, corporate taxes have produced far less revenue than individual income taxes. During World War I, World War II, and the Korean War, Congress raised additional revenues by imposing an excess profits tax to supplement corporate income taxes. But the excess profits tax did little to alter the basic ratio of individual to corporate income taxes. And an effort in the late 1970s to extract a sizeable tax from one part of the corporate sector—the oil industry—was also a failure.

In 1980 Congress approved President Jimmy Carter's request to levy a tax on the "windfall profits" that domestic oil producers were expected to earn as world oil prices surged after 1979. (In fact, the tax was not on profits, but on the difference between market prices for oil and a statutory "base price.") Domestic oil prices had been controlled, and the tax was tied to a plan to decontrol those prices to stimulate production. The caps were eliminated in Ronald Reagan's first act as president, moments after his inauguration in 1981, though they would have come off automatically by the end of the year.

The tax never generated the expected revenue. With oil prices soaring above $30 a barrel in the period just before decontrol, the tax was calculated to raise at least $227 billion. It was supposed to begin phasing out once collections reached that level, and in

no case was it to be in place after 1993. But the tax only raised $78 billion before market oil prices fell below base levels at the end of 1985, where they remained.

One key aspect of the 1981 tax law changes was a further shift of the tax burden off corporations and onto individuals, primarily through tax breaks aimed at encouraging corporate investment. The 1986 law had exactly the opposite effect, however, halting the trend since World War II of a declining corporate tax share. Instead, the law increased the corporate tax burden by $120 billion over five years.

Excise and Other Taxes

Excise taxes have always been a part of the federal tax system; they were mentioned specifically in Article I, Section 8 of the Constitution among the taxes that Congress was authorized to impose. The excises levied upon ratification of the Constitution included taxes on carriages, liquor, snuff, sugar, and auction sales. These and similar taxes have been controversial throughout the republic's history, in part because they were considered unfair and burdensome to the poor. Over the years, excises have been imposed and repealed or reduced; during every major war, the perennial liquor and tobacco taxes were supplemented by taxes on manufactured goods, licenses, financial transactions, services, luxury articles, and dozens of other items that lent themselves to this form of taxation.

The power of Congress to tax in other areas has become well established over the years. One of the most important areas has been payroll taxes, which financially underpin the Social Security and Medicare insurance and the unemployment compensation systems. Estate taxes date from the Civil War period and have been a permanent part of the national tax structure since 1916. The gift tax, levied to check avoidance of the estate tax, has been permanent since 1932.

Setting Public Policy through the Tax Code

From the beginning of the income tax, through its most recent and some believe most extraordinary transformation in 1986, tax law consciously and unintentionally has been a tool for economic and social change.

Even the act of raising revenue from one group to spend it on another—be it the poor, the elderly, homebuyers, university researchers, synthetic fuels producers, or arms makers—is itself a redistribution of income. But the intricacies of the tax code complicate that by establishing a "progressive" set of tax rate tiers designed to extract a higher percentage of the tax from wealthier taxpayers, while at the same time giving taxpayers at all levels varying deductions, exclusions, and credits to reduce the tax that they owe.

Such tax breaks are called by some economists "tax expenditures," because they reduce the amount of revenue the government would collect from an indiscriminate set of rates and result in increased money in the pockets of their beneficiaries. For every dollar exempted from tax, the government must either reduce direct outlays or find another source of revenue.

Tax expenditures are designed to achieve a specific purpose, perhaps the most visible of which is home ownership, supported by the deduction for mortgage interest. But critics of tax expenditures say they are a form of backdoor spending, uncontrollable and little different from any other entitlement, such as Medicaid health care benefits for the poor or farm price supports. Except, unlike most government entitlement programs, which tend to provide benefits to those less well off economically or otherwise, tax breaks tend to favor businesses and the well-to-do.

Perhaps the chief impetus for the 1986 tax changes was a widespread belief that the tax code had become too complex and too tilted to benefit the wealthy. Whatever ostensibly beneficial public purpose stood behind one individual tax expenditure, together they were seen to conspire against the public good. And elimination of dozens of tax breaks became the center of the 1986 tax debate, along with an offsetting change, the dramatic reduction of tax rates.

Growth of Federal Revenues

The federal tax system has steadily produced huge increases in government revenues. Even though Congress periodically cut taxes by reducing rates or enacting additional tax breaks, individual and corporate income tax revenues have risen almost without interruption as a growing population and expanding economy enlarged the base on which they were levied. In effect, tax cuts have most often been reductions from the level that would have been collected, not reductions below the previous year's collections—much as promises of spending cuts have most often been from a "baseline" of anticipated spending, not the real thing.

To help pay for the $1.064 trillion federal budget in fiscal 1988, individual income taxes were expected to provide $393.4 billion, more than double the amount collected just ten years before. Corporate income taxes nearly doubled in the same decade to an estimated $105.6 billion (although they had fallen to as low as $37.0 billion in the wake of the 1981 tax cut). Together, individual and corporate income taxes accounted for just over half the $909.0 billion in total federal revenues for 1988, which itself was more than twice the $399.6 collected in 1978.

Over the same decade, social insurance payroll taxes and contributions almost tripled to $331.5 billion, or 36.5 percent of revenues. Other federal revenues grew at rates closer to those for income taxes: Expected receipts for fiscal 1988 included $35.3 billion from excise taxes, $7.6 billion from estate and gift taxes, $16.4 billion from customs duties, and $19.4 billion from miscellaneous government activities, the bulk of which was earnings on Treasury bonds and notes held by the Federal Reserve System. (By law, the Fed's earnings on federal securities were returned to the Treasury.)

The growth of taxes as a share of the economy has not been as profound. From the Great Depression to the end of World War II, federal receipts went from less than 5 percent of gross national product (GNP) to more than 21 percent. Total receipts fell to 18.5 percent of GNP in 1946 and slipped to under 15 percent until the Korean War. Since 1952, however, revenues have hovered in a narrow range around 18.5 percent of GNP, rarely moving up or down by more than 1 percentage point, despite some deep recessions and strong boom times.

Individual income taxes have stayed rather steady over the last three decades—averaging between 8 percent and 9 percent of GNP—while corporate income and excise taxes have fallen, and social insurance taxes (particularly for Social Security) have risen. About half of social insurance taxes are paid by businesses, the rest by individuals. (See Table 4-2.)

Initial low rates kept revenues from federal income taxes at modest levels until the United States entered World War I. Then Congress sharply increased rates, stepping the revenue yield up from $360 million in fiscal 1917 to $2.3 billion in fiscal 1918. Since then, federal income taxes have produced more annual revenue than all excise and other internal revenue taxes combined—except for the nine fiscal years from 1933 through 1941 when the government levied numerous excise taxes to replace revenue lost as incomes sagged during the Great Depression.

In World War II high rates and a broadened tax base doubled and redoubled receipts from income and profits taxes. Those revenues fell off after 1945 and again after Korea as wartime rates were reduced. During the following decades, federal income tax revenues climbed year after year, even though taxes on corporate income occasionally fluctuated as Congress reduced rates and introduced new tax benefits to encourage investment.

Following the postwar tax reductions, Congress in 1964 approved an $11.6 billion tax cut designed to stimulate a lagging economy. Congress temporarily raised taxes in 1968 by imposing a 10 percent surcharge on personal and corporate income tax liabilities proposed by President Lyndon B. Johnson to finance the Vietnam War. But in 1971, with the economy in recession, Congress agreed to President Richard Nixon's plan for an $8.6-billion-a-year tax cut to renew growth. After the economy went into a deep recession in late 1974, Congress in 1975 approved an emergency $22.8 billion tax cut to bolster consumer and business purchasing power. Those reductions were extended through the end of the decade.

Congress in 1981 went along with President Reagan's request for massive tax reductions designed to slash individual tax rates 25 percent over thirty-three months and then, for the first time ever, to index the tax system to keep inflation from forcing taxpayers into higher brackets as their incomes kept pace with prices. Through fiscal 1988 these reductions were expected to have reduced federal revenues by more than $1 trillion.

Concern about the depth of the 1981 tax cut led Congress and the president the following year to roll part of it back. And Congress enacted additional sizeable tax increases in 1983 (to shore up the Social Security system) and in 1984. The 1986 tax law was supposed to neither increase nor reduce taxes over time. Instead, it had the

Table 4-2 Taxes as a Percentage of GNP

Fiscal year	Individual income	Corporate income	Social insurance [a]	Excise
1935	0.8	0.8	—	2.1
1940	0.9	1.2	1.9	2.1
1945	8.6	1.5	1.6	2.9
1950	5.9	3.9	1.6	2.8
1955	7.4	4.6	2.0	2.4
1960	8.0	4.2	2.9	2.3
1965	7.3	3.8	3.3	2.2
1970	9.1	3.3	4.5	1.6
1975	8.0	2.7	5.6	1.1
1980	9.1	2.4	5.9	0.9
1981	9.6	2.0	6.1	1.4
1982	9.5	1.6	6.4	1.2
1983	8.7	1.1	6.3	1.1
1984	8.1	1.5	6.5	1.0
1985	8.5	1.6	6.7	0.9
1986	8.3	1.5	6.8	0.8
1987	8.9	1.9	6.9	0.7

Source: Office of Management and Budget.

Note: GNP = gross national product.

[a] Includes Social Security, railroad, and other retirement programs and unemployment insurance.

unintended effect of adding $21.5 billion to fiscal 1987 revenues and cutting about that much over the following two years. As of 1988, the law was calculated to lose more than $23 billion over five years.

Before the 1981 tax cut was enacted, the Carter administration had projected that federal revenues would rise to $900 billion in fiscal 1984. In fact, total revenues barely exceeded two-thirds of that amount in 1984—$666.5 billion. It took four more years to reach the $900 billion threshold, and in 1988 the administration projected revenues would pass the $1 trillion mark in 1990.

Drafting Tax Bills

In both the House and Senate, powerful and prestigious committees control the complicated process of putting tax bills together. The collection of federal revenues affects virtually all Americans, along with a growing band of labor, industry, and public interest organizations. And the Internal Revenue Code over the years has evolved into more than one thousand pages of elaborate, often-convoluted law that probably no member of Congress fully understands.

Because of the complexity of the tax code, and the controversial nature of changes in it, senators and representatives are often hesitant to go on record for or against any but the most visible specific alterations. Most members prefer to let tax-writing committees handle the task of shaping revenue measures. Those committees—Ways and Means in the House and Finance in the Senate—as a result have accumulated vast power to design the federal revenue system and to influence the varied economic interests at stake in tax laws.

In the decades after World War II, the tax committees worked closely with the executive branch in drawing up tax measures. Before the 1970s, Treasury officials usually packaged tax proposals, and Congress acted on their recommendations. Congress itself initiated major tax-revision measures in 1948, 1952, and again in 1975 (enacted in 1976). But committee members, congressional staffers, and Treasury experts continued to consult throughout the process to reach agreement on tax-code changes.

The tax cut enacted in 1981 was largely designed by the administration, but the followup tax increase bills in 1982 and 1984 were congressional ideas. The comprehensive tax code overhaul enacted in 1986 was a hybrid. Conceived in the White House and Treasury, it was based on ideas embraced earlier by some in and out of Congress, and it was radically transformed on Capitol Hill.

Because the Constitution requires revenue measures to originate in the House, the Ways and Means Committee writes the first draft of virtually all tax bills. The House most often passes Ways and Means measures with few changes, then sends them to the Senate for consideration.

The Finance Committee may rework the House provisions—and often tacks on additional tax revisions. The full Senate customarily approves even more far-reaching changes before passing the measure. And as always, the House and Senate must resolve their differences in conference before sending a bill to the White House for the president's approval or veto.

Both committees are assisted by the Joint Committee on Taxation, which exists largely to provide the staff expertise and computer capability needed to analyze proposed tax law changes and their probable effect on the economy and revenue collections.

In both the House and Senate, influential tax committee chairmen have dominated congressional revenue deliberations. Carefully balancing competing interests during committee action, the chairmen usually have held firm backing from panel members to fend off floor amendments that would change the basic approach of the measure. Two former leaders—Ways and Means chairman Wilbur D. Mills, D-Ark., and Finance chairman Russell B. Long, D-La. (1948-1987)—were especially adept during the 1960s and 1970s at getting their way in committee and on the floor, and in hanging tough in House-Senate conferences.

Ways and Means Role

During Mills's tenure as chairman from 1958 through 1974, the Ways and Means Committee held virtually unchallenged control over the areas under its jurisdiction. The House created Ways and Means in 1802 and gave it authority over spending as well as taxes. In later years, the House gradually reduced the panel's control over spending until it set up a separate Appropriations Committee in 1865.

At present, Ways and Means considers revenue, debt, customs, trade, and Social Security matters, including Medicare. The committee traditionally was composed of senior House members with close ties to party leaders. Between 1911 and 1975, Ways and Means Democrats acted as their party's committee on committees and held political influence within the House by assigning other Democrats to positions on House panels.

Seven chairmen, including five Democrats and two Republicans, have led Ways and Means since 1947. But no one matched the extraordinary authority over tax matters that Mills exercised during his sixteen years as chairman. Mills's long tenure and command of complex tax laws won wide respect from House members. Mills also kept control over all tax measures by bringing them before the whole committee and refusing to establish permanent subcommittees to consider different issues. Most of all, Mills solidified his power by accurately sensing what House members wanted and drafting bills to suit them.

Through the years, Ways and Means members took pride in careful, professional work on tax bills. The committee's conservative leanings and cautious approach to tax-law changes for years reflected majority House sentiment on tax issues. House leaders sent Ways and Means measures to the floor under closed rules barring amendments, and the full House customarily passed the panel's bills by large margins.

By the mid-1970s, however, the House was changing. Democratic supporters of sweeping tax-law "reforms" grew restless with the power that Mills held. In 1974 Mills's self-confessed alcoholism and erratic personal behavior forced him to resign as chairman. House Democrats took the opportunity in October and December of that year to make the committee more liberal and break the chairman's grip over tax deliberations.

The changes included:

• Enlarging the committee from twenty-five to thirty-seven members, bringing twelve middle-level and freshman Democrats onto the panel. (In 1988 the panel had thirty-six members: twenty-three Democrats and thirteen Republicans, the highest percentage of Democrats on any major committee except Rules.)

• Requiring the establishment of subcommittees, and giving members of the committee the power to determine the number and jurisdiction of its subcommittees. Subcommittee chairmen and ranking minority members were each allowed to hire one staff person to work on their subcommittees.

• Providing that senior members of the committee would be allowed first choice for only one subcommittee slot and could not make a second choice until the junior members had each made one.

• Stripping Ways and Means of its Democratic committee assignment power and transferring it to the Democratic Steering and Policy Committee.

• Transferring legislative jurisdiction over revenue sharing from Ways and Means to the Government Operations Committee and national security export controls to the Foreign Affairs Committee.

Rep. Al Ullman, D-Ore. (1957-1981), took over from Mills and chaired Ways and Means from 1975 until his defeat at the polls in 1980. Ullman was considered a weaker leader than Mills, and the expanded committee proved too fragmented and contentious for Ullman to forge the consensus that Mills had constructed. As a result, Ways and Means suffered some embarrassing defeats during floor debate on its measures; and Ullman was unable to match Finance Committee chairman Long during House-Senate negotiations on tax bills. When Ullman was defeated, House Democrats named Dan Rostenkowski, D-Ill. (1959-   ), to chair Ways and Means. A more powerful presence than Ullman—both physically and politically—Rostenkowski had some early troubles, particularly when conservative Democrats deserted the party in 1981 and voted against his committee's tax cut proposals and in favor of the administration's. But Rostenkowski earned a reputation in 1985 and 1986 as a tough negotiator in dealings with the White House, the Republican-led Senate, and members of his own party.

In 1975 Ways and Means set up six subcommittees to handle welfare, trade, Social Security, unemployment compensation, health, and general oversight. A few years later, welfare and unemployment were combined in one subcommittee, and a new panel was created for so-called "select revenues," where special tax issues are considered at the chairman's discretion. But the full committee still considers most tax-law proposals, conducting lengthy hearings with testimony from the secretary of the Treasury and other expert witnesses. And tax bill drafting sessions—called markups—are still mostly done in full committee.

In recent years, markups have been "conceptual," instead of based on actual legislative language. This has been true even when the Treasury Department has submitted its own bill, or bills have been introduced by members. Preparation of legal language often is left to congressional and Treasury experts working together after the committee members have delineated the scope of the proposals to be put into a bill. Until 1973 markups generally were held in executive (closed) session, but following House passage of new rules on committee secrecy in March of that year, most of the markup sessions were opened.

That remained true through open-session markups on the 1982 tax bill. But members and some congressional observers complained that operating in full view of high-priced lobbyists, representing powerful home-state interests, did not produce bills most devoid of special-interest provisions. So, in 1985, the committee marked up the tax overhaul bill entirely in closed session. (With amendments limited on the House floor, the Senate Finance Committee markups held almost entirely in closed session, and the joint, House-Senate conference conducted in private, the only unfettered public debate on that bill occurred on the Senate floor.)

In 1987, Rostenkowski defended the closed meetings: "When we came to this glorious open, participatory government, you know, one of my members is sitting there looking at some labor skate and thinking, 'Oh well, how does he want me to go on this one?' Or the labor guy is running around, pulling him out to say, 'Wait a minute, you can't do this.'

"It's just difficult to legislate. I'm not ashamed about closed doors," Rostenkowski said. "We want to get the product out."

House Floor Action

Changed House procedures have also loosened Ways and Means control over the bills it writes and reports to the House floor.

Before 1973 the House took up tax measures under special procedures that had become traditional for Ways and Means bills and all but guaranteed acceptance of the committee's work without change.

Technically, under House rules, revenue bills were "privileged" business, which meant they could be brought up for consideration on the floor ahead of other measures and without a rule. In practice, the committee obtained from the Rules Committee a "closed rule" for floor action. Under this procedure, the bill was not open to amendment in the course of House debate; essentially, the House had to accept or reject the bill as a whole. The minority party had one opportunity, at the end of debate, to try to make changes in the bill, but significant revisions seldom resulted.

There was one exception to the prohibition against floor amendments. Amendments that were approved by the Ways and Means Committee (separately from the bill) could be offered on the floor by a committee member and voted on. This gave the committee an opportunity to backtrack on any provision that appeared to be in danger of drawing unusual House opposition.

Use of a closed rule was justified on the ground that tax, trade, and other Ways and Means bills were too complicated to be opened to revision on the floor, particularly because many of the proposed changes probably would be special-interest provisions designed to favor a small number of persons or groups; such floor proposals, it was argued, might upset carefully crafted compromises, as well as whatever balance between competing interests that the committee tried to build into the bill.

Nonetheless, the closed-rule tradition came under attack as members of the House began to criticize the powers of the Ways and Means Committee. Finally, in 1973, Democrats modified the closed rule by adopting a proposal that allowed fifty or more Democrats to bring amendments to

Ways and Means bills to the party caucus for debate. If the caucus voted to approve them, the Rules Committee was instructed to write a rule permitting the amendments to be offered on the floor. In 1975 the House went a step further by changing its rules to require that all Ways and Means revenue bills receive a rule prior to floor action and that they no longer have privileged status.

The impact of these reforms was vividly demonstrated in 1975 during consideration of two tax bills. The House February 27 passed a Ways and Means Committee tax cut bill but tacked on a provision repealing the oil depletion allowance, despite Chairman Ullman's objections. The issue was forced by the House Democratic Caucus, which voted to allow a floor vote on amendments repealing the depletion allowance offered by dissident Ways and Means members. In a long-sought victory for tax revision advocates, the full House accepted the amendment by a 248-163 vote.

Later that year, to assure committee approval of a tax revision package, Ways and Means Democrats agreed on floor procedures allowing their liberal members to offer floor amendments to tighten some provisions as written by the full panel. The House accepted three proposals, which further tightened the minimum tax provisions, deleted repeal of a withholding tax on foreigners' portfolio investments, and removed a controversial provision allowing capital loss carrybacks worth $167 million to wealthy investors.

Nowadays, most Ways and Means Committee bills come to the floor with "modified closed rules," allowing a limited number of amendments—often only substitutes for the entire bill. Even that procedure is fraught with trouble, however. In 1981, a bipartisan substitute to the committee bill was authorized by the rule. The committee bill represented a traditional Democratic tax cut that favored the lower end of the

economic spectrum; the substitute embodied the president's tax cut proposal, which favored the high end and corporations—as a way to boost investment. The substitute was adopted 238-195, with a sizeable number of Democrats defecting from their party.

Then, in 1985, disaffected liberal Democrats joined ranks with Republicans angered that the modified closed rule did not allow them much of an alternative to amend the bill. Together they defeated the rule allowing for floor debate on what was to become the 1986 tax overhaul bill. And it took an extraordinary effort by Reagan to change enough votes to keep the bill alive.

Finance Committee's Role

The Senate Finance Committee, created in 1816, has almost the identical jurisdiction as Ways and Means (health matters are one exception, where Finance's role is somewhat broader). But the Finance Committee's influence on revenue matters in the past has been more limited. Because Ways and Means normally drafts tax bills, Finance usually takes on a review or appellate role for interests trying to change House-approved provisions.

Through the years, Finance acquired a reputation as being receptive to special-interest tax schemes. That trait may trace to the Constitution and the second part of Article I, Section 7, which declares that "the Senate may propose ... amendments" to revenue measures. At times, the Finance panel has had little to do except tinker with the House-passed bills and add provisions in which individual senators take special interest.

The committee eventually will go into markup session and make changes it deems necessary in the House bill. It may, and sometimes does, write basic changes into the measure sent to it by the House, but its revisions often will be primarily addition of new material. The committee, like Ways and Means, is assisted by congressional and Treasury Department experts.

In 1981 and 1986, Finance departed somewhat from its past practices.

The Senate had switched to GOP hands with Reagan's election in 1980. Under the leadership of Chairman Robert Dole, R-Kan., Finance in 1981 marked up its own version of the tax cut bill, attached it to an unrelated measure raising the ceiling on the federal debt, and sent it to the Senate floor—before Ways and Means acted. (The committee avoided the constitutional proscription against the Senate originating tax bills by amending the debt-limit increase, which had originated in Ways and Means.)

And in 1986, instead of settling for crafting amendments, Finance chairman Bob Packwood, R-Ore., turned the House-passed tax bill on its head. (Dole had been elected to majority leader.) Instead of the more traditional-appearing measure that emerged from Ways and Means, Finance produced a much more expansive version of "reform." And it did so, uncharacteristically, in closed sessions.

Senate Floor Debate

Senate floor action on tax bills often dramatically departs from the limited and careful consideration that the House gives revenue proposals. The Senate has no procedures or rules to ward off floor amendments. And at times senators have used their prerogative to rewrite House bills substantially or to load them with unrelated provisions.

Senate tax-bill debates often have evolved into legislative logrolling and mutual accommodation, particularly late in congressional sessions when members try to push through favorite proposals before adjournment. Given the nature and often late-in-the-session timing of these amendments, they have turned many tax measures into "Christmas-tree bills" bestowing benefits on varied economic interests.

The Senate sometimes approves popular amendments in full knowledge that

House conferees will insist that they be dropped. Finance Committee leaders sometimes accept amendments out of courtesy to a sponsoring senator. As Finance chairman, Long frequently agreed to take amendments to conference with the House as bargaining chips that could be discarded in trade-offs for other provisions that senators considered essential. Senate floor maneuvering on tax bills often lasts several weeks.

Floor action on the 1986 bill closely resembled the norm, except for one key respect. The bill was on the floor for three weeks, comprising thirteen days and not a few nights of debate. And, in the end, it was loaded with numerous ornaments, many of which were predestined to fall off in conference. But the difference was that the bill's sponsors were able to hold off virtually all amendments that would have had an important negative impact on it, perhaps even threatening its survival.

The informal pressure of the Gramm-Rudman antideficit law and the president's aversion to tax increases conspired against any amendment that would increase or reduce taxes. That more or less voluntary restraint by the Senate was virtually unheard of before—but it succeeded. (One amendment was defeated by invoking a "point of order" based on the 1974 Congressional Budget and Impoundment Control Act. That law said no amendment increasing or reducing revenue was in order until a budget for the effected fiscal year had been adopted. The budget process was ongoing while the tax bill was on the Senate floor.)

Conference Maneuvers

Like other acts of Congress, most tax law is put in final form by a House-Senate conference committee. But tax-bill conferences, because the economic stakes are high, have produced intense and dramatic bargaining.

Conference sessions usually have been held in a small room maintained in the

Capitol off the House floor by the Ways and Means Committee. The conference committee is presided over by either the Ways and Means or the Finance chairman; they alternate turns. As a rule, there are three members from the majority and two members from the minority from each panel, although the number may be enlarged for major bills. A larger number of one side or the other theoretically makes no difference because each side votes as a unit with the majority vote controlling each group.

However, the outcome can be affected by the selection of conferees. In 1986, Rostenkowski and to a lesser extent Packwood violated tradition in selecting junior members of their committees to serve on the conference, while skipping over some more senior members. The intent—and the result—was to give the two chairmen greater control over the conference and to avoid members who might not have favored their own views of "reform."

A conference may last from a day or two to several weeks on major or controversial bills. Congressional and Treasury tax experts are present to assist the conferees—although Rostenkowski and Packwood made some of the most important compromises on the 1986 bill in private with no other members, no staff, and no Treasury aides around.

Once all differences are resolved, the bill is sent back to each chamber for approval of the conference agreement. The House files a conference report (for both chambers) listing the differences and their resolution; it is a rather technical document and of most use to experts. Often only the simpler explanations of conference decisions given on the floor by conferees are available to guide members on final action. If the conference agreement is approved by both chambers, the bill is sent to the president for approval or veto.

House action and lengthy Senate debates in some years last most of the congressional session; the 1986 bill took two full years from the time the Treasury Department first released a draft bill until it was signed into law. So conferees often negotiate their differences under tight deadlines as members prepare to leave Washington, D.C., to vacation or campaign for reelection.

Astute conference leaders such as Mills and Long have used the pressures of time to strengthen the case for their positions. And the final products, sometimes negotiated in all-night sessions, usually represent careful compromises that take account of House and Senate politics. The bills that conferees fashion also may determine how much money the government collects for years to come.

During conference negotiations, Treasury officials and Joint Taxation Committee staff aides help members keep track of the revenue impact of their decisions. But except in the extraordinary case of 1986, conferees have often given revenue gains or losses only secondary consideration.

Economic Intervention

Virtually since its inception, the tax code has embodied two primary economic goals: a progressive rate structure that was designed to tax more those who could afford to pay more, and a means of encouraging businesses to upgrade their factories and equipment by allowing them to reduce their taxes as their existing equipment began to deteriorate with age and use.

The goal of a progressive tax system was accomplished by setting very high rates on the earnings of upper-income taxpayers. Even in 1913 the rate structure had a progressive cast to it. Although the top rate was only 7 percent, on income above $500,000, the rate for most taxpayers was 1 percent. By the end of World War II, the top rate was 90 percent on income of $400,000 (although the nominal rate was 92 percent, the law offset some of that to cap the effective rate at 90 percent). (See Table 4-3.)

Table 4-3 Top Individual Tax Rates

Year	Top marginal tax rate	On taxable income over
1913-1915	7 %	$ 500,000
1916	15	2,000,000
1917	67	2,000,000
1918	77	1,000,000
1919-1921	73	1,000,000
1922-1923	56	200,000
1924	46	500,000
1925-1928	25	100,000
1929	24	100,000
1930-1931	25	100,000
1932-1935	63	1,000,000
1936-1939	79	5,000,000
1940	81.1	5,000,000
1941	81	5,000,000
1942-1943	88	200,000
1944-1945	90 [a]	400,000
1946-1947	85.5 [a]	200,000
1948-1949	77 [a]	400,000
1950	87 [a]	400,000
1951	87.2 [a]	400,000
1952-1953	88 [a]	400,000
1954-1963	87 [a]	400,000
1964	77	400,000
1965-1967	70	200,000
1968	75.25 [b]	200,000
1969	77 [b]	200,000
1970	71.75 [b]	200,000
1971-1978	70 [c]	200,000
1979-1980	70 [c]	212,000
1981	69.125 [b,c]	212,000
1982	50	82,200
1983	50	106,000
1984	50	159,000
1985	50	165,480
1986	50	171,580
1987	38.5	90,000
1988 and after	28 [d]	29,750 [e]

Sources: Joint Tax Committee, Treasury Department.

Note: Table does not account for alternative minimum tax.

[a] Maximum effective rate allowed; marginal rate was technically higher.
[b] Accounts for surcharges or credits against total tax bill.
[c] Earned income was subject to maximum rate of 60 percent in 1971 and 50 percent from 1972 to 1981.
[d] Marginal rate was 33 percent for high-income taxpayers who were subject to phase-out of personal exemption and the 15 percent tax bracket.
[e] Tax brackets were indexed with inflation beginning in 1989.

The concept of a progressive rate structure means that each taxpayer's first dollar earned is taxed at one rate and, as more is earned, the rate on higher earnings is taxed at higher rates. The so-called marginal rate is that paid on the last dollar earned.

Since 1945, the marginal rate has declined to 28 percent, except that some very-high-income taxpayers are subject to a 33 percent rate that has the effect of phasing out the tax benefit of the lower rate and the personal exemption. But the marginal rate reverts to 28 percent for the wealthiest taxpayers who have no benefit from the low rate or personal exemption.

Liberal critics of the 1986 law argued that it was abandoning the historic progressive aim of the income tax code. But supporters of the law countered that many wealthy taxpayers escaped most tax liability through tax breaks that did not benefit poorer persons. By eliminating those tax breaks and reducing rates, the argument went, the aim of progressivity could still be maintained.

The second major goal—reducing taxes by allowing for depreciation allowances—created one of the original tax expenditures. Depreciation allowances have been altered over the years through formulas designed to give taxpayers more of the tax benefit of the cost of their equipment, factories and other buildings, and other assets sooner. The intent was to grant a higher tax value to the asset through some method of accelerating the depreciation.

The 1981 tax law, for instance, assigned artificially short depreciation periods for most assets, so they would still be functional long after their owners had recovered their worth through tax deductions. And from time to time, the tax code has granted an investment tax credit for spending on equipment that was often in addition to available depreciation.

Such tax incentives have often been controversial. President Dwight D. Eisenhower's belief in the private sector led him to propose, in 1954, business tax cuts to reward investment. But Democrats scorned the idea, saying it mainly helped the wealthy, and that the poor would only receive the meager breaks that would "trickle down" to them as a result of greater spending by the wealthy.

Eight years later, President John F. Kennedy proposed a package of tax cuts that resembled the program Eisenhower had backed, only to be accused of advocating "trickle-down" policies. But among Kennedy's proposals was an 8 percent tax credit on new investment and liberalized depreciation allowances, and Congress approved both.

Kennedy's investment tax credit was enacted January 1, 1962, and it stayed in the tax code for four years before it was repealed. It has since been reinstated twice and repealed twice, most recently in 1986. The net economic effect of such a credit is to greatly increase the tax benefit, since the ordinary depreciation deduction is merely an offset against taxable income, while the credit reduces actual taxes owed.

Repeal of the investment tax credit was an obvious target of the "reformers" in 1985 and 1986. It had previously been increased to 10 percent, and many economists thought it had skewed investment benefits, especially when combined with the very generous depreciation schedule enacted in 1981. One abuse from the 1981 law, which allowed profitable companies to lease investment credits from firms that owed little or no tax, so that both could benefit, had already been repealed in 1983.

Before the 1986 law repealed the investment tax credit, it had been projected to cost the Treasury $38.6 billion in 1991, according to the Congressional Budget Office (CBO). After the provision was repealed, the 1991 revenue loss was set at $1.6 billion, resulting from unused credits that businesses were eligible to carry forward to future years.

Just as depreciation and investment credits are designed to stimulate business investment, various elements of the tax code are designed to spur savings and investment by individuals.

One central tenet of the code since 1921 has been a reduced tax on capital gains—income derived from the sale of an asset that had increased in value, such as real estate or artwork or stocks. As long as maximum effective tax rates were quite high, individuals were allowed to exclude from their reported income part of the gain from the sale of a capital investment.

In 1986, when marginal rates were cut back severely, Congress eliminated the so-called differential. Prior to 1986, a person taxed at the maximum 50 percent rate would have paid tax on only 40 percent of a capital gain; the result was an effective 20 percent tax rate on capital gains. That effective rate rose to 28 percent (or 33 percent for some taxpayers) in the 1986 law, which taxes capital gains as regular income. The effect of the 1986 change was to eliminate entirely what CBO had projected to be a $56.1 billion revenue loss in 1991 due to the capital gains exclusion.

Other provisions have been designed to encourage individual savings and investment: a $100 per taxpayer exclusion from taxable income of dividends earned from stock holdings and Individual Retirement Accounts (IRAs) to name two. The 1986 law repealed the dividend exclusion and the availability of all taxpayers to invest tax-free in IRAs.

IRAs were created in 1975 as a retirement option for persons not covered by a pension plan. Wage earners could put up to $1,500 annually into an account, where it could earn interest tax-free, and the amount deposited would be subtracted from taxable income. Therefore both principal and interest would be tax-free until the money was withdrawn at retirement, when the individual's tax rate presumably would be lower.

From 1981 to 1986, all taxpayers with earned income could put $2,000 into an IRA, whether they were covered by pension plans or not, and they could put another $250 a year into an account for a nonworking spouse. During that time, revenue losses from the IRA provision skyrocketed, however, and the savings rate fell from 7.5 percent to 4.3 percent. It appeared that most taxpayers were merely transferring their existing savings into tax-deferred accounts, and not increasing their savings as was intended.

So, in 1986, Congress rolled back the IRA deduction to allow only lower-income taxpayers, or those with no pension plan, to deposit tax-exempt dollars in an account. Other taxpayers, however, were allowed to deposit money on which they had already paid taxes into an account where the interest would be tax-exempt until retirement.

The IRA change was expected to be a net gain of $10 billion to the Treasury in 1991, according to CBO.

Social Intervention

There is another kind of tax expenditures, those whose intent is not merely economic, but social as well. These encompass deductions or credits that have been provided for individuals for child care costs and political contributions. And they include a tax credit for businesses that engage in research on "orphan drugs," those that have little possibility for widespread commercial application but might make a valuable medical contribution.

One such socially based tax expenditure—one of the very few that was expanded in the 1986 law—is the earned income credit. The credit was enacted in 1975 to aid those low-income persons with children who work. In 1987, the credit was a maximum reduction in taxes of $800 a year for persons with income of $6,500, and it phased out so that persons earning

$14,500 would get no reduction at all.

The earned income credit was designed to offset the bite that Social Security taxes take out of the paychecks of the working poor, who pay for Social Security even when deductions negate their income tax liability. As a result, the earned income credit was made "refundable," so that eligible taxpayers can get a check from the government, even if they owe no income tax. In 1991, according to the Joint Committee on Taxation, the combined revenue loss and spending cost of the earned income credit will be $1.5 billion.

Perhaps the most sacred tax expenditure, and the one the "reformers" in 1986 had no intention of touching in any major way, is the home mortgage interest deduction. The 1991 cost of the deduction will be $35.8 billion, according to CBO. Eliminating the deductibility of consumer interest was welcomed by those who argued that the nation cannot afford to continue to incur huge amounts of debt. But there is no doubt that the centerpiece of the American Dream is home ownership, and it seems that nothing Congress does to the tax code will limit that—almost.

In 1987, in a deficit-reducing reconciliation bill, Congress did vote to cap at $1 million the amount of home mortgage debt on which interest payments would be deductible. And interest would be deductible on up to $100,000 in principle on second mortgages (commonly in the form of "home-equity loans" in the late 1980s). Nevertheless, families could own two houses and deduct the mortgage interest on both (so long as the total mortgage debt was within the cap). And one of the two "houses" could be a boat or a motor home, as long as it had a bathroom, beds, and eating facility and was occupied a minimum amount of time each year.

One social expenditure that has been up and down in the code is the deduction for charitable contributions, presumably because of the overwhelming social benefit that is provided by service organizations, churches, and the like that gain from such donations. Formerly available only to those taxpayers who itemize their deductions, the charitable contribution deduction was also made available to nonitemizing taxpayers in 1982, but that provision expired in 1986, allowing only taxpayers who itemized after that year to claim the deduction.

Social Security

One major tax change over the last several decades is the growth of Social Security taxes. In 1973, 1977, and 1983 Congress enacted increases in the rate of tax and the level of income subject to tax for the Social Security retirement and disability and the Medicare hospitalization programs.

The biggest changes came in 1983, when, facing imminent bankruptcy, the programs were vastly overhauled, and large tax increases were put in place. Some parts of that increase will not be fully in effect until 1990.

The Social Security system's share of all federal taxes has grown tremendously—from 15.9 percent in 1960 to 36.5 percent in 1988. (That figure includes employee and employer share of Social Security taxes, as well as a relatively small tax to pay for unemployment and railroad retirement.) In the same period, individual income taxes have stayed roughly in the range of 44 percent of all taxes, and corporate income taxes have fallen from a 23.2 percent share to 11.6 percent.

And one effect, according to CBO, is that the tax code is overall becoming less progressive. Since half of all Social Security taxes are paid by individuals, since the tax rate is the same for all taxpayers, and since income above a certain amount ($45,000 in 1988) is not subject to the tax, the burden falls heavily on the poor and lower-middle

class. It is even possible for an individual whose wages are in the $15,000 range, and who has several dependents or major deductions, such as for interest payments on a mortgage, to pay more in Social Security taxes than income taxes. By 1990, all income up to $49,500 will be taxed at 7.65 percent for both individuals and businesses, for a total tax rate of 15.3 percent.

Moreover, that burden has increased as Social Security taxes make up a larger and larger share of revenues. But that is not surprising considering that Social Security and Medicare together are the largest slice of the government's spending pie (some of Medicare's costs for physicians' fees are paid by general revenues and premiums from beneficiaries).

In 1988, CBO said, the social insurance tax burden (mostly Social Security) on all but the wealthiest 10 percent of taxpayers will be higher than the income tax burden. That analysis follows the logic of many economists that the portion of social insurance taxes paid by employers is passed on to employees in reduced wages and benefits. The result, CBO reported, is that the tax code has become less progressive since 1977, despite some improvements as a result of the 1986 tax changes.

The Revenue-Neutral 1986 Tax Bill

The Tax Reform Act of 1986 was a radical departure from previous tax bills for several reasons. Chiefly it was viewed as different because Congress was willing to act against the special interests that over the years have been responsible for the tax code's tapestry of favors. Although the law had—and continues to have—its critics, it was hailed by a broad spectrum of economists and politicians as "real reform" of a tax system gone haywire.

Reagan, the top tax-basher in the country, called it "the best anti-poverty bill, the best pro-family measure and the best job-creation program ever to come out of the Congress of the United States."

Economist Henry J. Aaron of the liberal-leaning Brookings Institution in Washington, D.C., called it "the most important improvement in the broad-based taxes on individual and corporate income in at least two decades."

Reagan's point and Aaron's were not necessarily the same, but they were not far apart either. There was much to like in the bill: It greatly reduced tax rates, long the aim of supply-siders, but it also eliminated many corporate and individual tax breaks that were opposed by more liberal economists on the grounds that they mostly benefited upper-income taxpayers. And it shifted the individual tax burden up the economic ladder, limiting or eliminating taxes for poorer people, and reversing the forty-year trend of declining corporate tax liability.

The measure did all that without costing the government any revenue—at least in theory. Neither was it supposed to gain any. Increasing or cutting taxes were the only reasons Congress ever waded into the tax code thicket. But this "revenue-neutral" approach, as it was called, guaranteed a united front from conservatives and liberals who favored the low rates and fewer tax breaks the measure promised. And it protected the measure from amendments on the uncontrolled Senate floor that would have been its undoing.

The law's supposed revenue-neutral behavior was among the major complaints about it; liberal Democrats and even some conservative Republicans favored a tax increase that would help to reduce the budget deficit. That was a minority view, however.

In fact, the law eventually proved to be anything but revenue-neutral. Because many of its provisions were to be phased in

over five years, and because taxpayers reacted to changes in the code by significantly altering their economic activity—such as selling off appreciated assets in 1986 to avoid higher capital gains taxes in 1987—the act produced increased revenues in its first year and was expected to produce decreased revenues in later years. And those fluctuations, while predicted in part before the law was enacted, turned out to be much greater than expected. In 1988 the administration estimated that the law would result in a $23.2 billion revenue loss over its first five years.

The Supply Side's Legacy

The 1986 law began life in the minds of Rep. Jack Kemp, R-N.Y., and his supply-side allies. Kemp and Sen. William V. Roth, Jr., R-Del. (House 1967-1970; Senate 1971-), first began pushing a low-rate tax code in 1977 as an economic stimulus, but without the offsetting effects of reduced or eliminated tax breaks.

Some of what they advocated wound up in the president's 1981 tax proposal that was for the most part enacted into law. In 1982, two Democrats, Sen. Bill Bradley of New Jersey (1979-) and Rep. Richard A. Gephardt of Missouri, embraced the idea of a few very low rates, not to pay for a tax cut but to eliminate the incentive for massive adjustments to taxable income in the form of exclusions, deductions, and credits.

The plan was then adopted by Reagan, who in his January 1984 State of the Union address called for a wholesale simplification of the tax code. Kemp joined with Sen. Bob Kasten, R-Wis. (House 1975-1979; Senate 1981-), to offer in April 1984 a new tax simplification bill based on a single, flat rate. And the race was on.

Treasury secretary Donald T. Regan proposed a three-rate income tax system in November that would have curtailed many tax breaks and eliminated accelerated depreciation for business equipment, the centerpiece of the 1981 tax cut. Businesses reacted warily—and in some cases angrily—to what became known as Treasury I. Reagan, himself, was lukewarm and said he would have his own proposal later and would like to hear suggestions from others in the meantime.

Bradley, Gephardt, Kasten, and Kemp reintroduced their bills in January 1985, sharing the stage at a joint press conference where they played down their disagreements and promised to work together to "reform" the tax code. It was clear that, with White House support, the Ninety-ninth Congress would be in a unique position to challenge the special interests that had derailed prior reform efforts, including some dating to the early 1960s.

Meanwhile, Regan and White House chief of staff James A. Baker III decided to switch jobs as the administration began its second four-year term, leaving the task of revising the tax plan to a new Treasury secretary. After several fits and starts, Baker and Reagan finally had a bill they could call their own—and not break complete faith with the business community— that they offered to Congress in May 1985. It was known as Treasury II and drew the fire of liberal and conservative reformers. The liberals thought Reagan and Baker gave back too much to special interests— particularly the oil and gas industry—and did not enough to benefit the middle class. The conservatives bristled at the top individual tax rate of 35 percent the bill proposed. It was much higher than the Kemp-Kasten proposal for a flat 24 percent tax rate, and even higher than the Bradley-Gephardt top rate of 30 percent.

The Ways and Means Committee, after a summer of hearings, got around to markups in September and reported the bill to the floor December 7. More than once during the closed-door markup, Rostenkowski had to engage in deal making with his members, offering special tax favors for their constituents in return for their promise to support the measure. In the early morning hours of November 23, just before the committee finished work, there was a final spate of deal making that ratchetted up the rates a notch to protect the tax-free treatment of employer-paid education, legal, and other fringe benefits.

Only five Republicans voted to report out the bill. And GOP discontent at the level of vote trading—and the higher than wanted rates (the top individual rate was 38 percent, the top corporate rate 36 percent)—boiled over the morning the House took up the bill. With the aid of fifty-nine liberal and Oil Patch Democrats (who opposed the "less-progressive" rate structure, new rules for public-employee pensions, and limits on deductions for oil drilling costs), a nearly unanimous block of Republicans succeeded December 11 in killing the rule that would have allowed the bill to come up for floor debate.

Reagan was by then deeply invested in the cause and had put his prestige on the line—even if he, too, disliked the Ways and Means bill. He traveled to Capitol Hill to plead for Republican support. Six days after the first vote, with more than fifty Republicans changing sides, the rule was approved by voice vote, and after adoption of two minor Democratic amendments, the bill was passed by voice vote—to nearly everyone's surprise. Opponents, for unknown reasons, failed to ask for a roll-call vote.

In the Senate, the Finance Committee got to business in mid-March in public session and with about the same degree of difficulty as Ways and Means in private at reaching consensus. A week or so earlier, fifty senators had signed a letter to Reagan opposing the emphasis on the revenue-neutral tax bill at a time when reducing the deficit was more critical. It was not that they all supported a tax increase instead, although some no doubt did, but rather that they did not want the attention of Congress and the White House diverted from what they considered to be the real priority. But Packwood was not deterred.

Instead of working from the Ways and Means bill, Packwood proposed his own that varied from the House measure in several important respects: somewhat lower rates, more favorable business depreciation deductions, and repeal of the deduction for state and local sales, personal property, and income taxes. He had already cut deals with members, unlike Rostenkowski who had not done so before markup. So, when the markup began—and senators began demanding that even more tax breaks be retained—Packwood's bill began falling apart.

The Finance Committee's open markup was almost a perfect example of Rostenkowski's admonition about members fearing to vote against special interests in public. After not quite three weeks of markup, the committee had voted to restore so many tax breaks that it would have produced a tax cut of $29 billion over five years. Packwood suspended the markup the morning of April 18. That afternoon, over lunch and couple pitchers of beer, Packwood and his staff director, William Diefenderfer, devised a strategy that was not only to reverse the direction the Finance Committee was taking but also to define the terms of the bill that was enacted into law.

Working over two weeks with Treasury officials and a bipartisan "core group" of seven senators—liberal and conservative, urban and rural—Packwood produced a bill that had only two individual tax rates, 15 and 27 percent, instead of the fourteen existing rates that ranged from 11 to 50 percent. At least 80 percent of all taxpayers would have paid at the 15 percent rate, and six million working poor persons would have been taken off the tax rolls.

Other major changes were to tax capital gains as regular income, to repeal the use of most tax shelters that relied on paper losses, and to create a stiff minimum tax for corporations and individuals.

In barely two days of markup beginning May 5 and extending to just past midnight May 6, the committee ratified the Packwood proposal, making a few dozen minor changes and one big one: exempting oil and gas investments from the crackdown on tax shelters. That provoked the only public fight, when Bradley tried to roll back the oil and gas exemption.

In the end the committee voted 20-0 to send the bill to the floor, which some people told Packwood was "a miracle." Said the chairman, "If you don't believe in miracles, you're just not a realist."

During the three weeks that the bill was on the Senate floor, Packwood was able to hold off virtually all amendments that would have jeopardized the measure's success, by insisting that amendments—like the bill—be revenue-neutral. The key test came on a plea by Alfonse M. D'Amato, R-N.Y. (1981-), to restore the tax break for IRAs, which the bill would have eliminated for any taxpayer covered by another pension plan. When that amendment was defeated, though narrowly because it was supported by all nine Democrats and half of the eighteen Republicans facing reelection in 1986, it was clear sailing for Packwood.

Although dozens of amendments were adopted, few were significant and many fell in conference. The bill passed the Senate 97-3 June 24.

It took conferees on the bill a month, from July 17 to August 16, to negotiate the sizeable differences between the House and Senate versions—particularly how much taxes should be increased on businesses. But it took no time to figure out the merits—political and economic—of the Senate's two-tier rate structure for individual taxpayers. By trying to adhere to such low rates, as well as eliminating some extremely costly tax breaks, such as special treatment for capital gains income and tax shelters, conferees believed they could produce a bill that granted ample tax relief to the lower and middle classes and increased fairness in the tax code, if not much simplicity.

Leveling the Playing Field

Despite Reagan's initial 1984 call to simplify the tax laws, Congress in 1986 did not really do so, except by reducing the number of persons eligible to itemize their deductions.

The tax code was still thousands of pages long, with countless provisions affecting all manner of activities in different ways. But persons with average incomes were expected to benefit from efforts to make the law less complex for them: Individuals had fewer items with costs that were tax-deductible; therefore, record keeping for them should be simpler. For high-income persons and corporations, a new, stiffer minimum tax was expected to make record keeping and tax calculations more complex, but the trade-off was considered necessary to ensure that those taxpayers with the most income paid their share.

Most observers said the 1986 tax law went a long way toward making the code more equitable for all classes of taxpayers. As Packwood put it, during final Senate debate on the conference agreement on the bill: "Taxes are about money, they are about more than economics. They are about fairness—and this bill is fair."

That assessment was in no small part based on an economic judgment. Some critics maintained that the law's deep cuts in tax rates were a step away from a historical tendency toward progressive rates. But traditional tax law also offered complex strategies for individuals and corporations to reduce their tax burdens by engaging in certain kinds of economic activity. To the extent that the 1986 bill eliminated provisions from the tax code that were deemed to stimulate those activities, despite their desirability or profitability, the bill was seen to be more fair.

Joseph A. Pechman, a tax expert at the Brookings Institution, wrote in 1987 that the 1986 law was a definite improvement. "While the tax law itself is not simpler, it is more equitable and distorts economic behavior much less than the old law," Pechman wrote in the fifth edition of his book *Federal Tax Policy*.

Certainly the 1986 law's restrictions on sheltering income were expected to eliminate large amounts of uneconomic investment. For example, taxpayers with sufficient income could buy into businesses—often limited partnerships—set up strictly for the purpose of taking advantage of tax breaks and without any regard for the profitability of the enterprise. Investment tax credits, accelerated depreciation schedules, particularly for real estate, and other benefits were used by these partnerships to create paper losses in excess of actual income. Since partnership income and losses are passed through to the partners, the paper losses could—before 1987—be deducted against an individual's wage income, thereby reducing tax liability. Often before a tax shelter used up its tax benefits and began earning real profits, the partners would sell their interests and move on to a newly formed shelter.

The 1986 law made it impossible to deduct paper or so-called "passive" losses against anything but "passive" income—in other words real income from the same kind of investments that generated the paper losses.

Eliminating the special tax rate on capital gains earnings and the investment tax credit and altering the accelerated depreciation schedule also had their effect on the tax liability of various industries, as did numerous other changes to the treatment of oil and gas operations, timber, retailing and other inventory-sensitive industries, and research and development.

One study from the Congressional Research Service, an arm of the Library of Congress, found that overall the effective tax rate on corporations would increase under the 1986 law from 38 percent to 41 percent. But for industry the change was more dramatic: Agriculture, manufacturing, and trade, which paid the highest effective rates under the old law, would see no change or a slight reduction in their tax liabilities. But oil and mining, utilities, construction, communication, transportation, and services industries would see their effective rates climb from as low as 23 percent to as high as 41 percent.

When the study was applied to assets—equipment, structures, and inventory—the results were even more striking. The effective tax rate on equipment went from 11 percent to 38 percent; on structures from 35 percent to 39 percent; and on inventory from 58 percent to 48 percent.

It was no wonder that many U.S. businesses strongly favored the bill, while others opposed it.

Changing Corporate Share

Aside from making the tax code's impact on different types of businesses more economically neutral, the 1986 changes sought to reverse a trend since World War II that saw a greater percentage of the income tax paid by individuals, while the corporate share diminished.

The original House-passed bill would have shifted about $140 billion in taxes from individuals to corporations over five years, while the Senate version would have switched just over $100 billion. The final bill roughly split the difference at $120 billion. But despite the increased importance of corporate taxes, their share of the total income tax burden in 1988 was still expected to be lower than at any time prior to 1979. (See Table 4-4.)

Table 4-4 Individual and Corporate Share of Income Tax Payments

Fiscal year	Individuals	Corporations
1957	62.7%	37.3%
1967	64.4	35.6
1977	74.2	25.8
1978	75.2	24.8
1979	76.8	23.2
1980	79.1	20.9
1981	82.4	17.6
1982	85.8	14.2
1983	88.6	11.4
1984	84.0	16.0
1985	84.5	15.5
1986	84.7	15.3
1987	82.4	17.6
1988 [a]	78.8	21.2

Source: Office of Management and Budget.
[a] Estimate.

Throughout the tax debate in 1985 and 1986, attention was repeatedly focused on the corporate sector's tax burden. Two separate and somewhat different studies released July 15, 1986—both updates of earlier work—showed that one in six of the nation's largest, and most profitable, corporations paid no tax in 1985.

One study, by Citizens for Tax Justice, a group financed largely by organized labor, found that 42 of 250 corporations paid no tax in 1985, and more than half paid no tax in at least one of the five years from 1981 to 1985.

Tax Analysts, supported entirely by sales of its publications to businesses, tax lawyers, and accountants, found that 95 of the 604 corporations it studied paid no tax in 1985. Citizens for Tax Justice based its study on corporate annual reports and filings with the Securities and Exchange Commission (SEC). Tax Analysts used SEC filings and tried to get additional information from the corporations.

"For most of America's largest corporations, no-tax years are now commonplace," said Robert S. McIntyre, head of Citizens for Tax Justice. Thomas F. Field, executive director of Tax Analysts, said, "It is fair to conclude on the basis of our figures that the U.S. corporate income tax is seriously flawed. In particular, the finding that effective corporate tax rates continue to vary widely from industry to industry means that our tax system promotes misallocation of capital and losses of economic efficiency."

Commerce Department figures in early 1988 showed the effects of the law on corporate tax receipts. On pretax profits of $237.1 billion in calendar 1980, total corporate tax liability (including that paid to states) was $84.8 billion. In 1987, total tax liability was $137.5 billion on pretax profits of $274.6 billion. The change was from 36 percent of profits to 50 percent.

The Office of Management and Budget (OMB) painted a similar picture. In fiscal 1958, corporate income taxes were 25.2 percent of all federal receipts; in 1968, 18.7 percent; in 1978, 15.0 percent. After falling to a low of 6.2 percent in 1983 (after the 1981 tax cut), corporate taxes edged upward to 9.8 percent in 1987 and were expected to hit 12.5 percent in 1992.

The Fiscal Impact

Ultimately, the most direct economic impact of the 1986 tax changes may be on the deficit. The revenue fluctuation that the phase-in of the law's provisions guaranteed wound up being much more dramatic than anticipated.

To avoid the higher tax on capital gains income that would be imposed in 1987, many taxpayers unloaded stocks, real estate holdings, and other appreciated property in 1986, so they could pay a much reduced tax on the accumulated gains. For a tax bill designed to end such seemingly unsound economic decisions, it was an ironic twist.

When the law was enacted, the Joint Committee on Taxation projected a revenue gain of $11.4 billion in the first year, fiscal 1987, and losses the following two years of $16.7 billion and $15.1 billion. Over five years, the bill was projected to lose only $300 million—less than 0.1 percent of income tax collections, fairly close to revenue-neutral by almost any standards.

But in early 1988, OMB said the law was expected to lose $23.2 billion over the first five years it was in effect. And that was after a windfall of $21.5 billion in extra revenue the first year. The revenue loss expected in fiscal 1988 was only $4.5 billion, but that loss was anticipated to grow to $17.2 billion, $13.5 billion, and $9.5 billion in subsequent years.

Even so, in a tax system that collects upward of $500 billion in income taxes, the five-year loss was only 1 percent or less. Though $23 billion meant little to the overall revenue picture, it became an imposing sum next to $150 billion deficits. When a small increase in the deficit has the potential to trigger Gramm-Rudman's automatic, uniform spending cuts, a small revenue loss takes on greater meaning.

Some members of Congress—notably Sen. Pete V. Domenici, R-N.M., who was Budget Committee chairman in 1986—worried about the revenue fluctuations. But Domenici could do little to persuade his colleagues to do anything about it. At his urging the Senate adopted by voice vote an amendment that in effect would have ignored the volatile revenue curve. For Gramm-Rudman deficit calculations under Domenici's amendment, the revenue effects of the 1986 tax law were not to be considered. The intent was to prevent large revenue increases resulting from the bill from allowing Congress to avoid its obligation to take action to reduce the devicit. And Domenici was equally concerned that in later years a revenue loss might trigger automatic Gramm-Rudman cuts. However, the amendment was dropped in conference.

5

Experiments in Budgeting

Critics of the congressional budget process can point to its first years as a time of failure; supporters can find evidence of its success. But there is one obvious lesson in Congress's longest sustained experiment in comprehensive, thoughtful budgeting: The process is adaptable.

As embodied in the 1974 Congressional Budget and Impoundment Control Act, the budget process is a creature of compromise. It was created to flow with, not against, the myriad political and jurisdictional currents that cascade down Capitol Hill. Flexibility has been its virtue, allowing Congress to continue to produce budgets even when the results please few in or out of government. Yet, because the process has not yielded the desired reward of a reduced deficit, its flexibility, which accommodates political pressures, threatens to be its undoing. By devising budget procedures that gave free play to conflicts, "Congress institutionalized its own ambivalence over budget policy," as budget expert and University of Maryland professor Allen Schick has noted.

One clear indication of just how frustrating the budget process can be came in 1983, a year of limited budget success. Early in the year, defense secretary Caspar W. Weinberger urged President Ronald Reagan to eschew compromise as part of a broad strategy to defeat congressional attempts to write a budget. If Congress failed to formulate a budget plan, Weinberger and others believed, limits on appropriations for defense spending would not be adopted, and there would be no rolling back of the administration's military buildup.

Congress eventually adopted its budget but was unable to take further action to reduce spending and increase revenues. Then, the frustration of budget making was even more visible. "As we leave Washington, word of our impotence will precede us," said House Ways and Means chairman Dan Rostenkowski, D-Ill., expressing a widely held belief. "We have confessed to an already doubting nation that we are ruled by political fear rather than economic courage."

Understanding Terms

Over time, the words "budget process" have become almost synonymous with "deficit reduction," particularly in the public's mind. But they are not the same things. The former really has no relation to the latter. When it was first being considered in the early 1970s, the process that now governs congressional budget behavior had little to do with deficits and everything to do with regaining control over spending. Only in the

1980s has deficit reduction become the most important budgetary goal confronting Congress and the president. It may be a subtle distinction, but the process was supposed to be equally well suited to increasing as well as decreasing spending. Budgetary control was the key objective.

In this book "budget process" is used to mean the way Congress adopts the budget resolutions that set overall taxing, spending, and deficit goals for the federal government. And budget process includes the enacting into law of "reconciliation" bills that were designed as the means to enforce the budget resolution's goals—but that have become the legislative means to deficit reduction.

Budget resolutions, like laws, are adopted by both chambers of Congress. Differences between the chambers are worked out, as is the case with laws, in joint House-Senate conference committees. And compromises agreed to in conference are returned to each chamber for final adoption. But budget resolutions are not laws, because they do not go to the president for approval or veto. As one of the two legislative tools of the budget process, budget resolutions are strictly a device of Congress, expressing its wishes, but not those of the president.

As they have evolved, budget resolutions are supposed to bind Congress to broad spending, revenue, and deficit totals, but these budgets are binding only insofar as Congress is willing to be bound from day to day. The fact that Congress often ignores the mostly voluntary restraints of budget resolutions is one explanation for why actual deficits have exceeded targets year after year.

Reconciliation bills are the other chief tool of the budget process. They are the means by which existing programs, particularly entitlements and taxes, are changed—reconciled—to conform with the goals expressed in the budget resolution. Because

they must be signed into law by the president, reconciliation bills do have an effect on the deficit, and their impact on budget decisions is significant and lasting.

But decisions made in the crafting of budget resolutions and reconciliation bills are not the only decisions made by Congress that affect spending and tax policy. Appropriations bills move separately from the budget resolution, though in theory somewhat after the resolution and in compliance with it. And free-standing tax bills (like tax decisions made through reconciliation) are supposed to follow the budget's revenue guidelines. Authorization bills that create new entitlements and other spending programs that are not subject to direct, annual appropriations also are supposed to observe budget limits.

Yet, to the degree that political currents change, budgetary decisions have changed with them. And, over the years, members of both parties and of every political stripe have found cause to complain about the budget process, that it failed to prevent some abuse—or itself became the means of abuse.

In the early years of the budget process, conservatives took issue with the free-spending Budget committees that merely added up whatever requests for spending they were given by the authorizing and Appropriations committees and thereby found a bottom line.

Liberals, whose favored spending programs have suffered at the hands of budget cutters since fiscal austerity took hold at the end of the 1970s, found a ready target for their complaints in reconciliation. In 1981, the reconciliation procedure was used to make wholesale changes in the way government was structured—and without much deliberation or conscious thought about the outcome. But in time, even liberals found ways to use reconciliation to their advantage. These "must-pass" bills are protected against dilatory tactics even in the Senate where debate usually is unrestrained. As a result, since 1981, reconciliation has become the main vehicle for expanding eligibility for Medicaid, the health-care program for the poor, among other things.

An Evolving Process

One measure of the success of the budget process is the degree to which it has enabled Congress to set its own priorities despite the desires of the president—even a popular one like Reagan, whose two-term mandate presumably included an assault on government spending.

In virtually every year since 1975, when the current budgeting process began, Congress has adopted budgets that vary from the president's budget request and from eventual reality—both in absolute terms of tax dollars received and spent, but more importantly in the ways that those dollars were spent. The only deviation from that trend was the fiscal 1982 budget adopted in May 1981, five months into Reagan's first term. That budget, much more so than any other, closely tracked the president's blueprint for a tax cut and companion spending cuts. In the end, however, the reconciliation bill designed to implement the budget resolution fell short of the mark. (For a summary of budget requests, budgets adopted, and actual revenues and outlays, see Table 5-1.)

Budgets are adopted in the calendar year preceding the fiscal year for which they are intended; a fiscal year runs from October 1 through September 30. A review of the budgets adopted since 1975 reveals ways in which the process has varied. For instance, in the early years Congress annually adopted at least two budget resolutions. (The 1974 budget law assumed at least two budget resolutions a year, but as with many of the law's "requirements," this one could not be enforced and later came to be ignored.) One was prepared in the early part

of the year and was not binding; the other was adopted later—near to the start of the fiscal year—and theoretically was binding. Once, in early 1977 just after Jimmy Carter took over the White House, Congress prepared a third budget resolution for the ongoing year, to accommodate Carter's desire to give individuals a tax rebate. That third resolution had to be revised once more after the rebate plan was dropped a few months later.

By the end of the 1970s, however, adoption of the second budget was becoming a pro forma action with little meaning. The task of adopting two budgets also expended inordinate time and energy and cost considerable political capital since budget battles had to be fought out twice. So, when Congress adopted a second resolution for fiscal 1982 that was completely unchanged from the first, the practice was doomed. Thereafter, Congress agreed that the first budget resolution would become binding if there were no second budget by the start of the fiscal year. With enactment of the Gramm-Rudman antideficit law in 1985, the requirement for a second budget was shelved altogether, though adoption of additional budgets was always permitted.

One other twist developed in the early years of the budget process: revising budget resolution totals midyear. The adoption of binding budget resolution totals establishes a floor procedure whereby any senator or member of the House may object to consideration of a subsequent appropriations, authorization, or tax bill that breaches the spending, revenue, or deficit totals set for the year. The process is somewhat different in each chamber and is quite complicated—involving "scorekeeping" by the Congressional Budget Office and each chamber's Budget Committee of how much the year's congressional activity has changed revenue, spending, and deficit expectations. But the general principle exists that a member may raise a "point of order" that a bill is—in

Table 5-1 Budgets Requested, Adopted, and Actual (in billions)

	Revenues	Outlays	Surplus or deficit
Fiscal 1976			
Ford budget request	$297.5	$ 349.4	$ −51.9
First resolution	298.2	367.0	−68.8
Second resolution	300.8	374.9	−74.1
Actual	299.2	364.8	−65.6
Fiscal 1977			
Ford budget request	351.3	394.2	−43.0
First resolution	362.5	413.3	−50.8
Second resolution	362.5	413.1	−50.6
Third resolution	347.7	417.5	−69.8
Revised third resolution [a]	356.6	409.2	−52.6
Actual	356.9	401.9	−45.0
Fiscal 1978			
Ford budget request	393.0	440.0	−47.0
Carter revised budget	401.6	459.4	−57.7
First resolution	396.3	461.0	−64.6
Second resolution	397.0	458.3	−61.3
Actual	401.1	449.9	−48.8
Fiscal 1979			
Carter budget request	439.6	500.2	−60.6
First resolution	447.9	498.8	−50.9
Second resolution	448.7	487.5	−38.8
Revised second resolution [a]	461.0	494.5	−33.4
Actual	465.9	493.7	−27.7
Fiscal 1980			
Carter budget request	502.6	531.6	−29.0
First resolution	509.0	532.0	−23.0
Second resolution	517.8	547.6	−29.8
Revised second resolution [a]	525.7	572.7	−47.0
Actual	520.1	579.6	−59.6
Fiscal 1981			
Carter budget request	600.0	615.8	−15.8
Carter revised budget	628.0	611.5	16.5
First resolution	613.8	613.6	0.2
Second resolution	605.0	632.4	−27.4
Revised second resolution [a]	603.3	661.4	−58.0
Actual	602.6	660.5	−57.9
Fiscal 1982			
Carter budget request	711.8	739.3	−27.5
Reagan revised budget	650.3	695.3	−45.0
First resolution	657.8	695.4	−37.6
Revised second resolution [a]	628.4	734.1	−105.7
Actual	617.8	728.4	−110.7

Table 5-1 *Continued*

	Revenues	Outlays	Surplus or deficit
Fiscal 1983			
Reagan budget request	666.1	757.6	−91.5
First resolution	665.9	769.8	−103.9
Revised second resolution [a,b]	604.3	807.4	−203.1
Actual	600.6	796.4	−195.4
Fiscal 1984			
Reagan budget request	659.7	848.5	−188.8
First resolution [c]	679.6	851.2	−171.6
Revised second resolution [a]	672.9	845.6	−172.7
Actual	666.5	841.8	−175.3
Fiscal 1985			
Reagan budget request [d]	745.1	925.5	−180.4
First resolution [d]	750.9	932.0	−181.2
Revised second resolution [a,e]	736.5	935.9	−199.4
Revised second resolution [a,e]	736.5	946.3	−209.8
Actual [d]	734.1	936.8	−202.8
Actual [e]	734.1	946.3	−212.3
Fiscal 1986			
Reagan budget request	793.7	973.7	−180.0
First resolution	795.7	967.6	−171.9
Actual	769.1	989.8	−220.7
Fiscal 1987			
Reagan budget request	850.4	994.0	−143.6
First resolution	852.4	995.0	−142.6
Actual	854.1	1,002.9	−148.8
Fiscal 1988			
Reagan budget request	916.6	1,024.3	−107.8
First resolution [f]	932.8	1,040.8	−108.0
First resolution [g]	921.6	1,055.4	−133.8
Actual	909.0	1,064.1	−155.1

Source: Congressional Budget Office.

Note: Tables may not add due to rounding. Amounts are adjusted to subtract spending and revenues associated with functions that from time to time—principally before 1985—were considered "off-budget" (such as the Federal Financing Bank and the Postal Service) and to account for other differences in the treatment of spending in budget resolutions. Therefore, deficit amounts may not agree with those officially reported or found elsewhere in this book.

[a] Revised resolutions were adopted as part of the first budget resolution for the following fiscal year. A second resolution for fiscal 1982 merely reaffirmed the figures in the first resolution. No second resolution was adopted for fiscal 1983-1985, and in each year the first resolution became binding at the start of the fiscal year.
[b] Amounts for proposed reserve fund are excluded.
[c] Amounts are adjusted to account for partial enactment of reserve fund.
[d] On-budget only.
[e] On- and off-budget combined.
[f] Using administration economic assumptions.
[g] Using Congressional Budget Office economic assumptions.

essence—over budget. That has prompted Congress repeatedly to revise its budget resolution totals for the ongoing year, particularly its deficit estimate, when considering the budget resolution for the following year.

This happened not only in 1977, after Carter's abortive push for tax rebates, but in each year from 1980 through 1985. Once Gramm-Rudman—with its mandatory deficit targets—was enacted in 1985, however, it was no longer feasible to revise deficit estimates upward, so the process fell into disuse.

Missing Dates

The federal government would not halt in its tracks if Congress simply stopped adopting budget resolutions. Indeed, preventing adoption of a budget has occasionally been fostered as a good idea. But in Congress there is an almost religious devotion to the budget process. That has remained true, even though conflicting political pressures have at times threatened congressional faith that the beleaguered system could keep working. One sign of those pressures is the degree to which the House and Senate have slipped badly behind the timetable established for adoption of budget resolutions and enactment of appropriations and reconciliation bills.

For the first four years after 1975, and in that one anomalous year of 1981 when Reagan had Congress doing much of his bidding, the House and Senate managed to produce budgets on time, or nearly so. But the budget law's May 15 deadline for the first budget resolution notwithstanding, getting the budget adopted proved to be much more difficult and time-consuming after 1978. (See Table 5-2.)

Not only was adoption of budget resolutions put off until June or even August, but action was then necessarily delayed on second budget resolutions and reconciliation

and appropriations bills, often until after the fiscal year had begun October 1. And twice, in 1983 and 1985, reconciliation bills that had been mandated by the budget resolution were not enacted before Congress quit in December to go home for the year. In both instances, the held-over bills were enacted the following spring, but their presumed savings had greatly diminished over time.

In 1984, Congress did not even attempt to write a budget until the end of the process, after it had already adopted a deficit-reduction bill for the coming fiscal year—sort of a before-the-fact reconciliation bill. Having thereby reversed the process, the budget resolution that year merely ratified the spending and revenue changes accomplished by the deficit-reduction measure. The budget was adopted October 1, the day it was to take effect.

Congress changed the deadlines somewhat in enacting Gramm-Rudman. For instance, the budget resolution deadline was moved up to April 15, in an effort to encourage earlier action. But in the first three years after the deadlines were changed, Congress did little better at meeting them. It did meet one politically significant deadline in 1988: All required appropriations bills were passed before the October 1 start of the fiscal year to which they applied. It was only the third time since 1948 that all appropriations had passed on time.

Missing Fiscal Targets, Too

Deadlines were not the only thing Congress missed. Since 1980 Congress repeatedly missed meeting the reconciliation requirements of the budget resolution. And the actual yearly totals for spending, revenues, and deficits were often very different from those proposed in Congress's budgets.

That was partly due to the way that budgets are calculated and the long time

Table 5-2 Budget Resolution, Reconciliation, and Appropriations Dates

Year	First budget resolution [a]	Second budget resolution [b]	Required reconciliation bill [c]	Final appropriations bill [d]
1975	May 14	December 12	[e]	December 12 [f]
1976	May 13	September 16	[e]	October 1 [f]
1977	May 17	September 15	[e]	December 7
1978	May 17	September 23	[e]	October 15
1979	May 24	November 28	[e]	December 13
1980	June 12	November 20	December 3	December 16 [f]
1981	May 14	December 10	July 31	December 11 [f]
1982	June 23	Not adopted	August 19	December 20
1983	June 23	Not adopted	April 5, 1984	November 12
1984	October 1	Not adopted	June 27 [g]	October 11
1985	August 1	Not adopted	March 20, 1986	December 19
1986	June 27	—	October 17	October 17
1987	June 24	—	December 22	December 22
1988	June 6	—	[e]	September 30

Note: Calendar year dates conference agreements adopted or cleared for president's signature.

[a] For 1975-1985, the first budget resolution deadline was May 15; after 1985, the deadline was April 15.
[b] For 1975-1985, the second budget resolution deadline was September 15; after 1985, no second resolution was required.
[c] For 1975-1985, the reconciliation deadline was September 25; after 1985, the deadline was June 15.
[d] For 1975-1985, the deadline for all appropriations was seven days after Labor Day (roughly by mid-September); after 1985, the deadline was June 30 for the House to complete action on all appropriations bills. The fiscal year has begun October 1 since 1976. It began July 1 in 1975.
[e] Reconciliation not required by budget resolution.
[f] Part-year continuing appropriations resolution enacted to allow Congress to adjourn. Additional continuing appropriations resolutions were adopted later in the fiscal year (during the following calendar year).
[g] Deficit-reduction bill in 1984 predated budget resolution, and therefore was not technically a reconciliation bill.

span between adopting a budget and the end of the fiscal year that the budget governs. Congress and the administration calculate their budget decisions on "baselines" that are mostly drawn from the previous year's budget, then adjusted to reflect expectations about possible changes in federal programs and in the economy. Concerns such as a rise in unemployment that will increase costs and reduce tax revenues or a fall in interest rates that will reduce the cost of paying for the federal debt have a tremendous bearing on spending, revenues, and deficit. And they are tough to predict accurately.

Baselines are the projections against which the budget is compared. And since baselines almost universally assume increases in spending and revenues—owing principally to inflation and a larger population—suggesting that the budget will "cut" spending or "reduce" revenues does not always mean just that. A spending "cut" from baseline budget projections might still mean an increase in spending, just not as much as it might have been.

Not only do changing economic conditions affect the success of setting and meeting budget targets, the process itself lacks any significant means of enforcing those targets. Budgets are built on assumptions other than those incorporated in baselines. Congressional budgets "assume" that authorizing and Appropriations committees will take certain actions. If those committees fail—or refuse—to comply with the budget's assumptions, there often is little that can be done about it.

Moreover, although budget totals are in theory binding, they are fixed in about twenty "functional" categories that do not correspond directly with either authorizing committees or the thirteen Appropriations subcommittees. That makes comparisons between authorization or appropriations bills and the budget difficult, if not impossible. (The number of budget functions changes periodically. It was twenty in 1988.)

To the degree that the budget only assumes certain actions will happen, it is easy to see how the end result could differ markedly from the blueprint.

Partisanship Prevails

Throughout the early period of congressional budgeting, the nation's economy was in a slow and halting recovery from the steep 1974-1975 recession. Federal fiscal policy, while calling for an eventual balanced budget, gave Congress considerable latitude to increase spending even while budget deficits persisted. But the lack of real fiscal pressure in those early years did not mean Congress had no trouble adopting budgets. Usually just the opposite was the case. The newness of the budget process, the degree to which it imposed even small limits on the actions of previously independent committees, and conflicts with the Ford and Carter administrations over policy choices all contributed to discord. But compared with the 1980s, disputes in the late 1970s were a cakewalk. Nevertheless, early jurisdictional and partisan battles provided a prelude of things to come.

Before 1981, the Senate, with a forceful Budget Committee chairman and a bipartisan tradition of legislating by consensus, used the budget process much more smoothly than the deeply divided House. Even with Democrat Carter in the White House and both chambers in Democratic hands, it was typical to get a majority or

near majority of Republicans to vote for budget resolutions before they went to conference.

In the House, the rotating membership of the Budget Committee meant that the panel developed less budget expertise. And members' loyalties to the other legislative panels on which they served further limited the Budget Committee's political clout in House maneuvering. In addition, House Democratic leaders were unable to count on backing from more than a handful or two of the disgruntled Republican minority. So they were forced to barter with urban liberals and Southern fiscal conservatives to gain support for budget resolutions.

By the end of the 1970s, the game changed. The national inflation rate soared above 20 percent, and federal outlays were growing by roughly $50 billion a year, far outpacing revenues and driving the deficit higher and higher. Voters turned to Republican Reagan, who promised to curb inflation and bring the budget into balance. And the 1980 elections also gave Republicans control of the Senate and weakened the Democratic majority in the House.

Reagan's election—and its obvious political message—forced Congress to bring the discipline of fiscal scarcity to the budget. The results were the 1981 budget resolution and a subsequent reconciliation bill, both largely written by Republicans and abetted by the votes of conservative Democrats—most of them Southerners, hence their name, the Boll Weevils.

But Reagan's fiscal success was short-lived. The Boll Weevils did not stay in the GOP camp forever; steadily rising deficits—cresting over $200 billion in 1985—disenchantment with the rest of the Reagan program, and accommodations granted to them by the Democratic leadership all helped bring the wayfaring conservatives back on the reservation.

A backlash also arose among members—particularly those from powerful committees—who believed that wide-ranging reconciliation bills abused normal congressional procedures. Sen. William Proxmire, D-Wis., warned that "unless we stop short, take stock and revise some of the procedures, the budget reform act itself may die, or worse may destroy the Senate as a distributive body."

And House Rules Committee chairman Richard Bolling, D-Mo. (1949-1983)—in a *Washington Post* editorial-page article written with John E. Barriere, a Democratic staff assistant who helped write the 1974 budget law—protested at the time that continued use of reconciliation as it was practiced in 1981 "will be a gross distortion of the intent of those who wrote the Constitution and the Bill of Rights, as well as the intent of the 1974 Budget Act."

But despite the distaste for reconciliation after 1981, it remained an element of the budget process thereafter; the size of the deficit demanded it. And the congressional partisanship evident before Reagan's election remained as well. With the Senate in Republican control from 1981 to 1987, the partisan nature of the budget process became more visible than ever, and compromise with the White House on budget issues proved elusive.

The consequence of that partisanship was heightened frustration as the budget process appeared to be disintegrating. Not only did Congress stop adopting second budget resolutions, but it also failed in 1983 and again in 1985 to enact a reconciliation bill.

Finally, at the end of 1985, came the first major revision to the 1974 budget law. Gramm-Rudman, with its deficit targets and automatic spending cuts, was designed first and foremost to force more discipline on federal budget making. But all the new law really did was require Congress to find other means of avoiding difficult decisions. Eventually, Gramm-Rudman was revised to make it less painful.

The Ford Years: A Process of Accommodation

In the early years after creation of the new budget process, congressional budget making largely relied on accommodating various congressional interests, if not the White House. It was not surprising, given that one of the original reasons for the 1974 budget act was to wrest control of spending away from the president, that Congress was unwilling to cede authority back right away, leading to confrontations with the new president, Gerald R. Ford, over policy. And, while such conflicts were nothing new, for a time Congress—in the firm control of the Democrats—clearly had the upper hand.

Ford, a Michigan Republican, had served in the House almost twenty-five years and was minority leader when President Richard Nixon tapped him in late 1973 to be vice president, following the resignation of Spiro Agnew. When Nixon himself resigned August 9, 1974, Ford succeeded to the presidency, having never been elected to national office. Though his nomination as vice president was hailed by his fellow members of Congress, Ford suffered for having been an unelected president, without a popular mandate. And that, coupled with a resurgent Congress, contributed to his troubles.

Clear evidence of the conflicts between Ford and Congress was the frequency with which he refused to sign congressionally initated bills into law. Ford vetoed 66 bills in his two years and six months in the White House. That is more than any president since Dwight D. Eisenhower, who vetoed 181 over eight years, except for Reagan, who had vetoed 70 through October of 1988. Adding to the conflict, Ford's vetoes were overridden by Congress twelve times, matching the experience of Harry S Truman but short of Andrew Johnson's record of fifteen veto overrides. Four of Ford's vetoes—and three overrides—were on appropriations measures he considered over-budget. Congress also overrode Ford's veto of a public works jobs bill that the president said was too costly.

While Ford and Congress were squaring off, there was little desire for acrimony within the walls of the Capitol, and creeping deficits had not yet frayed political nerves enough to require fiscal restraint. So House and Senate leaders, anxious to make the new budget process work, steered away from proposing budget resolutions that would force legislative and appropriating committees to compete openly for budget resources. Instead of setting an overall spending total, the House and Senate Budget committees first considered the spending needs for each of twenty-one functional budget categories. According to Schick, "At no time during the first five years of budgeting did either committee vote explicitly to take from one function in order to give more to another."

As long as Congress remained in an expansive mood, the House and Senate were able to construct budgets in a piece-meal fashion that satisfied the particular interests of various committees and groups. Only when Congress tried to shift toward fiscal austerity in mid-1979 would members encounter much rougher going.

1975: Congress Tries Its Wings

Democrats, eager to rewrite the restrictive budgets that Ford's Republican administration drew up, put the new congressional budget procedures into use in 1975, a year ahead of schedule.

The budget law mandated that Congress start using the process for fiscal 1977, which started October 1, 1976. The law allowed Congress a year to get the feel of the procedures in 1975, if it chose, by putting the fiscal 1976 budget through a trial run. House and Senate leaders, determined to rework that year's budget to step up stimulative spending to counter a deep 1974-1975 recession, agreed to implement key parts of the process.

The 1975 proceedings waived some budget law deadlines and left out potentially controversial budget targets for program categories. But in December legislators adopted a second, binding budget resolution in which Congress for the first time (except for a couple abortive efforts in the late 1940s and early 1950s) specified the total size of the federal budget. The congressional budget boosted Ford's proposed level of spending by almost $18 billion and projected a $74.1 billion deficit, which would have been the largest in the nation's history. As things turned out, fiscal 1976 outlays fell short of the congressional budget ceiling, but the $65.6 billion deficit still was the largest ever.

The budget totals dismayed fiscal conservatives and displeased some prospending liberals who wanted Congress to take stronger action to reduce unemployment. In spite of their differences, influential conservatives and liberals in both the House and Senate supported the new system at critical points and kept it from collapsing.

Budget Committee leaders were particularly effective in forcing Congress to pay attention to its budget goals. In the Senate, Budget Committee chairman Edmund S. Muskie, D-Maine (1959-1980), gained key support from the committee's top-ranking Republican, Henry Bellmon of Oklahoma (1969-1981), a fiscal conservative. The going was tougher in the House; Republicans were more resistant to the new process, and liberal Democrats challenged the Budget Committee's recommendations as too restrictive.

Brock Adams, D-Wash. (House 1965-1977; Senate 1987-   ), had been elected House Budget Committee chairman when Congress convened, as Al Ullman, D-Ore., chose instead to take over the Ways and Means Committee.

With the vigorous backing of the House Democratic leadership, Adams evenutally won narrow House approval of both fiscal 1976 resolutions.

Early in the year, the budget process was handicapped by lack of a functioning Congressional Budget Office (CBO). House and Senate leaders had been fighting a protracted battle since the budget law was passed over filling the potentially influential post of CBO director. Finally, on February 24, Congress swore in Harvard-trained economist Alice Rivlin, a senior fellow at the liberal-leaning Brookings Institution in Washington, D.C., as the first CBO director.

Before the 1975 session ended, Congress stuck by the new process in a dispute with Ford over fiscal 1977 spending. Democrats fended off Ford's demand, backed by House Republicans, that Congress specify a fiscal 1977 spending ceiling without waiting for the budget procedures to operate in 1976.

Ford had proposed a $394.2 billion spending limit, which would have cut estimated fiscal 1977 outlays by about $28 billion, offsetting a $28 billion tax-cut package Ford had also requested. Rejecting the tax package, Congress enacted a six-month extension of 1975 tax cuts and worked that revenue loss into its second fiscal 1976 budget resolution. Because Congress had refused to consider his spending restraints, Ford vetoed the tax-cut extension.

House Republicans, with help from Democratic fiscal conservatives, upheld that veto. But House and Senate leaders, with Muskie and Adams in the forefront, refused to consider a spending limit proposal, contending it would short-circuit the budget process before the president submitted specific reductions in his fiscal 1977 budget.

The issue finally was resolved when Congress, pledging to consider spending restraints for fiscal 1977, won Ford's approval of a six-month tax-cut extension.

1976: A Tax Bill Challenge

The budget law went into full effect in 1976, and Congress met its requirements in approving a binding, $413.1 billion fiscal 1977 budget, which included a $50.6 billion deficit.

As expected, Congress paid scant attention to Ford's $394.2 billion budget request. Members nonetheless approved virtually all of the president's $101.1 billion defense spending projection and carved significant amounts from potential and proposed domestic outlays.

Debates on budget resolution spending and tax targets again produced sharp differences with Budget committee recommendations from both liberals and conservatives. But the Senate continued to back its panel, and the House demonstrated increasing acceptance of the new process by adopting budget resolutions with more comfortable margins.

And although the outcome was in doubt until the end of the 1976 budget process, Congress fulfilled a self-imposed budget resolution goal by enacting a tax increase of $1.6 billion, despite persistent resistance by powerful Senate Finance Committee chairman Russell B. Long, D-La.

In May, both the House and Senate approved a first resolution setting targets for fiscal 1977. Each version contemplated extension of the temporary tax cuts through fiscal 1977 and recommended that Congress revise tax laws to pick up $2 billion in additional revenues. But in trying to follow the first resolution's requirements, the Senate got tangled in profound jurisdictional disputes that cut to the heart of the weakness of the budget law—its ability to force congressional committees to bend to the budget's will.

The Senate Finance Committee set up the most serious showdown in May when it reported a tax bill that complied with the budget resolution's revenue target merely by juggling the expirations dates of specific tax-cut extensions.

Democratic Budget chairman Muskie and ranking Republican Bellmon quickly challenged the cost-trimming device as a threat to the fiscal policy assumed in the budget resolution. In a June 16 letter to their colleagues, Muskie and Bellmon argued that revenue losses in later years could keep the budget in deficit.

Finance chairman Long and ranking Republican Carl T. Curtis of Nebraska (House 1939-1954; Senate 1955-1979) retorted in their own letter that the bill and accompanying committee amendments provided tax cuts that were consistent with the budget goals. It was the Finance Committee's province, they argued, to decide what specific provisions should be used to meet the budget requirements.

When the full Senate took up the Finance Committee bill, Muskie took the dispute to the floor and, in a major defeat for the budget law, he lost.

But Congress salvaged the fiscal 1977 budget in September by enacting a second budget resolution that called for an additional $1.6 billion in tax revenues and enacting a tax bill that met the requirement.

This second budget measure moved in tandem with the tax bill, which was by then in a House-Senate conference committee. As conferees from Finance and Ways and Means negotiated a tax compromise, the House and Senate Budget committees drew up binding budget resolutions that scaled down the revenue gain to the level anticipated from the tax bill's provisions. Congress adopted its final fiscal 1977 budget resolution September 16, the same day it finished work on the tax bill.

The Carter Years: Unfulfilled Promises

The 1976 elections turned Ford out of the White House and brought in Democrat Jimmy Carter. The new Carter administration, which would enjoy continued Democratic majorities in the House and Senate, promised to end nearly a decade of budget battles between Congress and the executive. But cooperating with the White House proved more difficult for Congress than confronting it. Carter and the Congress never settled on a tax and spending strategy to fulfill the president's campaign pledge to restore the government to fiscal balance.

In the end, the Democrats wasted an opportunity to establish a consistent budget policy. Carter wavered during his four-year term between spending restraints to curb inflation and stimulative measures to fight unemployment. House Democrats remained badly divided over federal budget priorities, while a defense-minded Senate pushed hard to boost military spending to counter an arms buildup by the Soviet Union.

The four-year fiscal policy turmoil severely tested the budget process. With Carter in the White House, the House and Senate remained receptive to tax cuts and spending initiatives designed to fine-tune economic growth. But the budget process nearly foundered at times when changing economic conditions forced Congress to shift toward fiscal restraint through politically difficult spending reductions.

Under Muskie's leadership the Senate Budget Committee often forged consensus support for the panel's fiscal policy recommendations. The committee pushed hard for spending cuts, although it yielded to conservative senators' demands for stepped up military spending while the controversial SALT II arms limitation treaty was being debated in 1979.

Several times during the four-year period, Muskie took on influential chairmen of other Senate committees, notably Appropriations Committee chairman Warren G. Magnuson, D-Wash. (House 1937-1944; Senate 1944-1981), and Finance chairman Long, in efforts to force those panels to comply with budget resolution limits. The fight to put teeth into budget goals paid off at the end of 1980, when Congress for the first time put together a reconciliation bill incorporating spending cuts and revenue increases that its first fiscal 1981 budget resolution had ordered congressional committees to prepare. By then, however, Muskie had resigned from the Senate to serve as Carter's secretary of state.

In the House, budget making during Carter's term usually was fractious, even chaotic. Several budget resolutions went down to defeat, opposed by Republicans and liberal Democrats alike. Budget Committee chairman Robert N. Giaimo, D-Conn., labored to devise budget totals that could satisfy a majority of House Democrats, including conservatives who wanted to spend more on defense and liberals who fiercely resisted limits on the Great Society programs of the 1960s.

Outnumbered House Republicans pushed for spending cuts, permanent tax reductions, and an end to chronic deficits, which were then in the range of $50 billion to $70 billion a year. On most House votes, Republicans united against budget resolutions, preferring to saddle Democrats with the blame for the deficits they envisioned. That stance may have helped to push deficits higher, as House leaders accommodated the spending demands of liberal Democrats in an effort to hold onto their votes and keep the process working.

During the debate on the first budget resolutions in 1975, House Democratic leaders offered floor amendments to make budgets more palatable to liberals. But that approach put Democrats in the position of openly promoting larger deficits, so leaders began cutting their deals during the less-public Budget Committee markup sessions on budget resolutions. To ease the way in 1977, as the Ninety-fifth Congress convened, the leadership accordingly changed the Budget panel's membership to give it a more liberal majority.

By 1980 critics charged that the congressional budget process was little more than a meaningless exercise of adding up separate spending proposals, not a way to restrain them by adhering to overall budget goals. Congress strengthened that impression during that year by approving disingenuous balanced budget targets in June, in a first budget resolution, and then putting off until after the November election the chore of approving a second and final budget that showed a deficit of $27.4 billion.

In both 1979 and 1980, Congress began missing the budget law's deadlines. And in both years, in its second, presumably final budget resolutions, Congress approved unrealistically low deficits that had to be revised upward a few months later.

Congress's budget-making problems were compounded by uncertain, often inaccurate, economic projections. CBO projections frequently were less optimistic than administration economic forecasts, used to predict different outlays and revenue figures. But, in fact, both White House and congressional experts misread economic trends, and Congress in midstream found itself forced to make big changes in budget estimates that dramatically altered expected deficits. (Like the problem of missed deadlines, this was a condition that only deteriorated after Reagan took office.)

1977: An Expansive Budget

Carter entered office in 1977 with a plan to pump up the sagging economy, in part through individual $50 tax rebates. Congress responded eagerly, shifting federal fiscal policy toward economic stimulus. And by September, Congress had also substantially enlarged the fiscal 1978 budget that Ford had requested three days before his term ended in January. But in the intervening months, Carter's sudden policy shifts—including his abandoning of the tax-rebate plan—and deep House divisions nearly threw the budget process into chaos. As Congress set targets for fiscal 1978, dissatisfied Democratic liberals and disgruntled Republican conservatives combined in the House to defeat a budget resolution for the first time.

In response to Carter's tax plan, Congress March 3 adopted an unprecedented third fiscal 1977 budget resolution, adjusting previously approved spending and revenue limits to accommodate the administration's economic proposals for the year that was by then half over. The third resolution encompassed Carter's full $13.8 billion tax cut package, even though doubts were growing in Congress about how much stimulus $50 tax rebates would generate. Convinced that direct government spending would create jobs more quickly than the administration's proposal, Congress nearly doubled the budget's assumed outlay increases for jobs and countercyclical assistance.

But barely a month after Congress put revised fiscal 1977 budget goals in place, Carter abandoned the $50 tax rebates. He told reporters April 14 that improving economic indicators since the stimulus package was planned in December had made it unnecessary. The administration reversed itself five days before the Senate took up the Finance Committee's tax-cut package in a climate of growing hostility to the rebates from Republicans who favored permanent tax cuts and Democrats who thought spending increases would be a more effective stimulus.

Carter's surprising withdrawal of the rebate plan—which also incorporated some business tax credits—left the third fiscal

1977 budget revenue assumptions far too low, and the projected deficit too large. In adopting a first fiscal 1978 budget in May, Congress once more revised the fiscal 1977 figures. The final revision set the fiscal 1977 deficit estimate at $52.6 billion, just $2 billion more than Congress had approved in the second budget resolution adopted the previous September.

Seemingly continual revision of the fiscal 1977 budget was not Congress's only problem that year. Legislators approved fiscal 1978 compromise budget targets only after the House resoundingly rejected a budget that displeased both liberals and conservatives. House backing for the first budget resolution, usually tenuous at best, unraveled on the floor after adoption of an amendment that would have restored defense spending to the level in Carter's budget. That action undercut the Budget Committee's effort to balance defense and domestic spending and cost moderate and liberal support for the budget.

Budget Committee chairman Giaimo maintained that those members "felt that the restraint they had showed with respect to spending for urgent domestic needs was not going to produce a similar restraint on the part of the defense establishment." On the other hand, the defense increases failed to win support from Republicans who remained concerned by the size of the deficit. The amended resolution satisfied neither side, and it went down to defeat, 84-320, with only five Budget Committee members supporting it.

The outcome left in doubt whether the House was committed to making the budget process work. Defense secretary Harold Brown's lobbying for defense increases angered House leaders, while Carter's abrupt withdrawal of his tax rebate plan stirred discontent about shifting administration policy. Administration projections that fiscal 1977 spending would be $6.1 billion less than previously expected further confused the budget outlook. The changes, Muskie complained, had "created a crisis of confidence and competence for the budget process."

Congress eventually settled on a revived first budget resolution only after House-Senate conferees spent one full day and half of a second negotiating a compromise defense target that Senate leaders felt was large enough and that House leaders thought was small enough to draw sufficient liberal votes to pass the measure. The resolution, adopted 221-177 in the House, won support from twenty-nine Republicans; that was twice as many House GOP votes as any budget resolution had received in the past.

Congressional action on final fiscal 1978 budget totals generated less heated debate over defense spending, but other issues bubbled to the surface. The House and Senate committees, in drafting a second budget resolution in August, made important adjustments to accommodate pending energy bills and higher spending than previously anticipated for farm programs. Both Budget panels were unhappy that Congress had ignored preliminary budget targets in drafting a major reauthorization of federal farm programs. But the Senate committee's attempt to order farm spending restraint was rejected.

1978: Coping with Fiscal Austerity

Congress's expansive mood carried over into the next session, and the House and Senate began writing fiscal 1979 budget resolutions with high unemployment and a possible recession in mind. But inflation soared again during the year, and an antigovernment spirit took hold in national politics after California voters in June approved a state constitutional amendment slashing property taxes.

By September concern about inflation and high federal spending had eclipsed the early focus on stimulative tax cuts and job-creating measures. As a result, Congress that month approved a second, binding fiscal 1979 budget that set spending at $487.5 billion and sheared Carter's proposed $60.6 billion deficit to less than $39 billion. The budget took account of congressional actions that limited Carter's proposed $24.5 billion tax cut for 1979 to $18.7 billion. And it reflected smaller-than-expected outlays for defense procurement, medical costs, and unemployment assistance.

In the process, Congress scaled back the $50.9 billion deficit projected by the first fiscal 1979 budget resolution adopted in May. And the Senate, demonstrating support for its Budget Committee's position, held firm in September against House Democratic leaders' pressure to leave room in the budget for $2 billion in new spending for public works projects. The dispute delayed approval of binding budget totals until September 23, a week after the deadline set by the 1974 budget law.

With negotiations stalemated, Muskie asked the Senate to back up his stand against compromising with the House. By a 63-21 margin, the Senate complied September 14 by instructing its conferees to insist on no new public works spending at all. Conferees finally broke the impasse by adopting a face-saving solution that allowed the House and Senate to interpret the budget limits differently.

1979: Guns versus Butter

Congressional budget making faltered badly in 1979 as conflicts between defense and social spending grew. Congress managed to hold its binding fiscal 1980 deficit estimate to less than $30 billion, meeting a goal that President Carter had set the year before. But the fiscal 1980 budget tied Congress in knots, straining longstanding political coalitions and slowing action so that the budget law timetable was seriously breached. Congress finally adopted a second budget resolution on November 28, two months after fiscal 1980 began.

In the Senate, the Budget Committee continued to make impressive strides in encouraging fiscal discipline. But the House, sharply divided over where spending should be cut, defeated two budget resolutions before settling on a compromise. As it was, the final budget resolution met Carter's own deficit goal, but only because inflation-generated revenues partly kept pace with rising outlays.

Pressure to balance the budget built up early in the year. Some state legislatures and potential presidential candidates clamored for a constitutional amendment forbidding federal deficits, and conservatives stalled a needed increase in the ceiling on the federal debt until congressional leaders assured them a chance to vote on balancing the budget.

Congress responded, after a long and arduous battle, by writing a first budget resolution that promised to bring the fiscal 1980 deficit down to $23 billion, $6 billion less than Carter proposed. In the process, the Senate Budget Committee laid out a strategy for balancing the fiscal 1981 budget—but only if Congress provided no tax cuts until 1982.

The $23 billion fiscal 1980 deficit target was set even though the Senate insisted on approving most of Carter's defense spending request. House Democratic liberals, who had persuaded the House to include substantial defense reductions in its original budget resolution, mounted a successful campaign to defeat the initial conference report. They demanded that money be shifted from defense to social programs. Senate conferees refused to budge, although they mollified the House by accepting increased appropriations targets for education, training, employment, and social service programs.

In the same resolution, Congress re-

vised the binding fiscal 1979 budget figures it had set the previous September to make room for nearly $7 billion in higher-than-expected outlays and supplemental appropriations for defense and other programs. But because estimated revenues had jumped more than $12 billion, Congress was able to reduce its previous deficit target by $5 billion.

The budget process bogged down in the fall as the House and Senate worked on a binding fiscal 1980 budget measure. The House September 19 rejected its Budget Committee's initial binding recommendations, the first time either the House or Senate had turned down a second budget resolution. The House accepted a revised measure eight days later but conferees then haggled a record twenty-three days before agreeing to increase both defense and domestic spending.

The compromise second resolution, finally adopted November 28, raised the fiscal 1980 outlay ceiling to $547.6 billion but kept the deficit at $29.8 billion by assuming rising revenues. Work on the budget was finished only after the House rejected the Senate's proposal to force Congress for the first time to reconcile existing laws to the budget resolution limits.

The Senate backed its Budget Committee's plan to invoke the reconciliation process, never before used by Congress, when it first approved the binding budget resolution in September. The committee recommended that defense spending should rise dramatically, at least in fiscal 1981 and 1982. But, to keep fiscal policy steady, the panel agreed on budget totals that were lower than the sum of the authorizing and appropriations measures that Congress was likely to approve.

The committee then voted 9-4 to use the reconciliation process to require other congressional committees to report measures to fit budget limits. The Budget panel proposed instructions to seven Senate committees to reduce fiscal 1980 spending by $4 billion. A likely floor fight on the issue was averted when Muskie negotiated a compromise with other Senate Democratic leaders that settled on $3.6 billion in reconciliation cuts.

The key to Muskie's success was an agreement he reached with Appropriations Committee chairman Magnuson. The agreement left the Appropriations panel free to decide later how to achieve $2.5 billion in spending cuts sought by the Budget Committee. Muskie cemented his agreement with Magnuson by successfully opposing a floor move by Budget Committee Republicans to clamp down more tightly on the Appropriations Committee. While placating Magnuson, Muskie apparently appeased Finance Committee chairman Long by reducing to $1.4 billion from $1.7 billion the amount of savings his panel would be expected to achieve under the reconciliation process.

Muskie then won direct floor battles with disgruntled members of the Agriculture and Veterans' Affairs committees.

In the House, however, Budget Committee Democrats rejected reconciliation in a September 10 caucus, backing away from tangling with other committees over budget-cutting instructions. But despite the House Democrats' adamant opposition, the House-Senate conference compromise on the second budget resolution contained reconciliation instructions that directed six authorizing committees to trim $1.8 billion from previously passed bills and ordered the House and Senate Appropriations committees to cut fiscal 1980 spending by $2.6 billion.

The Senate approved the conference version. But the House, at the urging of Budget chairman Giaimo, struck the budget-cutting directions from the resolution in a 205-190 vote. That fifteen-vote margin was firm evidence, Giaimo said later, of his panel's relative strength in the chamber. "I

can't take on seven committees in the House" over spending cuts, he said. "We've made Congress aware of reconciliation. But it's just too massive to achieve this year."

The House and Senate subsequently settled on a compromise resolution, with Budget leaders warning committees that Congress would not bail them out later by adopting a third fiscal 1980 resolution to cover spending increases. But federal spending bumped up against the fiscal 1980 limits by March of 1980. Forgetting the warning, Congress revised the fiscal 1980 budget while working on the fiscal 1981 budget and added $17.2 billion to the deficit projection to cover the increases.

1980: Reconciliation Gets a Test

The budget process all but fell apart in 1980, as Congress dealt with election-year politics instead of with economic reality. Democratic leaders, working with the White House, scrambled in the spring to produce a first fiscal 1981 budget resolution showing a balance between spending and revenues. Congress left to a postelection session the chore of writing a more realistic final budget resolution that predicted an inevitable deficit.

But in devising the balanced budget targets, Congress for the first time agreed to make use of the budget law's reconciliation provision. In December, long after springtime zeal for balancing the budget had faded, the House and Senate followed through by passing a reconciliation bill to cut back outlays for federal programs already on the books. The 1974 budget act required reconciliation instructions to committees be included in second, binding budget resolutions, as needed. But in 1980, by attaching reconciliation instructions to the first budget resolution setting fiscal 1981 budget targets, Congress established a precedent that it was to follow in 1981 and in later years to make wholesale budget reductions.

Alarmed by an election-year surge in prices, Congress and Carter worked hard in the spring to balance the fiscal 1981 budget. The president began the year in January by proposing a "prudent and responsible" $15.8 billion deficit. But even as Carter unveiled his budget, the January inflation rate soared to an annual rate of nearly 18.2 percent, and U.S. bond markets came close to collapse.

With Republicans blaming a Democratic-controlled government for driving up prices through continued budget deficits, Democratic congressional leaders quickly went to work with Carter officials to chisel away at the president's budget request. Even before the White House revised its budget proposal in mid-March, the House and Senate Budget committees were drafting budget targets to meet Carter's 1976 campaign pledge to balance the budget during his first term in office. Because Democratic lawmakers had taken part in spending cut negotiations, the budget resolutions followed the president's revisions closely on most matters.

Emboldened by budget-balancing pressures, the House committee for the first time agreed to try the budget reconciliation process, ordering eight authorizing committees in each chamber to make $9.1 billion in spending cuts to meet budget limits. The reconciliation instructions also directed the House Ways and Means Committee to draw up a measure adding $22.2 billion to fiscal 1981 revenues.

Six liberal Budget Committee Democrats opposed the budget-balancing plan. But the panel's Republicans for the first time backed Giaimo's proposals, assuring committee approval.

The Senate committee, like its House counterpart, included reconciliation instructions and allowed $10.1 billion for a possible 1981 tax cut. The panel's resolution ordered other committees to save $12.2 billion, including $2.6 billion through curtailed fiscal

1980 appropriations. It warned that the anticipated $10 billion tax cut would be reduced "on a dollar-for-dollar basis" for spending cuts that other committees refused to make.

During floor debate, Democrats and Republicans in the House voted to uphold the idea of using reconciliation. And the House adopted its Budget Committee's targets by a 225-193 vote. But final approval of the first fiscal 1980 budget resolution was delayed until mid-June after liberal House Democrats defeated a conference agreement that allowed $5.8 billion more for defense spending than the House had approved.

No sooner had the compromise been defeated, however, than the House turned around and voted to instruct its conferees to insist on retaining the conference report's record-high defense figures. Two weeks later, the conference agreed on a second compromise that increased outlays for transportation and low-income energy assistance by $300 million, cutting a projected budget surplus to $200 million from $500 million. In addition, conferees switched $800 million in budget authority from defense to social programs. The House June 12 accepted those changes, 205-195, and the Senate adopted the resolution by a 61-26 vote the same day.

Within a month, changing economic conditions made it clear that the budget-balancing struggles would prove futile. The administration's July budget reestimates projected a $29.8 billion deficit as a long-predicted recession took hold. Congress quietly adjusted its binding, second fiscal 1981 budget resolution accordingly, although it put off action until after the November elections.

The Senate Budget Committee had written a second budget resolution in August, figuring on a $17.9 billion deficit by betting that the downturn would end quickly. House committee Democrats, waiting until Congress convened a November session a week after the election, then put together a revised package that amounted to a political challenge to Reagan to make good on his campaign assaults on federal spending. By a party-line vote, the House approved a Budget Committee resolution built around a 2 percent across-the-board cut. The Senate adopted its resolution by an uncharacteristically thin 48-46 margin.

House-Senate conferees took only ninety minutes to compromise on a final resolution that predicted a $27.4 billion deficit. Both chambers gave perfunctory approval to the binding fiscal 1981 totals as Democrats prepared to turn over budget responsibilities to a Republican president and Republican-controlled Senate who were expected to push for wholesale cuts in spending.

The Ninety-sixth Congress then wrapped up its budget business by enacting the reconciliation bill that the first fiscal 1981 resolution had ordered. While falling short of the savings that had been targeted, the reconciliation measure contained $4.6 billion in spending cuts and $3.6 billion in revenue increases.

In its final form, the measure cut back spending for federal programs already on the books—for education, transportation, health, federal retirement, unemployment compensation, and other services. Its revenue-raising provisions were expected to yield $3.6 billion in added tax receipts through various tax-law changes, duties, and excise taxes. The one bill contained provisions that eight House and ten Senate committees had drafted to meet budget goals. And its approval, despite protests from some powerful committee chairmen, bolstered the House and Senate Budget committees' influence over authorization bills.

The Budget panels had less success trying to gain additional control over appropriations. The 1974 budget act had envisioned the use of reconciliation to make cuts in enacted appropriations bills. And the reconciliation instructions included in the first fiscal 1981 budget resolution had called for cuts in appropriations for fiscal 1980. Those cuts were never made, however, and the reconciliation bill was not enacted until after fiscal 1980 had ended. It was the only time that reconciliation of enacted appropriations bills was attempted.

The Budget in 1981: A Reagan Revolution

Ronald Reagan brought to the White House a promise to transform the government: to make it smaller and more efficient; to get it out of activities in which he thought it did not belong; and to bring spending in line with revenues, while cutting back on the tax burden.

Whether Reagan managed that transformation is debatable. The federal government was bigger and more costly as his presidency drew to a close than when he was first elected. Few social programs were ended outright during his administration, although the burden of meeting some social needs, particularly education and welfare, was shifted more onto the states. Tax rates were cut, however. And, after enactment of more than a dozen laws over eight years changing the tax structure or seeking to improve collections, government estimates of tax revenues were far below what they would have been absent any change.

But, overall, federal revenues equaled 19.4 percent of the gross national product (GNP) in 1987, the same rate as in 1980. And spending stood at 22.8 percent of GNP in 1987, compared with 22.1 percent in 1980. Significantly, the deficit had grown from 2.8 percent of GNP in 1980 to 3.4 percent in 1987 (and stayed above 5.0 percent for most of the period between those years).

It is worth noting that spending for all federal government activities—except for net interest on the debt—was projected to be roughly equivalent to revenues in the late 1980s. That means that the budget was nearly balanced, except that the government was forced to borrow every dime it needed to pay interest on the federal debt. Moreover, both the debt and the interest payments were sizeable and growing amounts, even if the deficit was stabilized in the range of $150 billion a year.

Nevertheless, Reagan had managed a small, overnight revolution in the way budgets were written, with the aid of David Stockman, his budget director, and a second-term House Democrat from Texas named Phil Gramm (House 1979-1985; Senate 1985-).

Reagan took office with a popular mandate to turn around the economic calamity that befell the nation in the late 1970s. He attacked tax rates and social programs, linking the two as a way to boost support for cutting both. He promoted a huge increase in defense spending on top of growth in the Pentagon's budget begun the year before by his predecessor—more than a 10 percent increase over what Carter requested just before leaving office. And much, if not quite all, of Reagan's first-year fiscal program was enacted into law by a Congress whose Democrats were in disarray and incapable of stopping it.

The means to the end was the successful use of Congress's own budget process, particularly reconciliation.

At the end of 1980, the budget process was being dismissed by some members of Congress as irrelevant to fiscal discipline. Democratic leaders' politically motivated delay in considering a final fiscal 1981 budget resolution—which eventually acknowledged the growing deficit—gave opponents more fuel for attacking the process. They charged that it had declined into a meaningless exercise producing little change in federal spending. James Hedlund, the House Budget Committee's minority staff director, noted that Republicans believed the process "makes very little difference in what Congress would have done anyway."

Still, by putting the reconciliation mechanism to use in 1980—at the end of a year in which budget-balancing efforts had collapsed—Congress salvaged some hope for the process. By following through on reconciliation, Congress set a precedent for Reagan's sweeping 1981 budget-cutting feat, which gave the budget process unexpected, some say unintended, power to change the whole course of government.

Immediately after taking office in January 1981, Reagan asked Congress to cut Carter's proposed fiscal 1982 budget by $41.4 billion through spending reductions in eighty-three federal programs. (It was too late to make many changes in the budget for the ongoing year, fiscal 1981.) Stockman, who had come to head the administration's Office of Management and Budget after serving two terms as a House Republican from Michigan, masterminded the campaign. And Republican leaders, who had taken control of the Senate after the 1980 elections, agreed to consolidate the spending cuts in one reconciliation measure early in the 1981 session. By packaging the cuts, then forcing the House and Senate to vote on a single measure, Republicans hoped to prevent congressional committees and interest groups from chipping away at the plan through piecemeal changes.

The strategy worked, far better than many dismayed Democrats could have imagined. By August 13, Reagan signed into law a deep tax cut and a far-reaching package of spending cuts. Not until the "budget summit" of 1987 did any budget-cutting exercise approach the 1981 effort. The final 1981 reconciliation measure, curbing outlays for hundreds of federal programs, was calculated to reduce fiscal

1982 spending by nearly $35.2 billion—$130.6 billion through fiscal 1984.

Pete V. Domenici, R-N.M., the Senate Budget Committee chairman, proclaimed that "the entire reconciliation process has done two crucial things: It has strengthened the legislative process, and it has restored confidence in Congress among the American people."

Early Warnings

Despite the political connection between the tax cut and the spending cut, there was a hint of discontinuity between them and the defense increase that dated back to the 1980 presidential campaign. Although the tax and spending cuts were roughly equivalent in size for the first year, the likelihood that they would balance out over the longer term was in doubt. And it was obvious to many that with higher military spending added to the equation there was a great threat the deficit would increase, not decrease as promised.

But the political impetus behind Reagan's fiscal program was strong. The right-wing Heritage Foundation in Washington, D.C., had published its call to arms, *Mandate for Leadership,* shortly after the election. The book detailed hundreds of legislative and administrative changes needed to make the revolution presumably called for by the election happen. Many of the shock troops of the incoming administration were followers of the views expressed in the book. And they set about following its prescriptions. But the new administration enjoyed mixed success, according to Stockman, because not everyone was on board for the same trip, including—perhaps—the president himself.

Reagan's supply-side rhetoric during the early days of the 1980 campaign had drawn fire even from his challengers for the GOP nomination. George Bush, before his campaign faltered and he was tapped as Reagan's vice presidential running mate, denounced Reagan's economic platform. Reagan's adopted notion of tax cuts leading to a balanced budget was "voodoo economics," according to Bush. By 1988, when he was running to succeed Reagan in the White House, Bush was endorsing the same antitax position that was Reagan's supply-side hallmark, and his 1980 quip was ignored.

Sen. Howard Baker, R-Tenn. (1967-1985), another of Reagan's failed 1980 challengers, was just as harsh during the campaign. To Baker, who ultimately would join the president's team in 1987 as White House chief of staff, Reagan's economic proposals were a "riverboat gamble."

Even true believers were not sure that cutting taxes, cutting social spending, and increasing defense spending—even if it could all be accomplished politically—would yield the desired budgetary results. Stockman, who privately expressed his skepticism to *Washington Post* reporter William Greider during the spring and summer of 1981, saw his doubts disclosed in an *Atlantic* magazine cover story that November. The article was published after the main budget fights of the year were over, and it revealed that the architect of the Reagan budget himself did not believe that the numbers behind the tax and spending cuts and defense increase added up.

Stockman survived the scandal and stayed on as budget director until August 1985, when he left for a new career on Wall Street. In a subsequent memoir, *The Triumph of Politics: Why the Reagan Revolution Failed,* he detailed just how much in 1981 the administration's budget relied on sleight of hand. The tricks included "magic asterisks"—footnoted promises to Congress of billions of dollars in spending cuts to be specified at some future time—the "visceral computer" of Murray Weidenbaum, chairman of the president's Council of Economic Advisers and the administration's chief economic forecaster, and "Rosy Scenario," the 1981 economic forecast that did not fit reality.

From the start, the administration's economic forecast was derided by some and more modestly challenged by others as overly optimistic. "The economic assumptions . . . are optimistic but not impossible," said CBO director Rivlin in March 1981. "If the administration's economic scenario is not attained, however," she warned, "the consequences for the budget are troubling."

In his memoir, Stockman acknowledged that the administration's "Rosetta stone was a fake"; the economic forecast failed to anticipate the deep recession that ran from July 1981 until November 1982 and turned expectations that the deficit would be reduced into fears that it might not stop growing. As for the president and his chief White House aides—other than Stockman and Weidenbaum—they were "almost entirely innocent and uninformed" of the degree to which the numbers were pulled from thin air, Stockman wrote.

Crafting a Budget

The success of Reagan's first-year budget proposals is attributable to several factors: his stunning electoral victory; the GOP's taking control of the Senate; and the ascendancy of conservatives—Democrats and Republicans—in the House. But the cleverness of Stockman, Howard Baker (then Senate majority leader), Robert Dole (then chairman of the Senate Finance Committee), and others in bringing the proposal to a quick vote gave it a needed political boost. They vaulted traditional congressional methods of making tax and spending decisions by employing the leverage of the largely unused budget process. But even that process was used in ways never before contemplated.

House Democratic leaders, by far the biggest losers in 1981, were taken totally by surprise. That a budget process they had helped create to wrest control from a president could be turned against them was inconceivable. But turned against them it was, by strong-willed and in-control Republicans in the Senate and renegade Democrats in the House.

The outcome shook Democrats' confidence in their leaders—and suggested that the drive to cut spending was encouraging fundamental realignments of power in a chamber no longer dominated by liberal, prospending sentiments. And, in fact, the success of Democrats in wooing their more conservative colleagues back into the fold after 1981 was due in no small part to unprecedented accommodations made by more liberal elements in the party.

The Spending Cut

Both Republicans and Democrats saw the need to move quickly on Reagan's budget proposals. House Democratic leaders, including newly selected Budget Committee chairman James R. Jones, D-Okla. (1973-1987), began drawing up plans that scaled down the president's suggested spending and tax cuts.

But the Republican Senate moved out front. The Senate Budget Committee March 23 voted to require fourteen Senate committees to make changes in existing programs to chop more than $36 billion from anticipated fiscal 1982 spending and cut roughly $145 billion over three years. The committee acted on a resolution that was not itself a budget, for it lacked overall spending and revenue totals, among other things. But it was, in effect, the reconciliation instructions that a budget might contain. The Senate adopted the resolution April 2 by a vote of 88-10, after rejecting dozens of amendments to limit the cuts.

The House Budget Committee moved next, agreeing to a budget resolution April 16 that anticipated spending cuts of just under $16 billion in fiscal 1982 and $61 billion over three years. The House committee's budget included reconciliation instructions, though obviously more limited ones than those adopted two weeks earlier by the Senate. Nevertheless, even that gesture by the Democratic House was an acknowledgment of where the budget fight was headed that year. Reconciliation was previously presumed to be an end-of-the-line procedure, called into play by a second budget resolution after a year's worth of authorization and appropriations bills had been considered and just before the fiscal year began. For the House Democratic leadership to concede the need for early reconciliation was evidence of the power of the idea of spending cuts, as well as the deteriorating nature of the budget process.

Despite the House Democrats' seeming willingness to participate in an exercise of budget trimming—and despite Jones's own more moderate-to-conservative tendencies—their effort was deemed unacceptable by Republicans and the emerging Boll Weevils.

In a major defeat for the leadership, the House overturned the Budget Committee's proposal May 7. Leading the charge to adopt instead a Reagan-styled budget proposal were Boll Weevil Gramm and Republican Delbert L. Latta of Ohio (1959-   ), both Budget Committee members. The Gramm-Latta budget, approved by a 253-176 vote, drew the support of sixty-three House Democrats and ordered fifteen House committees to cut more than $36 billion from expected fiscal 1982 spending.

(That Gramm was accorded first billing on the measure was significant and a sign of his future legislative flair. Latta actually offered the substitute budget, and he was the Budget panel's ranking Republican; Gramm was a very junior Democrat, but he wound up with most of the credit. Later in the year, the two teamed up to offer a substitute for the Democratic-proposed reconciliation bill, drafted to put the adopted budget resolution into effect. Gramm-Latta II, as it was called, was equally successful on the floor. So, too, was Gramm's proposal to mandate deficit targets, enacted in 1985 as the Gramm-Rudman-Hollings antideficit law. By then, however, Gramm was no longer a Democrat and had moved to the Senate.)

While House Democrats struggled to hold onto the votes of their conservative colleagues, the Senate Budget Committee suffered a false start on April 9, when the panel rejected a draft budget proposed by chairman Domenici. All Democrats and the most conservative Republicans were opposed, but for different reasons. The proposed budget resolution failed to project a balanced budget in 1984, which had been Reagan's promise. Instead, it anticipated deficits in excess of $40 billion in three consecutive years. That caused some conservatives to break ranks. The Democrats saw, in defeating the budget, a chance to fight for less severe cuts in favored social programs.

To win the conservative Republicans back, Domenici found billions of dollars in savings from assumed reductions in waste, fraud, and abuse, and he adopted Stockman's magic asterisk of future, unspecified spending cuts of more than $40 billion. Together, these savings—which Democratic critics derided as "economic sleight of hand"—yielded an expected balanced budget in 1984 and picked up the votes of not only the GOP defectors but also three Southern Democrats.

The committee adopted its budget April 28, and the full Senate followed suit May 12. Efforts to restore some spending cuts for veterans, job training, education, mass transit—all heretofore sacred federal cows—failed. So, too, did efforts to reduce the defense spending increase and the tax cut. Perhaps most significantly, the Senate twice refused to restore full cost-of-living increases for Social Security recipients and federal civilian and military retirees. Most Republicans opposed restoring the benefits; most Democrats supported the idea. The inflation adjustment was preserved in conference committee deliberations on the budget. But it was an issue that, because of its potential for saving money and its high political profile, was to return again and again to budget debates in the 1980s.

The approved fiscal 1982 budget resolution included reconciliation instructions similar to those the Senate adopted in March. The measure was not too dissimilar from that adopted by the House, and conferees from the two chambers agreed May 14 on a compromise fiscal 1982 budget that specified a $37.6 billion deficit. The budget, with its instructions requiring $36 billion in reconciliation savings and its anticipated $36 billion tax cut, was finally adopted May 21.

The Tax Cut

Of all the elements of the fiscal 1982 budget proposal, the tax cut is the one that stands out for Republicans—and particularly for supply-side adherents—as most emblematic of the Reagan administration's achievements. Similarly, for many Democrats it is the tax cut that symbolizes the degree to which early Reagan-era policy was flawed. The tax cut was also the first element of the administration's economic platform put on the table—initially in 1977 by Rep. Jack F. Kemp, R-N.Y., and Sen. William V. Roth, Jr., R-Del.

Whatever the political perspective, the point is that a tax cut of $36 billion in one year makes a sharp impression on people's minds and has a enduring effect on the federal budget and the overall economy. That was particularly so with the Reagan tax cut. Federal revenues remained virtually constant as a percentage of GNP during the Reagan presidency—and taxes as a share of revenues remained constant as well. (The share of income taxes did fall slightly

after 1981, however, while Social Security taxes grew by an offsetting amount.)

Nevertheless, the reduction in anticipated tax collections has been dramatic. Taxes that would have been collected, had the law not been so significantly altered in 1981, would have totaled more than $2 trillion over the ten years 1982-1991, according to Office of Management and Budget projections. This presumed revenue loss is roughly equal to the increase in the federal debt over the same period. Even allowing for several hefty tax increases enacted after 1981, the net cost to the Treasury was projected to be $853.3 billion through the end of Reagan's presidency and $1.3 trillion over ten years. (See Table 5-3.)

No one predicted that the costs of the tax cut would be so high when it was enacted, however. In fact, the oversimplified initial premise of the tax cut was that revenues would go up as a result of business stimulus, higher productivity, and an increased desire of workers to work, because they would keep more of what they earned. Not everyone believed that, of course. As Ways and Means chairman Rostenkowski put it just before the final House vote on the tax cut, "This is . . . a bold—and risky—economic strategy. Only time will tell whether the risks involved . . . were worth taking."

Rostenkowski's relatively mild words disguised a genuine unhappiness over both the outcome and the way the bill was written. The Senate in 1980 had failed to consider a Finance Committee-endorsed tax cut that was broadly similar to candidate Reagan's own proposals. Then, in February 1981, when Reagan had been in office for less than a month, he proposed a 10 percent reduction in tax rates on individuals, and numerous business tax incentives, adding to a whopping $53.9 billion cut for 1982. Additional cuts were to follow in succeeding years. Four months later, in June, Reagan scaled back his plan to a 1982 tax cut of less

Table 5-3 Revenue Losses since 1982 (in billions)

	1982	1983	1984	1985	1986	1987	1988 [a]	1989 [a]	1990 [a]	1991 [a]	Total 1982-1991 [a]
Economic Recovery Tax Act of 1981	$-35.6	$-91.1	$-136.8	$-170.3	$-209.8	$-241.7	$-260.8	$-285.5	$-315.7	$-350.2	$-2,097.5
Tax Equity and Fiscal Responsibility Act of 1982	—	16.6	36.0	39.2	46.7	56.9	57.3	55.8	57.4	61.6	427.5
Highway Revenue Act of 1982	—	1.5	4.2	4.2	4.5	4.7	4.9	5.1	5.1	5.1	39.3
Social Security Amendments of 1983	—	—	5.7	8.7	10.2	12.1	24.6	31.0	23.9	23.9	140.1
Interest and Dividends Tax Compliance Act of 1983	—	-0.1	-2.6	-2.4	-2.1	-1.7	-1.8	-2.0	-2.5	-2.8	-18.0
Railroad Retirement Revenue Act of 1983	—	—	0.2	0.7	1.1	1.2	1.2	1.1	1.1	1.1	7.7
Deficit Reduction Act of 1984	—	—	0.9	9.3	16.1	22.0	25.3	27.7	31.0	34.0	166.3
Consolidated Omnibus Reconciliation Act of 1985	—	—	—	—	0.9	2.7	2.9	3.0	3.0	3.2	15.7
Federal Employees' Retirement System Act of 1986	—	—	—	—	—	-0.1	-0.2	-0.2	-0.3	-0.4	-1.2
Omnibus Reconciliation Act of 1986	—	—	—	—	—	2.7	2.5	2.0	1.0	0.2	8.4
Superfund Amendments and Reauthorization Act of 1986	—	—	—	—	—	0.4	0.8	0.8	0.8	0.8	3.6
Fiscal 1987 Continuing Resolution	—	—	—	—	—	1.9	2.7	2.6	2.7	2.8	12.7
Tax Reform Act of 1986	—	—	—	—	—	21.5	-4.5	-17.2	-13.5	-9.5	-23.2
Omnibus Reconciliation Act of 1987	—	—	—	—	—	—	9.1	14.3	16.2	15.6	55.2
Fiscal 1988 Continuing Resolution	—	—	—	—	—	—	2.4	3.1	3.3	3.4	12.2
Total	-35.6	-73.1	-92.4	-110.6	-132.4	-117.5	-133.7	-158.4	-186.3	-211.4	-1,251.2

Source: Office of Management and Budget.

Note: Totals may not add due to rounding.

[a] Estimated.

than $38 billion, as budget cuts to offset the revenue reduction failed to materialize. Later still, he added business incentives in several steps to win the support of corporate America.

While House Democrats debated how to counter Reagan, the Republican-led Senate Finance Committee voted 19-1 on June 25 in favor of a tax proposal almost identical to the president's. Somewhat eschewing tradition, which called for the Senate to defer debating tax bills until the House had acted, the Finance Committee moved first. The Senate's Republican leaders were anxious to move the president's proposal along, as well as to set the tone of the tax debate. So the full Senate took up the Finance Committee measure while Ways and Means was still working on the bill in the House. However, the Senate deferred a final vote until it had received the House bill. (The only Finance Committee vote in opposition to the measure came from Bill Bradley, D-N.J., who was a central advocate of tax-rate cuts during the 1985-1986 tax bill debate. But the 1986 bill had very different aims from Reagan's 1981 proposal.)

On July 22, Rostenkowski and his Ways and Means Democrats produced a counterproposal to the president's that would have cut revenues somewhat more sharply but concentrated the effects on individuals earning less than $50,000. Reagan's bill was aimed more at higher income individuals and corporations. Democrats criticized the president's corporate tax cut proposal for being excessive and favoring some businesses over others. But Ways and Means also played that game. At the last minute, by an 18-17 vote, the committee included a sweetener for oil producers—an exemption from the windfall profits tax on crude petroleum for each driller's first five hundred barrels of oil pumped a day. The provision was calculated at the time—when oil prices were well above the trigger for the tax, and were expected to stay there—

to cost the Treasury $7 billion over five years.

But Reagan went on television July 27 to promote his version of reduced taxes and prompted a flood of telephone calls to Capitol Hill offices, guaranteeing his proposal's success. When the House took up the Ways and Means bill two days later, forty-eight Democrats joined all but one Republican—James M. Jeffords of Vermont (House 1975-1989; Senate 1989-   )—to support a substitute that closely followed the president's proposal. The vote was 238-195 in favor; the Senate vote the same day was 89-11.

The few differences between the two bills were worked out in conference July 31. And there were some last-minute Democratic efforts to block it because of tax breaks for oil drillers. (The windfall profits tax provisions were limited somewhat from the House bill, but there were other incentives included for drillers.) Despite that, the final measure was easily passed August 4.

Seizing upon Reconciliation

In the month after the budget was adopted, Congress tackled the task of carrying out the budget resolution's reconciliation instructions. While the budget's spending totals merely assumed certain cuts, it was the reconciliation bill that actually was to contain the knife. Working separately, House and Senate committees drew up proposals to meet the budget's instructions, and its mid-June deadline. The House and Senate Budget panels then assembled the separate recommendations into a single bill for each chamber. (Although the budget act required reconciliation bills to be constructed without change for floor action, the House Budget Committee was forced to violate that rule, when the Energy and Commerce Committee failed to make a recommendation. The Budget panel used an informal recommendation from Energy and Commerce Democrats.)

The fourteen Senate committees proposed savings totaling $39.6 billion, more than the reconciliation instructions required. The fifteen House panels were more resistant, as some chairmen rebelled at making deep cuts in response to budget directives. For instance, House Education and Labor Committee chairman Carl D. Perkins, D-Ky. (1949-1984), who had personally guided many existing social programs through the House, protested that he had "never witnessed an action more ill-advised, more insensitive or more threatening to the rightful operation of the legislative process than these so-called reconciliation instructions."

But Perkins's committee reluctantly managed to find fiscal 1982 savings totaling more than $10 billion, including major reductions in college student aid and a public service jobs program. Republicans and Democrats on the panel refused, however, to go along with Reagan's proposal to combine dozens of elementary and secondary aid programs into large block grants to states and localities, both as a way to reduce costs and to limit federal control over the way the money was spent.

House Energy and Commerce Committee chairman John D. Dingell, D-Mich. (1955-), had even less luck than Perkins. His committee, with jurisdiction over many health programs, was expected to find 1982 cuts of more than $5 billion. But conservative Democrats on the panel, including Gramm, sided with Republicans, and Dingell could not get a majority. The panel, therefore, never made a formal reconciliation recommendation.

In the end the fifteen House committees called for $37.7 billion in fiscal 1982 savings. But Republicans and conservative Democrats charged that the authorizing committees had tried to undermine the reconciliation purpose by recommending cuts that were "false, counterproductive and unnecessarily severe."

Administration allies again took their case to the House floor where twenty-nine hard-core conservative Democrats joined Republicans on June 25 to engineer a critical procedural victory, whereby they could offer a comprehensive substitute amendment to the bill. The next day, by a 217-211 vote, the House adopted the Gramm-Latta II reconciliation substitute that projected cuts of $37.3 billion from fiscal 1982 outlays, following closely the administration's blueprint. The substitute, hundreds of pages long, was a rush job by Gramm, Latta, and their allies from the administration. And it made wholesale changes in federal programs with effectively no debate. Opponents criticized the way in which the pasted-together, scribbled-upon amendment was rushed to the floor.

The Senate had no difficulty passing its reconciliation bill June 25. After making a few minor changes, the measure was projected to save $38.1 billion in fiscal 1982. But the chamber also agreed in a series of floor votes to, among other things, reauthorize federal housing and community development programs, deny such aid to cities that maintained rent control programs, and reallocate television stations to New Jersey and Delaware, which had none. It was the first of many occasions in which reconciliation, because of its must-pass status and certain rules protecting it from Senate filibusters, became a vehicle to enact other measures that had no direct budgetary effect. The problem became so severe that the Senate eventually enacted a rule against putting extraneous matter on reconciliation bills.

It took Congress another month to work out House-Senate differences on reconciliation. More than 250 conferees, meeting in fifty-eight subconferences, shaped a compromise cutting $35.2 billion from the fiscal 1982 budget—and $130.6 over three years. Congress finally passed the bill on July 31, the House by voice vote and the Senate by an 80-14 margin. It was, Jones noted, "clearly the most monumental and historic turnaround in fiscal policy that has ever occurred."

Aftermath of the Cutting

The six-month budget struggle in 1981 left Congress exhausted and unsure of the long-term outlook for its budget-making process. Yet, in the following months, the administration attempted to cover at least a part of Stockman's magic asterisk, which had promised further spending cuts in the near future without specifying details. Reagan announced in late September that he wanted a new round of budget cuts that would focus on entitlements such as Medicare, the health care program for the elderly, and food stamps, and perhaps some limited tax increases, none of which was spelled out. The plan was that the spending cuts and tax increases would be enacted that fall as a means to reducing the deficit for fiscal 1982 and, more importantly, for 1983 and 1984.

But House members and senators of both parties clearly had little appetite for tackling a second round of spending cuts, and particularly not of entitlements. House Republicans, who Reagan needed badly if his plan had a chance of success, were especially unhappy at the thought of further social program cuts.

Through the fall, administration officials tinkered with alternatives, settling finally on a plan for reducing appropriations by about $10 billion. Even that seemed unrealistic at the time, and ultimately it did not succeed. It had become clear that the economy was headed into a recession (the downturn actually began in July, but statistical evidence often lags behind actual changes in the economy), making a tax increase an even more unpalatable option. At the same time, however, the recession guaranteed that the deficit would get worse

as tax revenues, counted on in the Rosy Scenario economic forecast, evaporated. Entitlement cuts, tax increases—even a balanced budget by 1984—all were forgotten. Reagan conceded as much in November 1981.

The president used his veto for the first time to reject a three-week continuing appropriations resolution that he said was a budget-buster. The late November veto, Stockman wrote in his memoir, resulted eventually in about $2 billion in spending cuts when Congress pared back the bill a bit to win Reagan's signature. It was virtually all the savings the administration netted from its plan for a second round of cuts.

Congressional leaders in the meantime were debating what shifts in power the year's budgeting experience brought both inside Congress and in relations with the White House. Many in Congress were concerned that the balance had shifted back to the White House; others worried that authorizing committees had been particularly sidestepped in the use of reconciliation.

For instance, with some hefty assistance from Stockman and his Office of Management and Budget, the Senate Budget Committee drafted reconciliation instructions that gave authorizing committees a detailed list of not only how much money to save, but also which programs and how they could cut. Although the panels were not compelled to adopt the suggestions, in the end many accepted in large measure the suggestions included in the blueprint.

As Domenici told reporters August 4: Reconciliation "is obviously now a tool—a process for budget restraint, inordinate budget restraint—that you use when you want to do something very different.... Absent reconciliation, [the budget process] is pretty damn weak," he continued. "With reconciliation, it will have a lot more teeth in it."

To some observers, Reagan displayed during the 1981 reconciliation and simultaneous tax-cut battles a kind of executive clout not seen in Washington since President Lyndon B. Johnson pushed Great Society programs through a compliant Congress.

"This is the most excessive use of presidential power and license," House Rules Committee chairman Bolling declared early in the reconciliation battle. "And reconciliation is the most brutal and blunt instrument used by a president in an attempt to control the congressional process since Nixon used impoundment."

Rostenkowski, in a floor speech after losing the fight over his alternative to Reagan's sweeping tax-cut program, told colleagues: "As one who served in Congress through a succession of administrations, I find it genuinely alarming to see a pattern developing on major pieces of legislation in which the work product of the committee system can be cynically discarded in favor of substitute legislation written in some downtown hideaway." The result, he maintained, "leaves [Congress] weaker, for it denies to Republicans and Democrats alike the opportunity to write and take responsibility for our work product."

Reconciliation, budget expert Allen Schick said in 1981, "has strengthened the president in that I can't envision him succeeding in making such large budget cuts without it." But the success was in large part a show of the president's "political skill and popularity," he said, "that positively made it work."

One other piece of fallout was a renewed effort to change the still-evolving budget process. Prior to 1981, the concern was that the process was ineffectual. Reagan's successes notwithstanding, those concerns remained.

Both Budget Committee chairmen, Domenici and Jones, were unhappy with the fact that the process required two budget resolutions—a first one that was not to be binding and a second that had become meaningless. Both launched studies of other

possible budget process changes, including ways to make spending ceilings in the budget binding on individual committees and subcommittees, not just an overall total, and strengthening the procedural tools for enforcing those ceilings. Scrutiny of such issues resulted eventually in enactment of Gramm-Rudman, which, along with its more famous deficit targets and procedure for automatic spending cuts, made those two changes. But it took four more years of frustrations before Congress got around to dealing with them.

Budgeting 1982-1985: Retrenching

Congressional budgeting would never be the same after the experience of 1981. Never again, House Democratic leaders vowed, would they be blindsided as they were in floor votes on the tax bill, the budget resolution, and the reconciliation bill. The early 1981 tidal wave quickly dissipated in the backwash.

The political fear that allowed Republicans to control the debate in 1981 was offset in Reagan's later years by a strong Democratic response. Conservative Democrats were accommodated more often; several eventually won seats on the House Budget Committee, for instance, although Gramm was kicked off the panel by angry Democratic leaders the day Congress convened in 1983. And liberals learned better how to play the game. The result was year after year of frustration on Capitol Hill and in the White House. Neither side seemed to gain an advantage, though Reagan and his congressional partisans complained that inertia favored the "tax and spend Democrats."

Nevertheless, it became clear that the magnitude of the spending cuts enacted in 1981 had lessened a general fear in Congress about using the budget process to tackle the deficit. This was true even though the enacted cuts did not in the end yield a net reduction in federal spending from the previous year and were never intended to. (Thanks in no small part to the severe 1981-1982 recession, the fiscal 1982 deficit was worse even than expected in late 1981. And it helped dash administration hopes that the tax cuts would stimulate sufficient growth and the spending cuts enough savings to reduce the deficit over time to zero.)

Several things happened to the economy after 1981 that confused the budget picture. First, there was the recession, which squeezed out the hyperinflation of the late 1970s and early 1980s but also sent deficits spiraling; then there was the recovery, which was as strong as the recession was devastating and which was sustained through 1988—and seemingly would continue well into 1989. Yet interest rates also remained relatively high through 1988. (See Table 5-4.)

The mixture did not make for easy policy choices, and Congress sometimes was unable to keep up with the changes, fighting a recession when a recovery was under way, enacting modest deficit-reduction plans even as projected deficits were climbing faster than anticipated. The same problems were seen in the White House, where traditional Republican sentiments against budget deficits clashed with antitax, supply-side enthusiasm. The president's Council of Economic Advisers under Chairman Weidenbaum was moved to write a lengthy justification of deficits in 1982, as the administration began to brace for the worst.

"When government's explicit debt is adjusted to take account of inflation and assets," the council wrote in its annual report, "its real net liabilities show a decline over the last twenty years. Official deficits that merely offset the devaluation of the debt due to inflation or that finance the purchase of assets

do not increase the government's claim on private resources." Buried in the dense words was essentially the argument that, relatively speaking, a dollar in 1982 was no longer worth what it once was, so the cost of borrowing that dollar was less.

Such justifications were not persuasive everywhere, and particularly not on Capitol Hill where supply-side thinking was less prominent. For congressional Republicans, who held a strong grudge against deficit spending, even tax increases eventually looked more palatable than uncontrollable red ink—especially once the recovery was under way. And Democrats—even more conservative ones who saw cherished social programs threatened—were not of a mind to go along with administration demands forever.

Ultimately, the political landscape changed, especially in advance of elections. There was political retrenching by both parties. When bigger social program cuts seemed politically infeasible, House Republicans challenged their Senate counterparts who seemed less concerned. Democrats seized the opportunity one year, only to give it back the next. Even the president was caught in the political ball game. In one action, by undercutting Senate GOP stalwarts, he prevented what may have been the best shot at an early reversal of the deficit spiral. He first agreed with Senate Republicans to cuts in cost of living adjustments for Social Security recipients; then he reneged and cut a deal with House Democrats—and some House Republicans—to take Social Security off the table. That was in 1985, but in 1988 it was still fresh in the minds of those GOP loyalists Reagan had abandoned.

1982: Rolling Back the Tax Cut

The ink was barely dry on the 1981 tax cut before it was clear to all but the most die-hard supply-siders on Capitol Hill that it

Table 5-4 Economic Statistics, 1980-1987

	1980	1981	1982	1983	1984	1985	1986	1987
Inflation-adjusted increase in gross national product	−0.2	1.9	−2.5	3.6	6.8	3.4	2.8	3.4
Consumer Price Index [a]	13.5	10.4	6.1	3.2	4.3	3.6	1.6	3.6 [b]
Civilian unemployment rate	7.1	7.6	9.7	9.6	7.5	7.2	7.0	6.2
Interest rate on three-month Treasury bills	11.5	14.0	10.7	8.6	9.6	7.5	6.0	5.8 [a]

Sources: Commerce Department, Labor Department, Treasury Department.

Note: Interest rates and unemployment are annual averages; others are percentage change from year to year.

[a] Computed for urban wage earners and clerical workers.
[b] Preliminary.

had been too much of a good thing. The recession had taken its toll, and Reagan's proposed spending cuts in the fall of 1981 had been rejected: the annual budget deficit was threatening to pass the $200 billion mark.

So, whether Reagan was on board or not, Congress seemed determined to enact a tax increase in 1982, and it did so with almost the same speed as it cut taxes the year before. By mid-August, a tax increase that eventually netted more than $16 billion in 1983 and $92 billion over the first three years was on its way to the president. The tax measure did little damage to the cuts enacted in 1981. For example, no change was made in the three-year personal income tax rate reductions encompassed in the earlier bill. Most of the revenues were achieved through the closing of loopholes and more stringent enforcement.

One provision that was expected to raise more than $20 billion over five years never took effect, however. The bill required banks and other financial institutions to withhold taxes equal to 10 percent of interest and dividend payments. Despite exemptions for certain low-income or elderly individuals, there was a groundswell of opposition, and the provision was repealed early in 1983. That canceled a significant amount of the new revenues that had been anticipated.

But the tax increase was not the only news in 1982. First, Reagan's proposed fiscal 1983 budget, which arrived on Capitol Hill February 8, was the first of a long string to be declared "dead on arrival" by congressional leaders. Second, Republicans continued to dominate the budget debates, as they had in 1981, but they fought more among themselves as Democrats let them take some of the political heat.

The reaction to Reagan's proposed budget was a sharp reversal from the previous year. But members of both parties were stung by the depth of his proposed domestic spending cuts—particularly after many of the same ideas had been rejected a few months earlier—and his continued large spending increases for the Pentagon. Moreover, despite his proposed cuts, Reagan's budget still anticipated a deficit approaching $100 billion in 1983, roughly the same as that projected for 1982. (The 1982 deficit eventually was reported as $127.9 billion, and that for 1983 would come in at $207.8 billion.)

As if to certify their disagreement with Reagan's priorities, the Senate Budget Committee voted unanimously on May 5 to reject the president's request for 1983. The following day the panel's Republican majority adopted a budget resolution that called for a three-year tax increase of $95 billion and three-year savings in the Social Security program—either through cutting benefits or increasing taxes—of $40 billion.

By 1982 the precarious financial underpinning for Social Security virtually mandated program changes of that nature, but there was intense opposition to using a rescue of the nation's largest benefit program as a way to reduce the budget deficit. The full Senate ultimately struck the anticipated Social Security savings, increased savings from defense, restored some Medicare cuts, and increased anticipated new taxes. But the budget resolution adopted by the Senate May 21 assumed a deficit of $115 billion. The numbers were creeping upward.

The House Budget Committee May 13 adopted a starkly different budget resolution, calling for a three-year tax increase of $147 billion, larger defense cuts, smaller domestic cuts, and no action on Social Security. The vote in the House committee was party-line, as it was in the Senate committee. But when the resolution got to the House floor, the tensions of the previous year boiled over. During a daylong session May 27 that spilled over into the early hours of the following morning, the House rejected the committee's budget, and seven other alternatives that were offered.

The gridlock sent Republicans and Democrats scrambling, and on June 10 the House accepted a GOP alternative that projected a deficit of just under $100 billion, anticipating a tax increase slightly larger than the Senate's and somewhat less defense spending. House and Senate conferees agreed a week later on a compromise drafted for the most part by Republicans on both sides of the table. It kept the House tax increase and in other respects mostly tracked the House measure, but the projected deficit crept back up to just over $103 billion.

Just as the budget resolution was largely written by Republicans, so, too, were the tax provisions in one of two reconciliation bills enacted to put the fiscal 1983 budget savings into law. The Finance Committee grafted its tax ideas onto a minor House-passed tax bill in mid-July, and the Senate sent the measure back to the House July 23. The bill also contained Medicare, Medicaid (the health care program for the poor), and welfare cuts that were in the Finance Committee's jurisdiction. The House chose to go straight to conference on the bill to avoid committee and floor votes that Democrats and some Republicans wanted to avoid in an election year. Conferees completed their work on August 19, the day after conferees finished a second reconciliation measure, which contained food stamp and dairy price-support cuts, among other savings, required by the budget resolution.

1983: Frustration Mounts

Congress worked hard at reducing the budget deficit in 1981 and 1982, but it did not pay off. And in the 1982 elections, House Democrats picked up twenty-six seats, making it easier to hold onto their majority. Those two factors and a slow recovery from the 1981-1982 recession combined in 1983 to make budgeting a totally different exercise than in the first two Reagan years.

After two sessions of defeats that led many Democrats to sit out some budget battles, the party dominated the Republicans in the budget debates of 1983. The House Budget Committee, drawing on advice from the caucus of all House Democrats, adopted a budget in mid-March that for the second year in a row called for new taxes, sought a rollback in defense, and proposed restoring some social spending. It even called for a few new programs. The party-line vote in committee was essentially duplicated on the floor March 23.

Meanwhile, the Senate Budget Committee, though nominally in GOP hands, adopted a bipartisan budget April 21 that drew three times as many Democratic votes as Republican. The Senate committee budget was very similar to that adopted by the House in its promise of new taxes and its assault on defense spending. After much pulling and hauling on the Senate floor—and even back to the committee—Democrats prevailed with the aid of moderate Republicans May 19 and adopted a budget that lessened the tax increase and domestic spending a bit, while allowing somewhat more than the House or the Senate committee for defense. Nevertheless, the White House was adamantly opposed.

It took House and Senate conferees a month to split the difference, but eventually a budget emerged with a tax increase of $12 billion in fiscal 1984 and $73 billion over three years; a defense increase of 5 percent above inflation; and a bit more than $12 billion in domestic spending reductions over three years through reconciliation.

That, however, was the easy part.

By the time the budget was adopted June 23, House Republicans were in a uproar, as was the White House. There was a marginally more bipartisan mood in the Senate. But everywhere the atmosphere was soured by the budget's projected deficit of more than $170 billion. The prior years had taken their toll, and Reagan was of no mind to go along with another tax increase. Moreover, by summer, the pressure to increase revenues and reduce spending abated as recovery from the recession was well under way, and projected deficits declined slightly on their own.

Nevertheless, a series of reconciliation bills were drafted and moved partially through the legislative process. Only one measure passed either chamber, however—a House measure that would have cut spending by $10 billion over three years. The House refused to take up a three-year, $8 billion tax-increase bill by defeating the rule that would have allowed for floor debate.

The measure was far below the required reconciliation target of $73 billion. When the House failed to act, the Senate stopped working on its own three-year, $28 billion reconciliation bill. And with that, Congress went home for the year, essentially empty handed. Fiscal 1984 would close with a deficit of $185.3 billion.

1984: Deficit Reduction Gets Priority

In 1984, as the frustrations of the preceding year made the ever-increasing deficit a bigger and bigger concern, Congress abandoned the process established in the budget act. Though the budget process may be intentionally adaptable, Congress proved once more just how willing it is to do what seems appropriate at the time, rather than what its rules require. The first order of business in 1984 became enactment of a deficit-reduction bill. The budget resolution would have to wait.

The House actually wanted to do a budget first and adopted one in early April that called for $182 billion in savings over three years, including a $50 billion tax increase, a reduction of almost $100 billion in anticipated defense spending, and $15 billion in domestic program savings.

But the White House and Senate GOP leaders refused to go along. The same day the House adopted its budget, April 5, the Senate passed without amendment a House-passed reconciliation bill left over from the previous year. The measure promised savings over three years of $8.2 billion, down from the $10.3 billion it had promised six months earlier. It had been disparaged as "puny" by House Republicans in 1983. The savings came from the delayed payment of cost-of-living adjustments to retirees and disabled veterans, a federal worker pay increase capped at 4 percent, and limits on Small Business Administration disaster loans to farmers.

The Senate then went to work on approving a deficit-reduction bill incorporating the terms of a White House-Senate GOP agreement. It called for $140 billion in three-year savings, coming in roughly equal parts from a tax increase, a defense cut, and domestic cuts—a far cry from the proposal included in the House-adopted budget. Central to the plan were caps on both domestic and defense spending that were to be enacted into law, not merely adopted as part of a budget resolution that could be ignored. (The caps were eventually downgraded to "sense of the Senate" language. But the technique was to be successfully employed in 1987 to enact defense and domestic spending ceilings that were agreed to as part of a White House-Congress "budget summit.")

Following its action on the budget resolution, the House in mid-April adopted two bills, one raising nearly $50 billion in new taxes over three years, the other trimming $4 billion in domestic spending over the same period. The Senate followed suit, passing its own deficit-reduction bill in mid-May that adhered to the White House agreement. It was only after passing that bill that the Senate adopted its own budget resolution.

A month of negotiations later, Congress passed a final version of the deficit-reduction bill on June 27. Its $50 billion in tax increases provided the first real rollback of the 1981 tax cut, restraining some tax preferences but not touching the individual income tax rates. Its $13 billion in spending cuts included a freeze in Medicare payments to physicians and an increase in premiums paid by Medicare beneficiaries.

The surprisingly easy way in which all parties could agree to the deficit-reduction bill hid a bigger problem; that is, working out a defense cut. Ultimately, through the appropriations process, three-year spending for military programs was scaled back by $58 billion from previously anticipated levels. With that accomplished, and some other, smaller domestic savings incorporated into appropriations bills, Congress was finally free to adopt a budget resolution for fiscal 1985. It did so on October 1, the day the new fiscal year began.

It is important to note that, with all the savings enacted during 1984, the budget still assumed a fiscal 1985 deficit of $181 billion, and an even higher deficit figure of more than $200 billion by fiscal 1986. Congress still had its work cut out in the future.

1985: The Year of Gramm-Rudman

In 1985, as was often the case during the first six years of Reagan's presidency, it was the Republican-led Senate that opened the bidding on the budget. Dole, who was the Senate's new majority leader, wanted to produce a budget that might win some Democratic support. But his efforts—and they were repeated throughout the year—mostly failed. Congress struggled to adopt a budget, taking more time than ever (not counting the inverted process used the year before). Finally, on August 1, Democrats and Republicans reached reluctant agreement, but only after Reagan scuttled a last attempt by Dole to get the president's assent to a modest tax increase and a freeze in Social Security cost-of-living adjustments. Those politically difficult items were to have been packaged with a freeze in defense spending beyond a small amount to cover increases due to inflation.

The adopted budget did halt growth in defense spending for fiscal 1986, but Social Security escaped the knife and there was to be no tax increase. Early in the year there were bipartisan hopes of cutting the anticipated fiscal 1986 deficit by $50 billion to $60 billion. But those hopes faded when Congress adjourned without enacting a needed reconciliation bill. In fact, fiscal

1986 yielded the largest deficit on record, $221.2 billion, despite the defense freeze, whose effects were felt more in later years. Politics had prevailed again.

Except for enactment of the Gramm-Rudman antideficit law, the year was notable for what did not happen. At the end of a mostly disappointing legislative session, Congress turned to Gramm-Rudman, with its mandatory deficit targets and provision for uniform budget cuts, as a needed overhaul of the 1974 budget law. Coming on the heels of the protracted battle over the budget resolution, it was enacted in record time. But the days it took out of Congress's schedule may have contributed to the failure of the reconciliation bill. Moreover, Gramm-Rudman received virtually none of the usual scrutiny that any measure, let alone one so profound, would ordinarily receive. (For a detailed discussion of Gramm-Rudman's legislative history, see Chapter 7.)

Some in Congress—Dole and Domenici in particular—recalled the 1985 budget fights as pivotal and as a strong indicator of the degree to which the budget process was hamstrung by politics. The deficit for the then-current fiscal year—1985—was already headed for $200 billion, and it was clear to Dole and others that fiscal 1986 would only be worse. He started the year trying to get his Senate colleagues to agree on a package of spending cuts, and possibly tax increases, to staunch the flow. The scheme was to cut more than ever before, even more than Congress managed in the momentous fiscal 1982 budget and reconciliation bill enacted in 1981.

Dole and Domenici tried no fewer than five times through the year to win support for proposals that in different formulations entailed tax increases and freezes in Social Security and defense spending. The Senate by the slimmest of margins, 50-49, finally adopted such a budget May 10—Vice President George Bush's tie-breaking vote made

the difference. The budget cut the deficit sharply by eliminating Social Security and other pension and benefit program cost-of-living adjustments for one year and reducing domestic spending well below fiscal 1985 levels. The domestic cuts envisioned sharply curtailing some programs, such as farm subsidies, and eliminating thirteen others, such as the Commerce Department's Economic Development Administration, which had been on the White House hit list since 1981. Defense spending would have been allowed to increase only by the rate of inflation, and there would have been no tax increase.

House Democrats sought to seize political advantage by writing a budget that claimed identical savings, though it restored the Social Security cost-of-living increase and cut domestic spending much less. It also cut more deeply into defense. The Social Security provision, in particular, helped hold Democrats in line to support the budget, and a number of Republicans also came aboard. The May 23 vote to adopt it was 258-170.

An effort by several conservative Democrats to eliminate the Social Security cost-of-living increase and add a $12 billion, unspecified tax increase to further reduce the deficit won only fifty-six votes on the House floor, reflecting the degree to which Social Security was a heavily charged political liability. At the same time, however, support for the proposal from some corners was a sign of how intractable those closest to the budget process believed the deficit really to be. Former Budget Committee chairman Jones voted for the proposal, as did California Democrat Leon E. Panetta, who had lost a challenge for the Budget chairmanship in 1985. The then-chairman, William H. Gray III, D-Pa. (1979-), privately supported the idea, as well, and voted "present."

The conference proved to be as difficult as drafting a budget in the Senate.

Again, no fewer than five compromises were offered, with Social Security and defense the central, irreconcilable differences. But tax increases, too, reared their heads, only to be knocked down.

In July, Reagan weighed in at a White House reception with House Speaker Thomas P. "Tip" O'Neill, Jr., D-Mass. (1953-1987), and worked out an agreement whereby the House would accept more money for defense if the Senate would drop its Social Security freeze. Since Reagan had implicitly endorsed the Social Security plan through Bush's tie-breaking vote, it was seen as a slap at Dole and Domenici.

Significantly, opposition to the Social Security freeze from House Republicans, particularly Kemp and Minority Whip Trent Lott of Mississippi (House 1973-1989; Senate 1989-), was credited for Reagan's change of mind. And it infuriated Senate Republicans. Conferees eventually settled on a defense increase equal to inflation, full cost-of-living adjustments for Social Security, and no tax increase, although some additional revenues were expected from a variety of sources. Spending on domestic programs, except for those serving the poor, was to be cut 20 to 30 percent.

The most important element of the compromise was reconciliation instructions requiring more than $75 billion in savings over three years. Congress went to work on that package, and both the House and Senate produced bills that tried to meet the target. Significant savings in Medicare payments to physicians and hospitals, an income test for access to Veterans Administration hospitals, and curtailed spending on the Strategic Petroleum Reserve were just part of the proposals that House-Senate conferees eventually accepted.

But the bill was saddled with the excess baggage of the "Superfund" toxic-waste cleanup program. A long-delayed Superfund reauthorization bill was attached to the reconciliation measure, along with a controversial new excise tax on chemical manufacturers that the Senate wanted but the House did not. The two chambers battled over that issue until the Congress adjourned for the year, leaving the reconciliation savings unattained. By the time the bill became law the following April, its three-year savings was expected to be $18.2 billion, not the more than $74 billion originally claimed. Some of the savings were achieved in other bills, particularly one reauthorizing farm price- and income-support programs. Other savings were lost through the delay. The Office of Management and Budget, however, said that the bill never would have saved the amount its sponsors believed.

In the end, one thing stood out: The budget process once again in 1985 had failed to make it possible for Congress to reduce the deficit in a meaningful, permanent—and painless—way. It had become all too clear that politics and legislative inertia were more powerful than the desire of most in Congress to change spending habits. And, where there were too few members with the political will to make hard choices, there were enough to seize upon a change in the budget process—Gramm-Rudman's automatic mechanism of spending cuts—to heighten the pressure. Congress could do little to make the tough decisions any easier (although occasionally Congress surprised even itself with its ability to act). Instead, senators and House members decided to limit their options. It was a course that yielded only mixed results in the years immediately after 1985, though it also offered a glimmer of hope.

6

Testing Political Will

Throughout the 1980s, "hard choices" have been the bywords of budgeting. The Committee for a Responsible Federal Budget, a Washington, D.C.-based advocacy group led by former House Budget Committee chairman Robert N. Giaimo, D-Conn., started the trend. In mid-decade the group began sponsoring annual retreats for legislators, journalists, and others to take a close look at the options for bringing spending more into line with revenues. Congressional Democrats picked up the idea at their yearly spring meetings to plan for the upcoming session.

The format was simple: Examine the size of the deficit and, choosing from a long list of program cuts, tax increases, and other "reforms," find enough savings to balance the budget. Of course, the choices were not easy; that was the whole point.

In 1988, the National Economic Commission, which came to life during the post-stock-market crash, White House-congressional budget summit in November 1987, adapted the hard choices exercise for its own deliberations. The commission, headed by former Democratic National Committee chairman Robert Strauss and former Reagan administration transportation secretary Drew Lewis, was charged with reporting to Congress and the president about budget options early in 1989 (it abandoned plans to hurry its work to meet a self-imposed December 1988 deadline).

In September 1988, Strauss gave his own preview of just how difficult the task would be to a gathering of leading economists discussing the agenda facing whoever won the White House in November.

"This is the toughest job I have ever undertaken," Strauss said. He described the first time he sat down at a commission computer to "play" the hard choices game: "I increased the damn deficit," he said.

The intent of the National Economic Commission was to sort through the difficult options and to recommend choices to Congress and the president. "Critics say, 'All you're there for is to give cover to a bunch of politicians,'" Strauss noted. "That's not so inaccurate as to be all wrong." What the commission hoped to provide, he went on, was a "structure" for understanding how complex and politically charged the task really is, "so they can make those hard votes and still have a political life left."

What Strauss meant, but did not say directly, was that some recipients of the government's bounty would lose. Moreover, those losers were likely to be visible petitioners for a reprieve, because the *real* money in the federal budget goes for big-ticket items. "We have to go to Social

Security, Medicare and entitlements generally, and we have to go to defense," Strauss acknowledged. But the consequence could be, he warned, "withholding money from the sick, the elderly and the defense of the nation."

Most post-1930s social programs were intended to assist the poor and to improve public services in parts of the nation with hard-pressed regional or local economies, but many also benefited middle-income Americans, and even the wealthy. Moreover, state and local governments over the years had grown dependent on federal grants, although Reagan-era cuts and policy shifts have, to a degree, forced states and localities to look more to themselves for revenue. For instance, in the early 1980s states and localities were paying less than two-thirds of the cost of their construction projects, with the federal government picking up the rest; the state and local share rose to almost three-fourths by 1987. Nevertheless, the federal government still passed along more than $108 billion in 1987, much of it for assistance to individuals, and that money is sorely needed by state and local governments. "We have, in effect, created a special interest group that includes a majority of the population," contended Donald G. Ogilvie, in 1979 associate dean of the Yale School of Organization and Management.

As a political institution, Congress obviously is attuned to the broad appeal that its benefit programs carry. Beneficiaries of federal programs—state and local officials, teachers and students, social workers and welfare recipients, entrepreneurs who win government contracts, and not least among them, the elderly—long ago became adept at lobbying for more spending, and, in the 1980s, against cuts. Interest groups learned to work with agency officials who run the programs and with congressional committees that authorize them—creating so-called "iron triangles"—to preserve or increase spending.

Periodically, in the 1980s, Congress and the president have attempted to break those triangles. And occasionally, such as with the demise of federal revenue sharing in 1987, they have succeeded. But rarely have the two branches of government succeeded through cooperation.

In late 1987, the president sat down with Congress to talk seriously about budget priorities for the first time in the 1980s. Previously during the Reagan administration, attempts at negotiating differences between the two branches—differences that were often not partisan, but were nevertheless political—either failed or resulted in agreements that were unsatisfactory to all sides. But in the aftermath of the worst stock-market crash in the nation's history, Reagan and Congress were seemingly shocked into an agreement.

The first-ever Reagan-era "budget summit" was held shortly after the October 19 crash. Over the next four weeks, White House and congressional negotiators agreed to a two-year package of spending cuts—including some affecting the military—and tax increases. About five weeks later the specifics were enacted into law, lopping about $75 billion off the anticipated deficits for fiscal 1988 and 1989. Few truly hard choices were involved in that agreement, however. What remained to be seen was whether the newly created National Economic Commission would recommend any, and whether Congress or the new president would follow the advice.

Choosing among Limited Options

If political considerations make budget choices difficult, Congress in some instances has given itself an even more challenging task by insulating some programs against spending restraint.

Over time Congress has seen its ability to manage spending diminish, as the costs of government grew ever faster. In addition, costs rise and fall with changes in the economy. Those variables cannot be predicted with any degree of certainty, but nevertheless Congress and the administration each must estimate their impact when making budgetary decisions. The fact that economic forecasting is imprecise only makes the task of budgeting more arduous.

There are two key legislative tools for Congress to use in restraining spending: appropriations and reconciliation. Annual appropriations bills are used by Congress to designate money for hundreds of discretionary spending programs. That includes virtually all national defense endeavors, foreign aid, and some domestic activities. But changes in appropriations can do little to limit the growth of entitlements—domestic spending programs whose beneficiaries are "entitled" to the money by virtue of meeting certain criteria spelled out in law. Reconciliation bills are so named because they are used to "reconcile" the laws authorizing existing federal activities with changes assumed in annual budget resolutions. As a result, reconciliation is principally intended to change entitlements, since the only way such spending can be reduced is through changes in the underlying authorizing laws.

Indeed, reconciliation was invented as a tool to get a measure of control over entitlements, which comprise an ever-growing slice of the budget pie.

Spending: Controllable and Uncontrollable

By far the biggest obstacle to a wholesale assault on federal spending is the limited control Congress has on year-to-year budgeting. Congress does adopt an annual, "unified" budget resolution that covers the entirety of federal activities, but that budget does not itself spend money or raise taxes; it merely sets an agenda for Congress to follow.

The harsh reality is that Congress controls barely half of each year's new budget authority—that is, the new money that agencies are allowed to spend. Nearly half of all government spending is permanently appropriated for some entitlements—such as Social Security and interest payments on the national debt—and is politically far out of reach. What direct control Congress does have is exercised through the annual appropriations bills that provide the other half of what federal agencies have to spend.

But some of the money annually appropriated by Congress also goes for entitlements, such as farm price and income supports. The beneficiaries of those programs are entitled to the money, even if Congress must appropriate more. It is, for instance, an almost routine occurrence for Congress to pass a supplemental appropriations bill for the Commodity Credit Corporation (the federal agency that pays for farm programs) in time for spring planting.

Moreover, much of what is appropriated in one year is carried forward to be spent in the future; and some of what was appropriated in the past is not only earmarked for the current year but also is already committed through contracts for military equipment and the like. (For a detailed discussion of the flow of budget authority into outlays, or actual spending, see Chapter 3.)

Budget experts use the terms "relatively controllable outlays" and "relatively uncontrollable outlays" to describe the situation they face in trying to identify spending cuts, particularly the ones that can be fashioned through the appropriations process. But the jargon obscures the seriousness of the problem. In the now forgotten past, nearly all of what was spent in a given year was specifically appropriated for that year. But that was before the New Deal, entitlements, and the explosion of federal programs. By fiscal 1975, the year before Congress began using current budgeting procedures, about a third of all spending was relatively controllable. By 1987, only a fourth was in any way able to be limited by annual appropriations, and less than 10 percent was in the domestic sector of the budget that the administration wanted to attack. (See Figure 6-1.)

From 1975 until 1987, the combined costs of most other domestic spending—from Social Security to Medicare and Medicaid, the health programs for the elderly and poor, to farm programs—stayed roughly the same, or even shrank somewhat. (Some of those individual costs rose, while others declined.) But money that was previously committed through federal contracts grew as a percentage of all outlays, and interest payments on the national debt nearly doubled by the same measure.

That clearly has left very little room for maneuvering.

Control Is Elusive

Relatively uncontrollable does not mean, of course, that Congress cannot stop spending money on a special entitlement program once it is begun, or that it must build every ship or airplane the military desires. Cuts can be made in defense appropriations, but they are felt much more strongly in the second, third, and fourth years after the fact. At that point, previously appropriated construction money starts to run out, and there is less new money than anticipated for additional contracts. The terms of entitlement programs can also be changed; strikers and students can be made ineligible for food stamps, for instance. Congress did just that in 1981 and 1982, modestly curtailing those costs. Or Congress can limit payment increases for physicians and hospitals under Medicare. And it has done so periodically in the 1980s, significantly limiting the growth in Medicare spending, but not reducing it.

Rolling back entitlements, however, is a much more visible, long-lasting, and politically difficult task than is whittling away a few million dollars of appropriations. That is also why changing entitlements—often the real aim of the reconciliation process—has a more significant and permanent effect on the deficit.

It is really no wonder that so much attention should be focused on entitlements. Such mandatory spending is by far the largest component of the budget, and over time the fastest growing (though not so in recent years, when defense spending was growing faster). And it directly affects the largest single bloc of citizens. Even so, virtually all taxpayers have an ultimate claim on some part of this guaranteed government largess, either through Social Security, Medicare, and civil service or veterans' pensions, not to mention unemployment assistance, welfare, food stamps, and Medicaid for the less fortunate.

By far the largest share of entitlement spending is in aid to individuals (as opposed to corporations, which can benefit from farm programs, for example). But not all payments to individuals are entitlements. Student aid and housing subsidies are prime examples of nonentitlement assistance for individuals, which is controllable through increases and decreases in appropriations.

Prior to the 1960s, veterans programs, unemployment assistance, and Social Security provided the bulk of entitlement spending. Then came Medicaid in 1961 and the Great Society programs, such as Medicare, in 1965.

Entitlements cost less than $35 billion the year Medicare was enacted, accounting for about 27 percent of all federal outlays (not counting receipts for federal retirement programs, paid by the government). As a percentage of all outlays, entitlements grew steadily until the mid-1970s, when they

Figure 6-1 Controllable and Uncontrollable Outlays

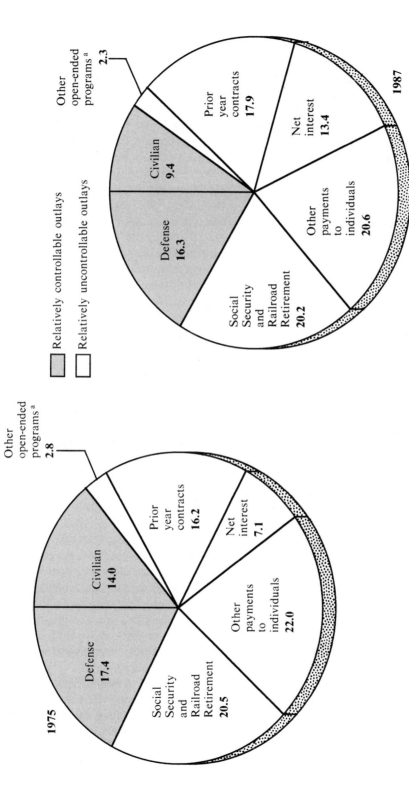

Sources: Office of Management and Budget, fiscal 1989 budget, fiscal 1985 budget.

Note: Percentage of total outlays, not accounting for undistributed federal employee retirement contributions made by the government. Totals may not add due to rounding.

[a] General revenue sharing, farm price supports, and other fixed costs, including payments to the government.

leveled off at between 44 percent and 46 percent. Entitlement spending peaked at almost 47 percent of the budget in fiscal 1983, which began just as the devastating 1981-1982 recession was ending. And, while the dollar amount continues to climb—reaching $474.1 billion in 1987, as a percentage of federal spending, entitlements are back below 45 percent. (See Table 6-1.)

Entitlement Costs Soar

One basic reason that entitlement spending expanded so rapidly was that Congress decided over the years that the federal government should provide more benefits to more people. One way it did that was by expanding government programs into areas, such as health care, that were previously beyond the scope of federal efforts. In 1965, before Medicare was under way, federal health care expenses came to about $1.3 billion, most of it for veterans. By 1987, the government spent $107.3 billion on the Medicare and Medicaid programs alone, and another $12.8 billion on veterans and other health care costs.

An even larger share of the growth in entitlement spending stemmed from Congress's efforts to protect recipients against inflation. Into the early 1970s, Congress periodically increased federal benefit payments to keep pace with rising prices. But by raising benefits on an ad hoc basis, Congress often approved increases that more than compensated for the rise in costs to beneficiaries. Between 1970 and 1972, for example, Congress increased Social Security benefits by almost 50 percent, while inflation was increasing at about 7 percent for food and 11 percent for health care.

Starting in the early 1960s, Congress began authorizing automatic increases by "indexing"—gearing the benefits paid by many programs to the rate of inflation measured by the government's Consumer Price Index (CPI). In 1962, civil service retirement benefits were linked to the CPI.

Military retirement pay was indexed in 1963, followed in 1969 by federal black lung compensation to disabled coal miners. Between 1971 and 1975, Congress indexed benefits paid under Social Security, food stamps, railroad retirement, Supplemental Security Income, and various nutrition programs. Veterans pensions were indexed in 1979, leaving veterans compensation, unemployment benefits, and Aid to Families with Dependent Children as the only major cash transfer programs not indexed to inflation. By 1980 benefits that rose automatically with the inflation rate accounted for 30 percent of all federal outlays.

Most indexed programs, such as Social Security, Supplemental Security Income, and railroad retirement, receive annual adjustments equal to the increases in the Consumer Price Index. (The law was changed in 1986. Prior to then, the adjustment was delayed for a year whenever the inflation rate fell below 3 percent.) For years, military and civil service retirement benefits were adjusted twice a year with no minimum, providing an even greater protection against inflation. As part of the major budget-cutting exercise of 1981, this semiannual adjustment was rolled back to once a year.

According to a study by the congressional General Accounting Office, indexing accounted for about half the increase in costs of Social Security between 1970 and 1977. However, given the earlier generous record of Congress, indexing—which allowed Congress to stay out of decisions to increase benefits above the inflation rate—actually may have helped to hold down costs by discouraging legislative interference with benefit levels. "On balance, indexation in the Social Security program has probably saved the trust funds money," Office of Management and Budget (OMB) official W. Bowman Cutter told the House Budget Committee in 1979.

In addition, the cost to the government for providing direct services has risen in

Table 6-1   Growth in Entitlements and Other Mandatory Spending (in billions)

Year	Social Security	Medicare/ Medicaid	Welfare and other means-tested programs	Nonmeans-tested programs[a]	Total
1965	$ 17.1	$ 0.3 [b]	$ 5.0	$ 12.1	$ 34.5
1970	29.4	9.5	7.4	19.9	66.2
1975	63.1	20.9	18.9	52.8	155.8
1980	117.1	47.9	32.6	80.6	278.2
1981	138.0	58.1	37.8	87.1	321.0
1982	154.1	66.6	38.1	98.7	357.5
1983	168.6	74.5	40.6	115.2	399.0
1984	176.1	81.1	41.6	96.1	394.8
1985	186.5	92.5	43.7	115.2	437.8
1986	196.7	99.2	45.9	113.5	455.4
1987	205.2	107.3	46.5	115.2	474.1

Source: Congressional Budget Office.

Note: Totals may not add due to rounding.

[a] Includes other retirement and disability spending, unemployment compensation, and farm price supports.
[b] Medicare began in 1966.

step with costs in the private sector. Medicare and Medicaid are not indexed, but their costs have been pushed up by increases in general health care costs.

Such services are known as in-kind benefits. Instead of making cash benefits to recipients, the government provides services through its own employees or by paying bills submitted by private providers, such as doctors, hospitals, and pharmacies. In 1960 government in-kind benefits were mostly limited to veterans' medical care and accounted for 1.4 percent of total outlays. Federal in-kind benefits rose to 7 percent of spending in 1970 and to nearly 14 percent by 1980. In-kind programs have been more costly to run than cash benefit programs because of the difficulty of enforcing eligibility standards and monitoring service levels. Combined with cash benefits often paid to the same recipients, in-kind services may also overcompensate for inflation.

In the 1980s particularly, Congress has tried to put a measure of control on in-kind benefits. The cost that must be borne by Medicare beneficiaries has risen, for exam-

ple, typically through an increase in the "deductible," the amount they must pay before the government begins picking up the hospital tab. And Medicare recipients pay higher "premiums" for coverage of physicians' costs. Congress also has established fee schedules for hospital and physician costs, and limited increases in those costs at a time when medical costs are rising at twice the rate of inflation generally.

The changing character of the U.S. population has also contributed to spending growth. Federal outlays, particularly for Social Security and Medicare, have risen as the nation's workers aged and retired.

In the first twenty years after Social Security was set up in 1935, relatively few retirees were covered by the system for all the years they worked. Between 1955 and 1986, however, the number of Social Security recipients more than tripled, from 4.8 percent to 15.4 percent of the U.S. population. During the same period the population grew by less than 50 percent, but the elderly population increased by more than 100 percent. In those three decades, federal Social

Security outlays increased from $4.3 billion to $193.9 billion, yet by one measure inflation was only 250 percent—a whopping amount but hardly the cause of the increase in costs.

The cost increase was mostly due to the fact that more workers were covered and most elderly persons lived longer after reaching retirement age. Social Security began paying for disability as well as retirement, and most recipients were eligible for higher benefits because they had been covered for a longer time and earned higher wages than earlier retirees. Similar demographic trends have driven up costs for military and civil service retirement and disability insurance programs.

Rejecting Some Solutions

One of the enduring images of the budget-cutting exercises of the 1980s was President Reagan's frequent trips to the dry well of domestic spending cuts. After his first-year successes, Reagan repeatedly proposed a series of program terminations, "privatizations," or cutbacks that Congress was simply unwilling to tolerate. Often, it was a strongly felt ideological difference of opinion that led to the impasse; sometimes it was more basic—constituent pressure to keep the money flowing.

Perhaps the most persistent White House advocate for domestic cutbacks was budget director David A. Stockman, whose own ideological predilection was to eliminate much of the government's social spending. "Forty years' worth of promises, subventions, entitlements and safety nets issued by the federal government to every component and stratum of American society would have to be scrapped or drastically modified," Stockman believed. In his 1986 memoir he described the unwillingness of other White House officials—including Reagan himself—to support such a radical revolution. Yet many of Stockman's propos-

als made it into the president's annual budget requests, only to be quietly ignored—or publicly rejected.

"Almost everything that was in the budget when we went to work in the Cutting Room in late January 1981 still remains," Stockman wrote.

It was true in 1986, and is so still. According to the Senate Budget Committee, for fiscal 1988 the administration proposed thirty-four different domestic spending cuts that had previously been rejected or ignored by Congress. Together they accounted for $19 billion of Reagan's proposed $42 billion in savings for 1988.

Some contend that the administration made little effort to sell these ideas. But even partisan Republicans, among them Sen. Pete V. Domenici, R-N.M., who chaired the Budget Committee from 1981 to 1986, rejected many administration budget requests.

In April 1986, for instance, Domenici bundled together forty-three of the president's proposed domestic spending cuts— worth about $4.5 billion in fiscal 1987 savings—and offered them as a floor amendment to his own proposed budget that the administration was opposing. Domenici encouraged "those who think it is the domestic, discretionary component of this budget that has run wild" to vote for the bundle of cuts. The amendment got fourteen "yes" votes; eighty-three senators opposed it, including Domenici, Senate Republican leader Robert Dole of Kansas, and assistant Republican leader Alan Simpson of Wyoming (1979-). Only one Democrat, William Proxmire of Wisconsin, voted for the amendment.

The previously failed budget-cutting proposals for fiscal 1988 involved a virtual Who's Who of domestic spending programs, ranging from the Legal Services Administration to Medicaid to the Strategic Petroleum Reserve. Given the constituencies they aided, and the programs' wide visibility throughout the nation, it seems hardly surprising that they were often spared the budgeteers' knives. What was surprising, if anything, was the administration's willingness to keep suggesting the cuts.

Take farm programs, for instance. Spending on price and income supports for farmers had increased tenfold during the Reagan presidency, from less than $3 billion annually in the 1970s to almost $26 billion in fiscal 1986. Such costs were clearly not sustainable in an era of huge budget deficits, and in 1985 Congress—in cooperation with the administration—reconfigured farm program spending in a effort to bring down costs. One change was to ratchet down income supports, cash assistance payments to farmers based on the difference between the market price for their crops and a statutory "target price." These target prices were to be frozen for two years and then reduced a total of 10 percent between 1988 and 1990, thereby reducing income-support payments a similar amount. Yet one year later, Reagan's budget for 1988 suggested further reductions. Congress, however, was not about to go along with another slice out of the farmers' hide. Despite the high cost of support payments, there was already a downward trend expected.

Consider, too, grants for economic development. Reagan regularly targeted the Commerce Department's Economic Development Administration and the program of Urban Development Action Grants (known as UDAG), both of which directed money to local public works projects and local businesses, but which the administration said served to "distort local priorities." And the administration also tried to curtail Community Development Block Grants, which even went to wealthy communities (although the weighted formula used to determine distribution favored poorer areas). But Congress just as steadfastly refused to touch these highly popular sources of fed-

eral bounty in any significant way. For instance, the House voted by three-to-one margins in 1986 not to touch either the Economic Development Administration or Community Development Block Grants. Despite the efforts of urban liberals, however, the UDAG program was ended after fiscal 1988, although some money for future grants remained to be distributed.

Then, again, there was Reagan's effort to cut federally subsidized transit. Congress did finally agree in 1986 to sell Conrail, the government-run freight railroad, but not to the Norfolk Southern Corp., as the administration wanted. Instead, over White House objections, Congress voted to sell the railroad through a public stock offering. But Congress would have nothing of the administration's similar desire to unload Amtrak, the national passenger railroad. Though federal payments for Amtrak were curtailed somewhat early in Reagan's term, Congress by wide margins rejected moves in 1985, 1986, and 1987 to slash subsidies or terminate the government's interest in the railroad altogether. Similarly, after Congress went along with a 32 percent cut in federal aid to urban mass transit projects in 1981, it refused to cut deeper, despite annual requests from the administration.

Some Budget-Cutting Successes

In the budget-cutting efforts of the 1980s, there have been a few notable decisions to cut or not to cut, with far-reaching implications: Some entitlements, like Medicare, have been pared, but the biggest of all—Social Security—has been made inviolate; the defense buildup of the early Reagan years was frozen and eventually rolled back; and on a several occasions, Congress slapped the hands of legislators reaching into the notorious pork barrel.

In what may be an archetypical case of Congress giving the deficit its due ahead of conventional politicking, federal revenue sharing was allowed to expire in 1986, despite the vigorous efforts of one of the most powerful members of the House.

General revenue sharing was born in 1972 as a product of the Nixon administration's efforts to give power back to the states and cities. Over fourteen years the program dispensed an estimated $83 billion with virtually no strings attached. State governments were weaned from the program beginning in 1981.

In the 1980s revenue sharing expenses averaged $4.8 billion a year, and as the program's authorization was about to run out in 1986, local governments began agitating strenuously for its renewal. They presumably could have had no better ally than Jamie L. Whitten, D-Miss., most senior member of the House and chairman of its Appropriations Committee. But Congress explicitly refused to renew the authorization for revenue sharing in its fiscal 1986, deficit-reducing reconciliation bill. Nevertheless, Whitten would not give up. In the final weeks of 1986, he tried to add $3.4 billion for revenue sharing to the fiscal 1987 continuing resolution, which contained all the year's appropriations. The House Rules Committee, which controlled the procedures under which most bills came to the House floor, refused to go along. Whitten was forced to back down.

In one final irony, a federal judge ordered the government to pay local governments $180 million in revenue sharing in 1987, after the program had expired. Congress had in essence exempted revenue sharing from automatic Gramm-Rudman cuts, by requiring that any money cut under Gramm-Rudman be returned to the revenue sharing trust fund. That was what had happened to the $180 million in 1986, the only year Gramm-Rudman cuts actually occurred. Since it was allowing the program to expire, however, Congress ordered the administration to pay out the last of the money. And Judge June Green agreed, but

only after a six-month court battle in which the administration argued that it no longer had authority to dispense the money. Green noted specifically that Congress "deliberately sought to protect the [revenue sharing] trust fund from at least some of its recent budget-cutting enthusiasm."

Defense Buildup Frozen

If an enduring legacy of the Reagan presidency is the sharp run-up of defense spending in 1981 and 1982, so, too, must be the cuts that the Pentagon endured in 1986 and 1987. For Reagan, who took office proclaiming his desire to put the military back on a solid footing after having been undercut during the Carter years, the reductions forced on him by Congress must have been particularly galling.

But, in fact, the record of defense spending was mixed during Carter's term, with a large increase in budget authority— or money that could be obligated—in 1977 that was double the rate of inflation that year. In the following two years, however, military spending grew by a factor somewhat smaller than inflation. And, as inflation peaked in 1980, a big increase in defense spending was barely large enough to offset it. (See Table 6-2.)

Congress, acquiescent in Reagan's spending requests in 1981, and still somewhat compliant in the next several years, allowed an increase in defense spending of 25.1 percent in fiscal 1981 (part of that came in a supplemental appropriation enacted after Reagan took office in January), 20.3 percent in 1982, and 13.6 percent in 1983. During that same three-year period, inflation (as measured for defense-related purchases) was 11.4 percent, 7.6 percent, and 3.6 percent. Together the annual increases amounted to almost three times what would have been required to keep pace with inflation.

The change came in 1985. As Congress became more and more concerned about the

Table 6-2 Growth in Defense Spending

Fiscal year	Budget authority (in billions)	Change from year to year	Inflation (GNP deflator) [a]
1977	$110.2	13.3%	6.9%
1978	117.2	6.4	6.9
1979	126.5	7.9	9.4
1980	143.9	13.8	12.4
1981	180.0	25.1	11.4
1982	216.5	20.3	7.6
1983	245.0	13.6	3.6
1984	265.2	8.2	3.5
1985	294.7	11.1	2.1
1986	289.1	−1.9	1.2
1987	287.4	−0.6	0.8

Sources: Office of Management and Budget, Commerce Department, percentage calculations by author.

Note: Totals may not add due to rounding. GNP = gross national product.

[a] Computed from the Commerce Department's constant weighted index for national defense purchases.

deficit's growth, and as it debated the Gramm-Rudman antideficit law, it decided the increase in defense spending had to come to an end. First, inflation had fallen dramatically, so the cost of holding the line would be less severe. Second, there was an enormous amount of money in the defense pipeline from big appropriations increases in prior years. Much of that money remained to be spent, so the immediate effect of a freeze in appropriations would not be a precipitous drop in actual spending. The shocking upshot was an actual decrease in defense appropriations for fiscal 1986 (after automatic Gramm-Rudman cuts took their bite in February 1986), and then again for fiscal 1987.

It was such a shock that the Congressional Budget Office (CBO) announced in August 1985 that the deficit had been set on a downward path. That projection turned out to be a bit premature, and the administration continued to put forward defense spending requests larger than Congress was willing to allow. But the trend was more firmly set in the 1987 budget summit, when Congress and the president agreed to hold

defense increases below the expected level of inflation in both 1988 and 1989—for a total savings of more than $13 billion. There was no doubt by 1988 that the then-measured decline in the federal deficit was in no small part due to savings from defense.

Putting a Lid on the Pork Barrel

An axiom of congressional life is that members do what favors they can for their constituents. It is called pork-barrel politics, whether earmarking appropriations for specific home-town construction projects, designating grants for the local university, or protecting military bases that even the Pentagon believes to be unnecessary (but that sit in one or another House member's district).

It is not that the money that such projects involve is so great. Most often the amounts are quite small. But for pork-barrel opponents such as James C. Miller III, director of Reagan's budget office, it is both the principle of the issue and the fact that there is so much of it that the dollars begin to add up. Miller urged in 1987 that the system be changed, "so we don't have so much porking."

There are few on Capitol Hill who believe that pork-barrel politics have been put to rest; the technique of including items of special interest to members in appropriations bills, for instance, has long been seen as necessary lubrication for the legislative process. But in the deficit-conscious days at the end of the 1980s, Congress began taking actions to limit (if not eliminate) certain kinds of pork.

In October 1988, for instance, Congress passed a bill that Reagan eagerly signed into law to put an end to pork-barrel military bases. A new, independent commission was to be created to recommend the closing or scaling back of obsolete bases. The defense secretary would then accept or reject the proposals en bloc. If accepted, Congress would have forty-five days to disapprove them, or they would take effect. It was expected that the process would tilt the political balance in favor of the base closings and against those members whose districts were expected to suffer.

But by far one of the largest cost-savings from an antipork move on Capitol Hill occurred in that most important year of 1985, when Congress finally voted to require states and localities to share significantly in the costs of water projects, including ports, dams, and inland waterways. One of the most time-honored means of awarding pork, water projects are also necessary for transportation, farming, and drinking water. They are also expensive. And until 1985, the federal government bore virtually the entire cost.

As part of a supplemental spending bill that included $48.8 million for forty-one individual projects, Congress also required that specific cost-sharing arrangements be negotiated for those projects, and that they be submitted to Congress for approval. A year later, Congress enacted a sweeping authorization bill for new water projects that wrote these new cost-sharing rules into permanent law to apply to all new construc-

tion. As a result, state and local governments would have to pay 25 percent, 50 percent, or even 100 percent of certain costs, where previously they paid as little as 5 percent.

The change was guaranteed to produce savings: Projects favored by a local House member or senator would suddenly get closer scrutiny because states and localities would have to invest some of their own money; and for those projects that do go forward, the absolute cost to the federal government would be less. In 1987, the first year after the authorization bill was enacted, Congress approved appropriations for forty new water projects, in part as a result of a backlog of requests. But in 1988, the energy and water appropriations bill contained no new water-project starts. It was the largest energy-water bill in history, but it was also the most austere. For the first time because of fiscal stringency no new water projects were started.

Expectations versus Fact

As hard as it is for politicians to get up the courage to cut spending or increase taxes to reduce the deficit, a mere blip on an economist's computer screen can make the task much more difficult.

Just as businesses must, of necessity, base their decisions on expectations about the future, the federal government's budget is tied closely to projections about the fate of the economy. A boom reduces costs for some "automatic stabilizers" such as unemployment insurance and "safety net" programs such as welfare and Medicaid—and it increases tax receipts. A recession has the opposite effect. It does not take a wide swing in economic performance to have a dramatic effect on a $1 trillion budget, however. Even apparently modest changes in economic growth, inflation, interest rates, and unemployment—on the order of a tenth of 1 percent, for instance—can increase or cut the deficit by billions of dollars.

One rule of thumb used by CBO forecasters is that a $10 billion overestimate of nominal, or noninflation-adjusted, GNP growth costs $2.3 billion in lost revenue. That is based on the assumption that economic growth directly affects employment and income and is reflected in taxes. For fiscal 1987, CBO miscalculated nominal GNP growth by $100 billion (about 2 percent in a $4.5 trillion economy); as a result it predicted an extra $23 billion in revenue.

Economic forecasting has been a tool of administration policy making since shortly after World War II, when the Employment Act of 1946 created the president's Council of Economic Advisers (CEA). The CEA forecasts are used by the administration's Office of Management and Budget in its budget work. Congress has had its own economic advisory group since 1975, when CBO was established.

But economic forecasting is an imprecise art at best. Though admittedly unreliable—a fact borne out in recent years—economic projections have nevertheless taken on an even more prominent role in the era of Gramm-Rudman and the threat of automatic spending cuts. Economic forecasts are used to predict deficits, and under Gramm-Rudman it is those deficit projections—not the actual deficits—that trigger automatic cuts.

Several times a year both CEA and CBO will take the economy's temperature and make estimates about changes in spending and taxes that are influenced by economic variables. At the beginning of the year, Congress must rely on those estimates to decide how close the projected deficit will come to the Gramm-Rudman target—and what fiscal policy adjustments, if any, will be needed to bring the projected deficit under the target. In late July, CEA makes

an even more important estimate of the economy's vital signs, because it forms the basis for ordering Gramm-Rudman spending cuts in August and again in October.

Problems arise when the forecasts that Congress uses to make its budget decisions, or those used by the administration to order automatic spending cuts under Gramm-Rudman, are flawed.

In 1988, Congress worked in the early part of the year with administration estimates about the economy's performance that were somewhat more optimistic than CBO's. OMB forecast a deficit of $143 billion; CBO said it would be $176 billion. There was obvious reward in following OMB's road map, if it proved to be correct. The OMB forecast allowed Congress to meet the $136 billion Gramm-Rudman deficit target (plus the law's $10 billion margin of error) without making any significant changes in fiscal policy. And in an election year, there was little sympathy to call for additional deep spending cuts or tax increases, as would have been necessary if CBO's numbers were used.

Congress was lucky; in fact, the economy did a little bit better than even the administration expected. And in July CEA and OMB continued to forecast good times ahead for 1989; no automatic cuts were necessary (although CBO strongly disagreed). But optimistic forecasts are not always accurate. A look at the economic projections for 1986 is a good example of where forecasts can go wrong. (See Table 6-3.)

In January 1985, CBO and OMB both said the economy would grow modestly the following year, 1986; they said inflation would be above 4 percent and that interest rates would stay on the high side. In January 1986, both agencies revised their estimates to account for reduced growth, and a related lessening of inflationary pressures and lower interest rates for the year that

Table 6-3   Economic Assumptions versus Economy's Performance, 1986

	Congressional Budget Office forecast		Office of Management and Budget forecast		1986 actual
	1985	1986	1985	1986	
Inflation-adjusted increase in gross national product [a]	3.2%	3.2%	4.0%	3.4%	2.9%
Consumer Price Index [b]	4.5	3.4	4.3	3.5	1.6
Civilian unemployment rate [c]	6.9	6.7	6.9	6.7	7.0
Interest rate on three-month Treasury bills [c]	8.7	6.8	7.9	7.3	6.0

Sources: Congressional Budget Office, Office of Management and Budget.

Note: Forecasts from January 1985 and January 1986.

[a] Percentage change year to year.
[b] Percent change year to year, computed for urban wage earners and clerical workers.
[c] Calendar year average.

was by then under way. In the end, economic growth, inflation, and interest rates were all lower still than either CBO and OMB had predicted. And the differences were not insignificant.

OMB and CBO both have uneven track records in projecting the direction of the economy, and therefore of the deficit. They have been far off the mark in some years and close in others. And at different times Congress has relied on both agencies to provide the estimates for its budget resolutions. Most often the forecast that provided the most favorable political opportunity—such as OMB's in 1988—has been used. On rare occasions, Congress has even used an amalgam of both agencies' forecasts, when that seemed most expedient.

The consequence of missing the mark with economic forecasts is that congressional deficit projections are also far off—and never on the high side. On average, from 1980 to 1987, congressional budgets have underestimated the deficit annually by more than $42 billion, but the swings have been extreme. For fiscal 1983, the budget resolution predicted a deficit of $103.9 billion; the actual deficit was $195.4 billion.

The following year, however, the budget resolution predicted a deficit of $171.6 billion, and the actual deficit was $175.3 billion. Those two years represent the high and low points of deficit estimating during the 1980s.

Since 1985, CBO has published an extensive analysis of deficit projections and has found that bad economic assumptions were the prime cause for mistakes—resulting in more than half of the average error in annual deficit estimates. Other causes were slip-ups in policy assumptions and in technical estimates, such as rates of spending. (See Table 6-4.)

Both CBO and OMB guessed wrong in most of the first seven Reagan years, 1981-1987. For example, in four of those years, CBO overestimated economic growth. In two, it underestimated growth and once—in 1984—it guessed right. During the same period, administration forecasters followed suit, except that in 1984 they undershot the actual figure. The result has been that neither CBO nor OMB has been able to claim that its estimates are more reliable that the other's. As a result, political posturing has affected this aspect of budgeting like all others.

Table 6-4 Effect of Economic Assumptions on Deficit Projections

	1980	1981	1982	1983	1984	1985	1986	1987	Average 1980-1987
Actual deficit	$-59.6	$-57.9	$-110.7	$-195.4	$-175.3	$-202.8	$-220.7	$-148.8	—
Projected deficit	-23.0	+0.2	-37.6	-103.9	-171.6	-181.2	-171.9	-142.6	—
Difference	-36.6	-58.1	-73.0	-91.5	-3.7	-21.6	-48.8	-6.2	$-42.4
Difference due to optimistic economic assumptions[a]	4.0	1.4	76.0	58.5	2.7	14.8	10.9	15.1	22.9
Percentage difference due to optimistic economic assumptions	10.9%	2.4%	104.1%	63.9%	73.0%	68.5%	22.3%	243.5%	54.0%

Sources: Congressional Budget Office, percentage analysis by author.

Note: Dollar amounts in billions; totals may not add due to rounding. The 1982, 1986, and 1987 budget resolutions were based wholly or in part on administration economic assumptions; the rest were based on Congressional Budget Office assumptions. Amounts are adjusted to subtract spending and revenues associated with functions that from time to time—principally before 1985—were considered "off-budget" (such as the Federal Financing Bank and the Postal Service) and to account for other differences in the treatment of spending in budget resolutions. Therefore, deficit amounts may not agree with those officially reported or found elsewhere in this book.

[a] The Congressional Budget Office's analysis also shows errors in deficit projection that can be attributed to mistakes in policy or technical assumptions (such as underestimating the revenue effects of the 1986 Tax Reform Act). Occasionally, bad economic assumptions are offset by technical and policy errors that reduce the actual difference between projected and actual deficits.

Using Politics
to Skirt the Issue

Needless to say, the intractable deficit dilemma has been compounded by politics. Blame for fiscal failures both past and anticipated is all part of the byplay between Congress and the White House, and between Republicans and Democrats. Budget politics has become such a popular game that at times it seems as if the deficit is too good a political foil to be gotten rid of.

The focus of the politicking has been on the deficit itself, and the policy choices that each side ascribes as the deficit's cause. That includes charges that administration economic forecasts have been "cooked" to yield more favorable results (allegations made all the more credible by former budget director Stockman's memoir-confessions).

Naturally, since it came to town with a mandate against excess, the Reagan administration has accused the Democrats—indeed, all of Congress—of being unwilling to cut unnecessary spending and too willing to increase taxes. Likewise, Democrats in Congress and a few Republicans have charged the administration with throwing money at its own favorite "problem," national defense, and with turning a blind eye toward the deficits that administration priorities have brought about. Neither formulation has allowed the other much latitude, which may account for repeated failures to find a common ground from which to attack the deficit.

The result, year after year, has been a virtual deadlock over major policy changes—to the extent that the more or less successful budget summit negotiations in 1987 surprised everyone, not least the participants themselves. The surprise was that they got together at all, not to mention that the outcome was an agreement that held together for two years.

All this failure to agree on substantive changes to address the deficit in turn has led to reliance upon gimmicks. Otherwise serious deficit-cutters have turned to the sales of government assets, such as entire federal loan portfolios, as a means to acquire quick cash to offset spending. Never mind that the long-term effect on the budget is negative, because of the loss of these revenue-producing assets. Indeed, objections to this particular gimmick were so loud that Congress, in reviving Gramm-Rudman's automatic spending cuts in 1987, forbade the counting of asset sales as a way to meet the law's deficit targets.

Politicians of all stripes also regularly proclaim a triumvirate of villains—waste, fraud, and abuse—as key culprits in the nation's fiscal mess. These rogues have been spied by Republicans lurking in social programs and by Democrats in the Pentagon. They are also seen in the revenue arena, and Congress with Reagan's blessing has nearly every year since 1981 increased spending on Internal Revenue Service agents—with the promise that they would more than pay for themselves with stepped up collections from tax cheats. The fact is, however, that sooner or later this gimmick, too, yields diminishing returns.

In 1984, Reagan campaigned for re-election on a platform that included well-publicized attacks on wasteful federal spending. The centerpiece of that effort was a forty-seven-volume report issued that January by the President's Private Sector Survey on Cost Control. Popularly known as the Grace Commission, after its chairman, industrialist J. Peter Grace, the panel listed 2,478 recommendations that it claimed would save $424 billion over three years through a shift to sound business practices to eliminate waste.

The CBO, in concert with the General Accounting Office, disputed the Grace Commission's claims. First of all, the two agencies said, actual budget savings would amount to only a third of that estimated by the commission. More importantly, most of the significant savings would come not from management changes targeting greater efficiency or from an end to fraud, but instead from making difficult policy choices. For instance, the commission proposed tying Social Security and Medicare to a means test, to see if beneficiaries really needed the money. And it proposed scaling back civil service and military retirement programs, which the commission said were three to six times more generous than the best private pensions. Together, the Grace Commission said these changes would save about $120 billion over three years, "without harming in any way necessary social welfare programs." Yet it goes without saying that Congress would not adopt such "reforms," at least not solely on the say-so of a presidentially appointed panel like Grace's.

Some suggestions that did not require congressional approval were put in place by the administration. These included paying government bills in a more timely fashion and depositing receipts more quickly: one saved interest costs; the other increased interest earnings. And Congress enacted other recommendations, such as giving the Treasury Department authority to collect unpaid government debts by deducting payments from individual tax refunds, or improving procedures for verifying eligibility for food stamps or the outside earnings of Social Security recipients. Together these changes amounted to several billions of dollars over a period of years, not inconsequential perhaps, but barely a drop in the very deep deficit bucket.

Changing the Constitution

For his part, Reagan maintained one consistent refrain throughout his time in the White House, and particularly in response to disputes with Congress: Use the Constitution to make the free-spenders behave.

Reagan's wish was for two specific changes to the Constitution that would severely tie the hands of Congress and give the president greater authority (beyond the veto authority already possessed) to reject congressional decisions. One change would be to mandate a balanced budget in which revenues were equal to or exceeded outlays. The other change would be to allow a president to veto specific items in appropriations bills, instead of forcing the president to accept or veto entire bills. (It was this last issue that was sharply focused upon during much of Reagan's two terms, as Congress enacted monstrous continuing resolutions that comprised four or five or even all thirteen regular appropriations bills.)

Balanced-Budget Amendment

Of the two proposals, the question of requiring a balanced federal budget clearly had the most support in and out of Congress, beginning as long ago as 1975. A statutory requirement that revenues equal outlays was seen as insufficient, since Congress can change laws as quickly as it enacts them. Suggestions that Congress vote to cap expenditures at some percentage of the gross national product also have received little support. Supporters of the notion of a balanced budget see a constitutional amendment as their only realistic hope of forcing lasting change in federal fiscal policy.

A change in the Constitution can be initiated by Congress with a two-thirds majority in each chamber. Or two-thirds of the states (currently thirty-four) can petition a constitutional convention to produce an amendment. In either event, three-fourths of the states (thirty-eight currently) must ratify a constitutional amendment before it takes effect. The process is arduous and often fails. Only twenty-six amendments have been adopted in the two-hundred-year life of the Constitution, including the first ten, known as the Bill of Rights. The most recent admendment, added in 1971, gave eighteen-year-olds the right to vote. In 1982 an amendment guaranteeing equal rights to women died after falling three short of the thirty-eight states needed for ratification.

Despite widespread concern about the growth in the deficit and the perceived need to control it, the permanence of a constitutional amendment gives pause even to those who believe strongly in balancing the budget. For instance, although the Eighteenth Amendment outlawing the sale, manufacture, or import of alcoholic beverages was eventually repealed, the repeal process took thirteen years after Prohibition went into effect.

In the case of the proposed balanced-budget amendment, there is widespread uncertainty as to the need for such a rigid formula, even one that might be waived in time of war. Opponents and even some supporters of Gramm-Rudman are troubled by its specific, mandatory deficit targets (phasing down to zero over time) and the threat that automatic spending cuts might be triggered without recourse by Congress. And then there is the complexity of the federal budget, with its multiple, self-financing trust funds for airport and highway construction and for Social Security and Medicare programs. Moreover, the proposed federal balanced-budget amendment would make no allowance for capital-cost financing, even though state governments that must maintain balanced budgets are usually not prohibited from some form of borrowing for purchase and construction of capital equipment, roads, and buildings.

The drive to adopt a balanced-budget amendment began gaining momentum in the late 1970s. By 1980, legislatures of thirty states had called for a constitutional convention to draft a balanced-budget amendment. Two more states did so by 1984—still two short of the minimum—and there was doubt that the state-passed ex-

pressions constituted a contemporaneous call for a convention, since many were a decade or more old and worded significantly differently.

But Congress responded to the pressure by acting on its own amendments. The Senate Judiciary Committee fell one vote short of approving a balanced-budget amendment in 1980. The measure, which was sponsored by Dennis DeConcini, D-Ariz. (1977-), would have required the president to submit a balanced budget, and the Congress to adopt one, unless three-fifths of each chamber voted to waive the requirement. Taxes would have to be kept to the same share of the gross national product as the previous year, but Congress could waive that requirement by a majority vote. The following year, with the Senate in Republican hands and Reagan in the White House, the committee voted for the amendment by an 11-5 vote. It was marginally different, having a specific waiver in time of war, and revenues could increase by the amount of increase in "national income," a somewhat different measure than that used the previous year.

The amendment did not reach the Senate floor until 1982, when it passed 69-31, two votes more than necessary. With time running out on the year, House Republican leaders, led by Barber B. Conable, Jr., of New York (1965-1985) and aided by Texas Democrat Phil Gramm, collected the signatures of a majority of House members on a petition to get the amendment out of the Judiciary Committee, where it had been bottled up by opposing Democrats. Both Reagan and Bush came to Capitol Hill to lobby hard for the measure. The House voted in favor of the amendment by 236-187, but that was forty-six votes shy of the needed two-thirds.

For the constitutional amendment, 1982 was the high-water mark. There was no real action in 1983 or 1984; although the Senate Judiciary Committee approved an amendment, there was no floor debate, and it died with the end of the Ninety-eighth Congress. The panel then approved the amendment again in 1985, this time with Paul Simon, D-Ill. (House 1975-1985; Senate 1985-), as sponsor. But when it came to the floor in early 1986, the amendment was defeated 66-34, one vote short of the necessary two-thirds majority. The issue was never raised again in the House.

Sponsors and critics of the amendment attributed the defeat to an increased Democratic presence in the Senate since the 1984 elections, and to enactment of Gramm-Rudman. "This amendment picks up where Gramm-Rudman-Hollings leaves off," said Simon during debate on the measure. But Daniel J. Evans, R-Wash. (1983-), who led the opposition, called the amendment "completely unworkable." Added Evans, "We should at least allow the Gramm-Rudman-Hollings plan a chance to work before we seek a constitutional amendment."

Line-Item Veto

The idea of allowing the president to veto individual items in appropriations bills gained prominence when Reagan asked for such authority in his State of the Union address in 1984. Although many governors have such authority, Congress has been unwilling to concede it to the president, chiefly because it was only in the 1974 budget act that Congress wrested back from the White House a measure of control over spending. And fights have broken out periodically during Reagan's years over his use of "deferrals," the permitted withholding of appropriated money for "management" reasons, which resemble line-item vetoes in effect. (See Chapter 3 for a detailed discussion of deferrals.)

Moreover, there is doubt that governors have made significant cuts in spending using the line-item veto, or that a president could do so—for the same reason that Congress has such a limited effect on spending by adjusting appropriations. As a case in point, Reagan objected strenuously in his 1988 State of the Union address to congressional padding of appropriations. But in March, when he finally specified what items he would have stricken if he had the use of an item veto, the cuts totaled only $1.5 billion—a mere 1 percent of the fiscal 1988 deficit, which eventually turned out to be $155.1 billion. Reagan listed 107 items he would have cut, including $6.4 million for a tourist gondola in Idaho, $4 million for soil-conservation flood control projects, and $100,000 for a local police force in Harpers Ferry, W.Va., a town that is encompassed by a national park. But much of the savings would have come from sales of Small Business Administration loans and user fees for certain federal programs, both of which Congress had forbidden.

There has been no serious effort to adopt a line-item veto as a constitutional amendment, as many scholars believe would be necessary. Instead, there have been tries at enacting statutory item vetoes, often for short, two-year trial periods. For example, in January 1984 the House rejected amendments to bills authorizing low-income weatherization programs and aid for libraries that would have established limited item vetoes for money appropriated under the two bills. And the Senate rejected an item-veto amendment to a deficit-reduction bill, sponsored by Mack Mattingly, R-Ga. (1981-1987). By a 56-34 vote, the Senate determined that the amendment was not in order because it was not in the form of a constitutional amendment.

Mattingly tried an unconventional ploy to get around the constitutional problem in 1985. He sponsored a bill that would have required all appropriations bills, after they are passed by Congress but before they are sent to the president for consideration, to be broken into individual paragraphs representing separate bills. Since each newly created separate bill could be vetoed, the effect would be to give the president a veto over each paragraph in an appropriations bill.

When the measure got to the Senate floor, a strong filibuster developed led by Rules Committee chairman Charles McC. Mathias, Jr., R-Md. (House 1961-1969; Senate 1969-1987), Appropriations chairman Mark O. Hatfield, R-Ore. (1967-), and Minority Leader Robert C. Byrd, D-W.Va. (House 1953-1959; Senate 1959-). Three separate efforts to break the filibuster failed, and the measure died.

There have been no further attempts to grant item-veto authority to the president. In 1987, in an effort to prevent enactment of omnibus continuing resolutions, Evans offered a similar amendment in the Senate to a bill raising the ceiling on allowable federal debt. The amendment would have for two years broken continuing resolutions into separate bills before they were sent to the president. The amendment was rejected 41-48.

When Negotiations Break Down

One consequence of all this political posturing is that since 1981 Congress and the White House have had inordinate difficulty getting together in a bipartisan way to work on the budget. Indeed, the 1987 budget summit was the only real negotiated success in seven years of the Reagan presidency.

Reagan saw budget request after budget request dismissed out of hand or go down in embarrassing defeat with only a smattering of GOP votes. Democrats merely scoffed at the idea that the president's proposals were serious or that he had the slightest intention to talk turkey.

But it was Senate Republicans who suffered the greatest frustration from failed efforts to devise a compromise budget that was acceptable to the White House and Congress. And, as the 1987 summit was getting under way, Dole and Domenici, in particular, painfully recalled budget agreements with Reagan that evaporated when put under a hot political spotlight. Following Reagan's 1981 budgetary blitzkrieg, there seemed to be little chance for a meeting of the minds.

In 1982, for example, talks to reduce the already mushrooming deficit collapsed under the weight of the two issues that would prevent compromise throughout the Reagan years: Social Security and taxes. Reagan refused to allow a breach in the huge individual income-tax cut of the previous year and House Speaker Thomas P. "Tip" O'Neill, Jr., D-Mass., refused to discuss limits on Social Security. In the end, Reagan accepted a three-year, $98 billion tax increase—based largely on closing loopholes and increasing excise taxes—coupled with spending cuts of $30.8 billion over three years.

Reagan was reluctant, to say the least. And afterwards he complained bitterly that he was promised three dollars in cuts for every dollar in new taxes, a promise that—made or not—was not fulfilled.

In 1983, Congress promptly rejected the president's budget request, and there was ultimately no agreement on how to implement a congressional budget that had no White House support. Then, in 1984, Reagan swallowed another deal with congressional leaders that included new taxes, some domestic spending cuts, and a rollback of his favored defense increase. Together the package promised $150 billion in savings over three years. Still, however, deficits grew, as did pressure on Congress and Reagan to work together.

The real turning point was 1985. Dole and Domenici tried repeatedly to craft a deficit-reduction compromise that would pass muster. But conflicting White House signals and Democratic opposition scuttled proposal after proposal. Finally, the Senate adopted a budget resolution by one vote—a tie-breaker by Vice President George Bush—that would have frozen Social Security cost-of-living increases, capped military spending growth at the rate of inflation, and terminated thirteen, mostly small, programs.

Only a few days later, however, Reagan and O'Neill together killed that deal, taking taxes and Social Security off the table. Congress ultimately adopted a different budget resolution that did allow for new revenues, but no Social Security savings. Administration opposition helped prevent passage of the necessary reconciliation bill to put the budget into effect, however. As a result of the year's frustrations, the Gramm-Rudman antideficit law was enacted.

The final straw was 1986, when Reagan refused to talk at all. House Democrats would not consider new taxes in that election year despite a bipartisan willingness in the Senate to raise revenues to reduce the deficit. And Congress on its own crafted an $11.7 billion deficit-reduction bill that barely met Gramm-Rudman requirements

and allowed all sides to declare victory and go home. Said Domenici: "We just can't do any more than the United States Congress lets us do and the president will support. That's it."

In the end, the few successes at enacting measures to reduce the deficit during those years had to be weighed against the overall failure to address the subject in a more forthright and aggressive manner. Until the 1987 budget summit, what high-level discussions had occurred were mostly like the one in 1985 that killed the Senate-passed budget. On that occasion, Reagan and O'Neill chatted under an oak tree on the White House grounds during a social reception; it was not a real negotiation where substantive ideas were addressed. In fact, such agreements mostly clarified what was not acceptable to both sides, rather than proposals that were. As a direct result, the deficit increased from less than $78.9 billion in 1981 to the record $221.2 billion in 1986.

7

Budgeting under Gramm-Rudman

The law that was supposed to balance the federal budget by 1991 saw much, but not all, of its promise go unfulfilled in its first three years.

That law, the Balanced Budget and Emergency Deficit Control Act of 1985—better known as the Gramm-Rudman-Hollings antideficit act—required a steady decline in the multibillion-dollar gap between the government's tax collections (plus other revenues) and its expenses. Gramm-Rudman was intended to force spending reductions and revenue increases. If Congress and the president could not agree, however, they faced the practical and political consequences of harsh, automatic, across-the-board cuts (except, of course, that most social welfare programs were exempted wholly or partially from the cuts). The law's methods were conceded to be extreme, but so was the problem. Gramm-Rudman's results were, from the beginning, mixed.

For example, on March 1, 1986, the first automatic cuts took effect, as had been expected. Those cuts were limited by the law to $11.7 billion. And they had effectively been mandated by the law, since the deficit target for the year, which had been enacted only months earlier, was intentionally set at a figure far below the anticipated amount of red ink. But the Supreme Court four months later eviscerated Gramm-Rud-man, striking down its method for computing automatic cuts as unconstitutional and taking away the law's bite for fiscal 1987.

Fiscal 1986 ended with a record deficit of $221.2 billion, well above the target of $171.9 billion, but, except for the relatively small automatic cuts required early in the year, there was little that Gramm-Rudman could have done about fiscal 1986 spending. Furthermore, although Congress expressed its intent to reduce the deficit by enacting Gramm-Rudman, it failed to enact a required, deficit-reducing reconciliation bill for fiscal 1986 until the year was half over and most of its savings had been lost. That was clear evidence of just how weak were the political sentiments behind Gramm-Rudman.

However, decisions made in 1986 for fiscal 1987 were a more crucial test for Congress, and that year's deficit came in at $150.4 billion, a dramatic improvement. In its first real test, Gramm-Rudman managed to keep a relatively tight rein on spending. Its deficit target and new procedures for floor action, particularly in the Senate, enabled deficit-minded members to resist legislative proposals that were considered too costly.

Moreover, the threat of Gramm-Rudman (if not the fact, since the mechanism for automatic cuts had been thrown out) helped keep on track the year's most significant legislative achievement—overhaul of the tax code. No tax bill amendment granting a new tax break, either in committee or on the floor, was in order unless it was "revenue-neutral," that is, unless it would have paid for itself with offsetting revenues, thereby not adding to the deficit. Had it not been for the political discipline forced by Gramm-Rudman, the tax bill might have been sunk by special-interest favors and the fiscal 1987 deficit might have been much larger.

Ironically, part of the fiscal 1987 success at trimming the deficit can be attributed to $21.5 billion in extra, one-time revenue collections generated the first year by the 1986 tax bill. That law was not supposed to increase taxes, but the phasing in of some of its provisions caused revenue fluctuations that reduced the deficit in 1987 and increased it for several years afterward. (Indeed, some analysts believed that the law would fail in its claim of being revenue-neutral and would cost money over the long term.)

In 1987, Congress reaffirmed its original support for Gramm-Rudman's battle ax by restoring, in a constitutionally acceptable way, the procedure for triggering automatic cuts when deficit targets are breached. But in the process, Congress relaxed the targets, mainly to take off some of the heat for further deficit reduction in the election year of 1988. And the law's principal objective—that is, a balanced budget—was put off for two more years until 1993.

At the same time, Congress made no progress through the spring and summer of 1987 toward reducing the anticipated fiscal 1988 deficit or meeting the deficit target, which, at $144 billion, was identical to that for the previous year. Eventually, automatic cuts were triggered in the fall. But almost simultaneously the October 19 stock-market crash grabbed the attention of Congress and the president. Policy makers at both ends of

Washington's Pennsylvania Avenue feared that their fiscal foibles were contributing to the financial markets' unease. So, after failing to find much common ground for budget negotiations in prior years, together they crafted a two-year budget agreement that significantly reduced the anticipated deficits for fiscal 1988 and fiscal 1989. And the previously triggered automatic cuts were repealed.

But after that momentous achievement, Congress and the president coasted. As a part of the budget summit agreement, Congress had put into law appropriations caps for fiscal 1989 for defense, foreign aid, and discretionary domestic programs. Those caps could have easily been voided during budget deliberations in 1988, had Congress chosen to do so and had the president gone along. But the political consequences of breaching the caps were deemed to be too high, and there was never serious talk of it.

Indeed, the caps had the salutary effect of eliminating some of the more difficult annual budget decisions. At the top of the list of moot questions for fiscal 1989 was: How much should Congress take out of the president's defense spending request to add to domestic programs? That question in every other Reagan-era year had been central to budget fights and setbacks. It was not so in 1988, since an agreement on the level of defense spending was already in place.

But the fact that most of the tough decisions had been made the year before did not help Congress to meet its deadline for adopting a budget resolution in 1988; there were plenty of lesser issues to quarrel about, mainly how to split up the already limited domestic spending pie between space exploration and programs for low-income individuals. But the spending caps did help Congress to complete action on all thirteen regular appropriations bills before the October 1 start of the fiscal year. It was the first time since 1976 (the first year the current budget process was in full effect) that Congress had made that deadline.

The budget summit agreement had one other effect: For the first time since 1980 Congress made no effort to take specific action to reduce the deficit. There was no reconciliation bill required by the budget resolution and there was no special concern given to appropriations bills to reduce spending, other than to hew to the line drawn by the summit agreement.

With the approaching October 15 deadline for calculating whether automatic Gramm-Rudman cuts would be triggered, some in Congress were concerned that the anticipated deficit for fiscal 1989 would exceed the law's magic number—that is, $136 billion plus a $10 billion margin for error. Triggering billions of dollars in cuts just weeks before the November 1988 elections was a prospect that neither Democrats nor Republicans savored. But the economy cooperated, staying strong; Congress did not get carried away in its last days with new spending ideas; and the projected deficit came in under the target by about $500 million. It was a slim margin, but it was enough to allow Congress to make still another last-minute appropriation—after the Gramm-Rudman deadline passed—to pay for an anti-drug-abuse bill.

Seizing a Political Opportunity

Back in mid-1985, with the fiscal 1986 deficit clearly headed for a record, it was no wonder that Congress went looking for new ways to constrain itself. Ordinary political pressure was not working, so some external control over the budget was needed.

The difficulty was in deciding what to do. The idea of giving the president authority to veto individual items in appropriations bills appeared to most members of Congress

to cede too much authority to the executive branch. That idea never did catch on. Adoption of a proposed constitutional amendment to require a balanced budget was stymied by the need for a two-thirds majority in each chamber of Congress, not to mention approval of three-fourths of the states. Those political hurdles were clearly too high. Absent any better ideas, Gramm-Rudman's mechanistic approach to reducing the deficit seemed not so radical, illogical, or otherwise flawed that members of Congress could easily dismiss it.

Budget attack-dog Phil Gramm of Texas, who in 1981 as a House Democrat had maneuvered Congress into making deep cuts in spending, was by 1985 a Republican senator. Gramm had long liked the idea of a mandatory deficit target and its companion enforcement tool of automatic spending cuts. Gramm saw an opportunity to change the budget process when Congress was confronted with the need to vote an increase in the government's borrowing limit—a measure that was directly tied to the deficit problem. He was joined in the process by a pair of equally strident budget-cutters: Warren B. Rudman, R-N.H. (1980-), and Ernest F. Hollings, D-S.C. (1966-), forming the now-famous budget triumvirate.

Gramm, Rudman, and Hollings were not the only members of the Senate to seize upon the debt-limit bill as an appropriate vehicle for change. The target was too tempting, since it was designed to allow the government to borrow more than $2 trillion; the bill was an official acknowledgment that the federal debt had already doubled during President Reagan's administration. But the Gramm-Rudman-Hollings proposal won the support of Majority Leader Robert Dole, R-Kan., and that was crucial.

Debt Limit as a Procedural Tool

One of Gramm-Rudman's more enduring legacies is the attention it focused on essential measures to raise the allowed limit on the federal debt. This happened not only in 1985 when Gramm-Rudman was enacted, but also in 1986 and 1987 when Congress worked to repair the mechanism for automatic cuts. The debt is the sum of accumulated deficits, and it grows bigger year after year as the government continues to spend more than it takes in. Because federal borrowing cannot exceed a statutory ceiling, bills to raise the ceiling were seen as among the most urgent in Congress.

If the ceiling is not raised periodically, so that new Treasury bills, bonds, and notes can be issued, the government must either shut down—forcing it into the awkward position of failing to make good on contract payments and other legally required disbursements—or it must default on its interest and principal payments—a nightmarish possibility for the world's financial system.

As a result, debt-limit bills often become political lightning rods. The party out of power in the White House routinely objects to increases in the debt limit, and, of course, there was no shortage of political irony in Reagan's requesting a debt-limit increase all the while he was blaming Congress for creating the deficit problem.

Such bills, because they must be enacted, also serve as magnets for controversial amendments. So it was natural for the debt-limit measure in 1985 to become host to the amendment known as Gramm-Rudman. The consequence, however, was protracted negotiations over a proposal that even supporters such as Dole and Senate Budget Committee chairman Pete V. Domenici, R-N.M., believed had serious flaws. And those negotiations delayed enactment of the debt-limit increase long enough to provoke a near crisis.

The Treasury Department had warned Congress that it would need an increase in borrowing authority by early October. The House in August had sent the Senate a simple bill raising the debt ceiling. Then, on October 10, the bill passed the Senate with Gramm-Rudman attached. But Gramm-Rudman and the permanent debt-limit increase underlying it did not become law until mid-December. While House and Senate leaders talked about changing Gramm-Rudman to make it more palatable to opponents, Treasury ran out of money. Even then, Senate supporters of Gramm-Rudman refused to allow passage of a short-term increase in the debt limit, fearing that to do so would ease pressure on Congress to act on the antideficit bill. That in turn forced Treasury to use a variety of tricks to keep the government from defaulting on its obligations, including making raids on the trust funds that finance Social Security, Medicare, and various government retirement programs.

The techniques employed by Treasury included substituting almost $15 billion in securities issued by the Federal Financing Bank for Treasury Department securities held by retirement trust funds. The financing bank is essentially a Treasury Department entity created to funnel borrowing by agencies such as the Rural Electrification Administration to the public. But its borrowing was not subject to the overall debt ceiling. That gave Treasury some breathing room in October. But with November approaching, and large payments due in the form of Social Security benefit checks and other commitments, Treasury secretary James A. Baker III wrote Congress that absent an increase in the debt ceiling, he would be forced to redeem Treasury securities held by the Social Security trust funds.

The practical effect of this so-called disinvestment would be to deny the trust funds earnings on the securities—earnings that easily could be restored later. But the political impact was enormous: It sounded like another assault on elderly pensioners by the government. When it became known that Treasury had disinvested the trust funds previously to cover cash shortfalls—

in September and October, and in October 1984—the negative reaction was swift. Congress did not act in time to prevent the November disinvestment, but a temporary debt-limit increase was enacted November 14 to prevent a recurrence. And the final version of Gramm-Rudman required that the trust funds be reinvested and that all lost earnings, including those from 1984, be restored. An effort to deny Treasury authority to disinvest in the future died quietly, however, perhaps because Congress recognized the utility of the maneuver in times of emergency.

Following the Supreme Court's rejection of Gramm-Rudman's procedure for automatic cuts, the Senate in 1986 tried unsuccessfully to use another debt-limit bill to restore the law. But opposition to the Gramm-Rudman "fix" tied the debt-limit increase in knots. The measure was never passed, and a provision to increase temporarily the debt ceiling until May 1987 was added to a pending deficit-reducing reconciliation bill at the last minute. A similar fix amendment was added by the Senate to a short-term debt-limit bill that became necessary when the larger increase bogged down. That amendment, too, was unacceptable to House Democrats; they stripped it off and the Senate acquiesced. Gramm, however, promised to pursue his fix when the debt-limit would again have to be raised.

In 1987, Congress did restore the process for ordering automatic cuts—again using a debt-limit bill, and again threatening the government's ability to stay in business in the process. As the debt-limit increase enacted the year before was about to expire in May, not only Gramm but also Rep. Buddy MacKay, D-Fla. (1983-1989), threatened to hold a new debt-limit bill hostage. Gramm's concern was his fix; MacKay wanted to force appointment of a bipartisan commission to study the deficit problem. (His was an idea that finally blossomed

after the stock-market crash five months later.)

Gramm and MacKay backed off their threats long enough to allow enactment of a two-month debt-limit increase, to last until mid-July. That was supposed to allow time for negotiation of an agreement on the Gramm-Rudman fix. But two additional short-term increases in the debt ceiling— one lasting until early August and another until late September—were ultimately required before a long-term increase could win passage.

Finally, on September 23, Congress signed off on an increase in the debt ceiling that was expected to last through May 1989, and that carried with it provisions restoring Gramm-Rudman's automatic cuts and stretching out until 1993 the law's mandate of a balanced budget. The increase allowed the government to borrow up to $2.8 trillion, exactly three times the $935 billion debt ceiling in effect when Reagan took the oath of office. And the increase also allowed Congress to avoid any more debt-limit battles, and related struggles over the budget process, until after the 1988 elections.

Gramm-Rudman: The Only Idea Around

Second only to Ronald Reagan, Phil Gramm was perhaps the most important person to federal budget politics and process in the 1980s. Gramm's significant role began with two rounds of congressional maneuvering over President Reagan's proposed spending cuts in 1981, and he enjoyed a reprise with the enactment of Gramm-Rudman in 1985 and the Gramm-Rudman fix in 1987. It is the rare person whose name is attached to some act of Congress, and Phil Gramm had four such credits after only nine years on Capitol Hill.

Gramm did not ever act alone, of course. He collaborated behind the scenes on the 1981 spending cuts with Reagan budget director David A. Stockman, a former House colleague. And he shared the public billing in 1981 with Delbert L. Latta, R-Ohio, and in 1985 and 1987 with Rudman and Hollings.

One measure of Gramm's effectiveness—and his fellow Democrats' unhappiness with him in 1981—was that in early January 1983 they stripped him of his Budget Committee membership. In retaliation, Gramm resigned his House seat, switched parties, was immediately reelected, and rejoined the committee as a Republican. In 1984 he was elected to the Senate, where he lost a bid for a Budget Committee seat to a more senior member who did not seek it. That, however, did not deter Gramm, who again seized the opportunity in 1985.

Gramm's two Senate colleagues—Rudman and Hollings—deserved a share of the credit for the 1985 antideficit law not only because they were early cosponsors, but also because, like Gramm, they had taken a special interest in the deficit in the 1980s. Hollings had pressed year after year for a flat freeze in spending, an idea that finally caught on enough in 1984 to win thirty-eight votes on the floor. And, while campaigning for president that same year, Hollings did not hide his view that every interest group—including Social Security recipients and the military—would have to sacrifice if the deficit were to be controlled. It was not a popular message, but it was more honest than that carried by many of his fellow contenders. As for Rudman, he was so disgusted with Congress's inability to control the deficit that in early 1985 he threatened not to seek reelection to a second term in 1986 unless there was some progress. Gramm-Rudman was that progress and Rudman stayed in the Senate, although it was Gramm's name that became synonymous with the budget and with deficit reduction.

Gramm-Rudman had a very short, and somewhat unorthodox, trip through Congress. Conceived by Gramm in his first years in the House (and in fact introduced as a bill in 1981 by Gramm and then-majority leader Jim Wright, D-Texas), the idea of automatic budget cuts was not really pressed until the waning days of September 1985, as work in the Senate on the debt-limit increase began.

The idea behind the law was seemingly simple: Congress would have to meet specific deficit targets each year until the budget was in balance, or federal spending would be cut by a uniform percentage across the board to achieve the required deficit reduction. In fact, the idea proved to be deceptively complicated, enough so that many Democrats, who knew they could not stop it from being enacted into law, worked overtime to make significant changes in Gramm's original proposal.

As first envisioned by Gramm, the measure would have vested virtually all authority for making automatic cuts in the Office of Management and Budget (OMB). Few specific exemptions from the cuts were allowed, but the cuts would have been limited to accounts specifically identified by OMB as "relatively controllable," a tiny share of the budget. Spending that was deemed by OMB to be "relatively uncontrollable" was exempt from the automatic cuts. Those designations, while intuitive at one level, turned out to hide significant aberrations. Fights developed on the Senate floor almost immediately after Majority Leader Dole offered Gramm's bill as an amendment to the debt-limit measure. Daniel Patrick Moynihan, D-N.Y., for instance, objected that price- and income-support payments to farmers, one of the fastest growing elements of the budget, as well as military construction contracts, would be out of reach as relatively uncontrollable expenditures.

Some Democrats mounted a filibuster of the measure to gain more time to understand it. To counter them, Dole kept the Senate in for a rare Saturday session, October 4, and an even rarer Sunday session the next day. Gramm negotiated some changes with Senate colleagues to pick up votes, including a provision to delay the automatic cuts in the event of a recession. And other changes were fought out on the floor. One of the most significant was an amendment offered by Carl Levin, D-Mich. (1979-   ), that significantly altered the method of calculating the automatic cuts. Levin's change required that cuts be apportioned uniformly among "programs, projects and activities" identified in appropriations bills, not the much broader spending categories used by OMB. The fear was that OMB could have adjusted the cuts within its broad spending categories to favor some activities over others, thereby thwarting congressional intent in appropriating money in the first place.

On October 9 the Senate voted 75-24 to add the Gramm-Rudman amendment to the debt-limit bill; the amended bill was then passed 51-37. But the negotiations had barely begun. House Democratic leaders, fearful that the House might jump on the Gramm-Rudman bandwagon before there was an opportunity to further refine the measure, pushed for a conference with the Senate. Over two weeks, fifty-seven House and Senate conferees met and talked about the intent of Gramm-Rudman and how it would work. Then, on October 31, after House leaders had developed and proposed an alternative that was sharply different from the Senate measure, the conference deadlocked over the differences.

The next day, the House voted 249-180 for the House Democratic alternative, setting the stage for a second conference. The House version differed in many respects, most importantly in the role it gave to the Congressional Budget Office (CBO) to help craft the automatic cuts; the steeper cuts it would have required in defense spending

(while limiting cuts in Medicare); and its insistence that there be cuts in fiscal 1986 (the Senate measure appeared to hold off cuts until after the 1986 elections).

A new conference of sixty-six members convened, but quickly a core group of twenty-nine began working on a compromise between the two proposals. Those talks lasted more than a month, and final details were not worked out until December 10. Both chambers passed the compromise the following day—the Senate by a 61-31 margin, the House by 271-154.

The overwhelming support for the final bill reflected the degree to which House negotiators—led by Majority Whip Thomas S. Foley, D-Wash. (1965-   ), and Leon E. Panetta, D-Calif.—had prevailed. For instance, a first round of cuts was specified for early 1986. Social Security was exempt from the cuts, as were many social programs that aided the poor, such as Medicaid, food stamps and nutrition programs, and welfare. Cuts in certain other programs—Medicare and Guaranteed Student Loans, for instance—were sharply limited. Half of all cuts were to come from defense spending and half from the remaining domestic accounts.

The bill also created a host of new rules for the existing budget process designed to make it more difficult for Congress to fudge its responsibilities. Presidential budget requests and congressional budget resolutions would have to comply with deficit targets; bills brought to the House or Senate floors could not breach deficit targets; and deadlines for congressional budget action were accelerated.

And a complex procedure was created in an ultimately vain effort to prevent a constitutional challenge to the automatic cuts. CBO and OMB would prepare a joint report estimating the deficit for the upcoming fiscal year and calculate the size of automatic cuts needed to reach that deficit target, if any. Where the two agencies disagreed, their results would be averaged and the differences split. Then the General Accounting Office (GAO) would review the CBO-OMB report, make changes where it disagreed, and issue a second report. It was to be the GAO report that the president would have to sign as an executive order instituting the automatic cuts. (For more detail, see Appendix A.)

Yet for all the work, few were really pleased with the end result. Sponsor Rudman called the measure "a bad idea whose time had come." And Reagan, who had embraced early versions of the measure, grew increasingly unhappy toward the end when it became clear that his cherished defense buildup might be jeopardized by the threatened automatic cuts. In fact, defense secretary Caspar W. Weinberger was one of the measure's most vocal critics. But Reagan signed the bill into law December 12, calling it "an important step toward putting our fiscal house in order." At the same time, he said he would not be railroaded into tax increases or defense cuts.

That caused many to believe that the law would never have the intended result of breaking the congressional-White House deadlock over budget priorities.

The First Years

If anything characterized congressional behavior after enacting Gramm-Rudman it was the degree to which members contrived to meet the letter of the law's requirements, but not the spirit. Federal spending programs were exempted from the reach of Gramm-Rudman's automatic cuts—sometimes for seemingly good policy reasons—just as the law as first enacted limited the way some spending was affected. Economic assumptions were selectively adopted to provide the most favorable conditions for annual budget debates. (It

must be noted, however, that "cooking the numbers," as it is called, was practiced long before Gramm-Rudman.)

But the biggest deception may have been in the way Congress—usually with the administration's assent—viewed the law's deficit targets. It was a critical element of Gramm-Rudman from the first that Congress could miss its annual target by $10 billion and not trigger cuts. The theoretical reason for allowing this cushion or "margin of error" was that deficit estimates were inherently error-prone: An honest attempt by Congress to meet the deficit target should not trigger cuts just because a later calculation shows that it missed.

Most observers—critics and fans of the law—conceded, however, that the effect of this cushion was merely to raise the annual target by $10 billion. In fact, Congress clearly acted year after year as though that were the case. This was true even though missing the deficit by one dollar more than $10 billion would have triggered cuts of more than $10 billion. Congress could miss the deficit target and not trigger the cuts, but if the cuts were triggered, they would have to bring the deficit down to the target. And that involved playing a serious game of chicken.

Fiscal 1986 Budget: A New Procedure

As noted, there was little that Gramm-Rudman could do about the fiscal 1986 budget. The budget resolution for the year was already in place when the antideficit law was enacted. And Gramm-Rudman adopted the budget's projected deficit of $171.9 billion as the target for the year. However, the time spent negotiating the details of Gramm-Rudman got in the way of other congressional budgeting activities. Only four of the thirteen regular appropriations bills were enacted before Gramm-Rudman. And Congress adjourned for the year without passing a reconciliation bill of historically large proportions that was required by the budget resolution.

Ironically, similar failures in prior years were in large part the motivation for enacting Gramm-Rudman in the first place. But for 1986 the consequence was that by the time Gramm-Rudman was law, experts anticipated that the real deficit would be much larger than the target.

The law's first direct effect was felt January 15, 1986, when CBO and OMB issued their required joint report calling for $11.7 billion in outlay cuts from fiscal 1986 appropriations. The date of the report, and even that precise number, had been specified in the law.

As part of the calculation, the two agencies jointly predicted that the fiscal 1986 deficit would come in at $220.5 billion (about $700 million shy of the actual number). If special rules had not limited the size of the 1986 automatic cuts to $11.7 billion, Gramm-Rudman would have required $48.6 billion in cuts to reduce the deficit to the target. That amount would have been enormous by any standard and would have thoroughly disrupted both military and nonmilitary functions of government. The 1986 cuts, which came in the middle of the fiscal year, were limited for that reason. But, also, many in Congress wanted the 1986 cuts to happen to prove that the process could be effective. Had the required cuts been larger, there would have been stiff pressure on Congress to repeal them. Such an early abdication could have been Gramm-Rudman's death knell.

The cuts were ratified by the GAO January 21. Although the GAO could have made major adjustments, the agency let stand the earlier report, after resolving a very minor dispute between CBO and OMB that had no real bearing on the cuts. Based on anticipated levels of defense and nondefense spending (outlays in each broad category, minus exempted programs, were to be reduced by $5.85 billion), the GAO report required a uniform 4.9 percent reduction in defense budget authority and a uniform 4.3 percent cut in nondefense budget authority to yield sufficient outlay cuts.

The cuts took effect temporarily February 1, when, as required by Gramm-Rudman, Reagan issued an order requiring them. They became permanent March 1, after Congress failed to enact an alternative method of cutting $11.7 billion from the deficit. There was an attempt February 5 to force House committees to report such alternative cuts. But an amendment to do so, which Republicans tried to attach to a resolution allocating money for House committee studies and investigations, failed on a mostly party-line vote of 146-255.

A special three-judge panel of the federal district court in Washington, D.C., dealt Gramm-Rudman a serious blow February 7. The court held that the GAO's role in ratifying the amount and scope of automatic, across-the-board cuts—which would have to be followed explicitly by the president in ordering the cuts—was unconstitutionally impermissible under the doctrine of separation of powers.

The Supreme Court agreed two weeks after the lower court ruling to hear the case April 23. And on July 7, the high court upheld the district court's ruling, using the same grounds.

The likelihood of a legal challenge was anticipated even before Gramm-Rudman was enacted. In response, a special procedure was written into the law to expedite a legal challenge. That procedure enabled the courts to rule promptly and not leave the question of the law's application unanswered for even a single cycle of the budget process.

The legal challenge to Gramm-Rudman was brought by Rep. Mike Synar, D-Okla. (1979-), the day Gramm-Rudman was signed into law. He was joined by eleven other members of Congress. A second lawsuit was filed by the National Treasury Employees Union, whose membership claimed injury through cuts forced by the antideficit measure. The Senate, Speaker of the House Thomas P. "Tip" O'Neill, Jr., D-Mass., and the GAO all joined in the legal action to defend the law.

The courts' decisions were based on a rather simple concept of constitutional law, that one branch of government should be able to act independent of the other two, except to the degree that the Constitution provided for direct "checks and balances." In this case, the courts found that the GAO, though it had some minimal executive functions, was essentially a legislative branch agency. As such, it could not bind the president, head of the executive branch. The crucial point for the court was the fact that Congress, not the president, had the authority to remove the comptroller general, head of the GAO, from office.

Interestingly, it was just the comptroller general's special place in the government that had prompted Congress to endow him with authority to make the ultimate decisions on the automatic cuts. Congress did not view the comptroller general as a legislative officer alone, because, for example, he had responsibility for reviewing disputes between the government and its contractors. In that sense, the GAO's role was more of a hybrid of several branches.

At the same time, it was clear to Gramm-Rudman's authors that authorizing CBO to tell the president how to act would have been an obvious separation of powers violation. And while OMB's authority was constitutionally clear, many members of Congress were unwilling to leave the task up to the president's own budget adviser. That was particularly true of Democrats, who believed that the president's budget agency could not be counted on to behave in a politically neutral way in crafting the automatic cuts. (This concern would dominate the debate over restoring the automatic cuts, yet in the end OMB was given the final say.)

So in drafting the final version of Gramm-Rudman in late 1985, Congress decided that the GAO was independent enough to withstand the constitutional test.

But the lower court dismissed the notion that Congress's ability to remove the comptroller general was merely a technicality that would have no bearing on his role in defining the automatic cuts. "The balance of separated powers established by the Constitution consists precisely of a series of technical provisions that are more important to liberty than superficially appears," according to the lower court. And, led by Chief Justice Warren E. Burger, in his last major opinion for the court, a majority of the high court agreed, although only five joined in the lower court's reasoning.

Two Supreme Court justices, Byron R. White and Harry A. Blackmun, dissented, arguing that the importance of Gramm-Rudman overshadowed a "distressingly formalistic view of separation of powers." White wrote that it was "eminently reasonable and proper for Congress to vest the budget-cutting authority in an officer who is to the greatest degree possible non-partisan and independent of the president and his political agenda, and who therefore may be relied upon not to allow his calculations to be colored by political considerations."

Neither the lower court nor the Supreme Court accepted one argument by Synar and the other plaintiffs. Beyond the separation of powers question, the plaintiffs argued that Congress had overstepped its constitutional bounds in delegating to an agency spending decisions that were supposed to be made by Congress. Instead, they said, spending decisions had to be enacted into law by the combined votes of a majority of both houses of Congress and the signature of the president, or a vote by two-thirds of both houses to override the president's veto.

Two justices, John Paul Stevens and Thurgood Marshall, agreed with that argument. But the lower court and a majority of the high court did not, paving way eventually for the procedure for automatic cuts to be restored.

In arguing that Congress could delegate its authority, the lower court opinion, written by Judge Antonin Scalia (who a year later was elevated to the Supreme Court) did take a jab at the apparent hypocrisy in Congress's decision to enact Gramm-Rudman.

Scalia wrote that a constitutional proscription against excessive delegation of legislative branch authority "is not a credible deterrent against the human propensity to leave the difficult questions to somebody else. The instances are probably innumerable, however, in which Congress has chosen to decide a difficult issue itself because of its reluctance to leave the decision . . . to an officer within the control of the executive branch."

The court decisions striking down the procedure for making automatic cuts had a second, related effect. The first round of cuts already in effect were also held to be invalid. Even then, however, there was never any doubt that Congress would vote to restore them. And on July 17 first the House by a 339-72 vote and then the Senate by voice vote confirmed the spending reductions ordered the previous spring.

The cuts were "history," in the view of Senate majority leader Dole, and had to be reenacted by Congress. "What's done is done," he said. A more prosaic reason was that the year's budget deliberations were by then months old, and nearing completion. The "baseline" from which the fiscal 1987 budget was calculated assumed the fiscal 1986 budget had been reduced by $11.7 billion. Had the cuts not been reinstated, the baseline, and the deficit for fiscal 1987, would have grown by $11.7 billion overnight. In other words, Congress would have

had to cut an extra $11.7 billion from fiscal 1987 spending on top of other cuts that it had to find for the year.

Fiscal 1987 Budget: Missing Deficit Targets

In their first full year of budgeting under Gramm-Rudman, Congress and the president did not even follow the letter of the law. On the same day in 1986 that a federal district court struck down Gramm-Rudman's procedure for automatic cuts, Reagan submitted a fiscal 1987 budget that, according to OMB, met the law's $144 billion deficit target. But CBO pronounced the deficit $16 billion over the limit, chiefly because of differences in the ways OMB and CBO calculated rates of defense spending.

That summer, Congress adopted a budget resolution that purported to meet the deficit target, and at $142.6 billion even provided some leeway for error. But with the budget based on a set of overly optimistic economic assumptions and a host of proposed but dubious savings from the sales of government assets, many in Congress knew the promise could not be fulfilled.

When the fiscal year began in October and the deadline passed for taking real steps to meet Gramm-Rudman's target, Congress had, in fact, done nothing to reduce the deficit. As had become routine, no appropriations bills had been passed, and a reconciliation bill required by the budget resolution was languishing.

And when CBO and OMB called on Congress to vote on across-the-board cuts—as specified by Gramm-Rudman in the event that automatic cuts were voided by the courts—Congress ducked.

"We've faltered and fallen all the way in just the first year of this march toward a balanced budget," House minority whip Trent Lott, R-Miss., lamented halfway through 1986.

Yet even with the procedure for automatic cuts gone from the law, and with it the club that was supposed to enforce frugality, Gramm-Rudman altered significantly the way Congress did its business of raising and spending the taxpayers' money in 1986.

During Senate floor debate on the tax overhaul bill, amendments were successfully opposed unless they were revenue-neutral; that is, they would have neither increased nor decreased revenues over five years. The tactic, an outgrowth of the Gramm-Rudman requirement that bills or amendments on the floor be "deficit-neutral," was successful even though for technical reasons the requirement probably did not apply to most tax bill amendments.

That was but one example of how congressional processes and attitudes adjusted in the wake of Gramm-Rudman.

More directly, a $1 billion spring drive to boost aid for economically depressed farmers was scotched by the new Gramm-Rudman politics. Senators used the law to raise an objection to floor consideration of the farm-aid measure; the objection was upheld on a 61-33 vote.

Even Jamie L. Whitten, D-Miss., the powerful chairman of the House Appropriations Committee who usually got his way, could not resurrect one of his favorite spending programs, general revenue sharing. It had been targeted for expiration, mainly because continuing the program would have cost $3.4 billion and many members of Congress simply did not want to cut other spending, or raise taxes, to pay for it. Unless they found offsetting cuts or taxes, however, Gramm-Rudman made it impossible to fit the money for revenue sharing back into the budget.

But, if Gramm-Rudman was seen as beneficial for focusing Congress's attention on the deficit throughout the year, it proved to be a big disappointment to those members who hoped it would serve to reduce the deficit by sizeable, predictable amounts each year. And the law was also was seen as contributing a greater than usual reason for delay to the overall budget and appropriations process. The deficit-reduction efforts in 1986 were a good case in point.

Congress waited in 1986 until the last minute to vote on appropriations for fiscal 1987. And when it finally acted, Congress rolled all thirteen regular appropriations bills into a single, unwieldy measure that was then the largest-ever single appropriations bill (which nevertheless managed to keep down the growth in spending). Congress also enacted an $11.7 billion deficit-reducing reconciliation bill, but it relied heavily on sales of government loans and other assets for its "savings," not permanent changes in spending programs that would result in savings in future years as well. The process delayed final action on the appropriations and reconciliation bills until after fiscal 1987 began, and the final deficit estimate after all budget work was finished was $151 billion, not $144 billion as specified in the law. But the figure was within the $10 billion margin of error that made $154 billion the year's de facto deficit target. (A major reason that the deficit target came in as low as it did was a one-year uptick in receipts expected from the tax bill. The revenue increase was forecast at $11 billion and eventually was calculated to have been $21.5 billion; the actual fiscal 1987 deficit was $150.4 billion.)

Also in 1986 Congress turned its back on the requirement for a vote on across-the-board cuts. When the courts deleted the automatic cut process, they left in place a "fall back" procedure, whereby CBO and OMB would still file a joint report anticipating the upcoming year's deficit, and the size of across-the-board cuts required to meet the deficit target. A special congressional committee was to meet to report those cuts to the floor of each chamber, where after only a short delay, votes could be forced on them. Gramm-Rudman contained the alternative procedure because many believed, when the law was being drafted, that the automatic cuts would be declared unconstitutional.

CBO and OMB first reported August 20 and then affirmed October 6 that the fiscal 1987 deficit would be $163.4 billion. The report specified across-the-board cuts of $19.4 billion to meet the target. But it also noted that pending appropriations and reconciliation bills would reduce the reported deficit to below $154 billion. That figure was within the $10 billion margin of error allowed by Gramm-Rudman, so Congress felt no pressure to vote on the across-the-board cuts identified in the CBO-OMB report.

Following the August CBO-OMB report, the special congressional committee did report a pair of resolutions (one in the House and another in the Senate) embodying 5.6 percent cuts in defense spending and 7.6 percent cuts in nondefense spending to reduce the $163.4 billion deficit projected by the two agencies to $144 billion.

The House never brought its resolution up for a vote; members argued that progress was being made on the deficit-reducing reconciliation bill. In the Senate, the resolution was defeated on a 15-80 vote, September 19. But Majority Leader Dole reserved a motion to reconsider, by which he hoped to keep up pressure to enact the deficit reduction bill.

The reconciliation measure finally became law October 21, after the required October CBO-OMB report renewed the original call for across-the-board cuts. No action was taken on this second report at all.

Gramm-Rudman Revived

After the disappointments of 1986, the first order of business for the next year was reviving Gramm-Rudman's procedure for automatic cuts. And some Democrats who had opposed the move the previous year embraced it in 1987 as a way to force President Reagan to the negotiating table. The budget process itself went into another typical stall in 1987. And efforts to agree on a method of restoring Gramm-Rudman's automatic cuts—which sponsors referred to as Gramm-Rudman II—were also stagnant for a time.

But eventually compromises were forged to reinstate the Gramm-Rudman automatic procedure, while pushing back the law's deficit targets. The bill that did so became law September 29, 1987, along with a promise that $23 billion in automatic cuts would be triggered unless Reagan and Congress produced an alternative. That prospect seemed dim.

But then there was the stock-market crash, which proponents of face-to-face negotiations between the president and congressional leaders on the deficit used to advantage. The long-sought budget summit was held, and an accord was reached on two-year spending ceilings for defense, foreign aid, and discretionary domestic programs (which is to say, everything except entitlements, which were most of domestic spending). Moreover, the president agreed to yet another tax increase, the fourth sizeable one since the 1981 tax cut.

The summit agreement produced a combined reduction of more than $75 billion from the anticipated deficits for fiscal 1988 and 1989. Calculations varied at the end of 1987, but the Senate Budget Committee projected that the fiscal 1988 deficit would be about $150 billion and the 1989 deficit would be a bit over $141 billion. Ultimately, the fiscal 1988 deficit turned out to be $155.1 billion, and when fiscal 1989 began, that year's deficit looked to be in the vicinity of $146 billion. If the projection for fiscal 1989 held, it would be the smallest deficit since 1982.

Fiscal 1988 Budget: More of the Same?

Were it not for two important events in the fall of 1987, the budget process could have withered away that year. In 1986 there was little enough progress toward reducing the deficit. And gridlock between the legislative and executive branches had perverted the appropriations process to the extent that only one appropriations bill, comprising the entirety of federal spending activities, was enacted in 1986—not thirteen as was the prescribed norm. Congress appeared to be on the same path again in 1987. But then came the renewal of automatic Gramm-Rudman cuts, and soon thereafter the market crash. With that, Congress and the president woke up.

But things had to get worse before they could get better.

Congress began the year facing a deficit target of $108 billion—a figure so unrealistic that members never seriously considered trying to reach it. The president, the House, and the Senate all produced budgets that on paper met the target. But all relied upon optimistic economic assumptions from OMB to do so. When the CBO reestimated all three budgets, the deficits were found to be more in the range of $135 billion.

The House adopted its version of the budget April 9, by a partisan vote of 230-192. Not a single Republican supported it, in no small part because it called for enactment of $18 billion in new taxes for fiscal 1988. The Senate adopted its version of the budget May 7, by a 56-42 vote. Three Republicans voted for the Senate budget, and it, too, called for about $18 billion in new taxes. But the two budgets differed significantly in the amount of new taxes they would raise in later years, and in levels of defense spending.

Congressional budget negotiators had trouble reaching a consensus on taxes and defense. It was not an uncommon problem, but the fact that the talks mostly involved Democrats—since the president and Capitol Hill Republicans for the most part were sitting out the process in 1987—made it seem strange that a compromise was so elusive. And meanwhile, all sides were gearing up for an expected July showdown on restoring the process for Gramm-Rudman cuts.

On June 23 and 24, the House and then the Senate adopted a compromise budget for fiscal 1988, with nearly all Democrats supporting it and nearly all Republicans opposed. The resolution called for $19.3 billion in new taxes in 1988 and allowed for defense spending to rise at the rate of inflation. The measure called for additional savings to reduce the anticipated deficit by a total of $30 billion. But Reagan began brandishing a "veto pencil" immediately, saying he would support no tax increase and that the level of defense spending was insufficient. It was clearly unlikely that appropriations and reconciliation bills translating the terms of the budget into law could be enacted.

Congress spent the rest of the summer talking and thinking about the deficit problem, but not doing much. During a month-long August recess, CBO and OMB released their required joint report on the anticipated deficit for the upcoming year, and the amount of across-the-board cuts that would be necessary to reach the deficit target, which was still $108 billion. The deficit projection was $153.4 billion, which would require cuts of $45.4 billion. But with Congress out of town, and negotiations more or less under way to restore the automatic cuts as well as to increase the deficit targets, the report fell on deaf ears.

Automatic Cuts Restored

Since failing in 1986 in their effort to resurrect the antideficit law's chief enforcement tool—the automatic cuts—Gramm and Rudman had been plotting how to move

Congress when the government reached its borrowing ceiling in May 1987. The 1986 effort failed because there was little support for the idea among Democrats, and because many in Congress were wary of ceding to OMB sole authority to determine the size and scope of automatic cuts. Yet clearly that would have to be done for any restoration of the cuts to pass constitutional muster.

But as early as February 1987, House Budget Committee chairman William H. Gray III, D-Pa., was talking about reenacting the automatic cuts in return for Republicans allowing some slippage in the deficit targets. It was a compromise that could not be turned down by either side. The futility of trying to meet the deficit targets originally enacted in 1985 was obvious; if the targets were not changed, Congress would just ignore the law, leaving Republicans with no lever to force down spending. And the deadlock between congressional Democrats and the White House over taxes and defense was becoming so ingrained that nothing short of a threat that defense spending would be cut deeply, indiscriminately, and automatically was expected to bring Reagan to the budget negotiating table.

Gramm and his allies allowed a short-term debt-ceiling increase to be enacted in May, pushing the showdown into July. He and former Budget chairman Domenici offered one proposal for restoring the cuts as an amendment to a long-term debt-limit increase; new Budget chairman Lawton Chiles, D-Fla., had another. A major difference between the two plans was the degree of authority that Chiles wanted to give the CBO—in an effort to dilute OMB's clout. But the Senate rejected Chiles's plan 25-71 on July 23. Despite his use of procedural tactics to delay the Senate's acceptance of the Gramm-Domenici proposal, it was adopted 71-21 on July 31.

But the House had never acted on the Gramm-Rudman fix amendment, and the

Treasury was running out of borrowing authority. Congress had to adopt another short-term debt-limit increase July 30 that was to last until August 6, to give House and Senate negotiators time to work out a compromise. But it was clear that process would take more than a week, and on August 7 yet another short-term increase in borrowing authority was enacted to last through September 23.

Negotiations stopped while members of Congress left town for its annual August recess. But upon their return after Labor Day, the talks picked up, an agreement was reached, and Congress approved it overwhelmingly September 23.

The central element of the procedure triggering automatic cuts closely resembled the original idea proposed by Gramm in September 1985. The CBO would still have a role in projecting the size of the deficit and the size of cuts, if any, needed to meet the target. But its report would be purely advisory. GAO would no longer have a role in making deficit projections. OMB was given sole authority to make the calculations that would be turned into automatic cuts; though it would have to explain any differences with CBO's projections.

Democrats, particularly, had been opposed in 1985 to vesting that much authority in an agency controlled by the White House, a position that did not change in 1986. But given the views of the Supreme Court on separation of powers, there seemed to be no other solution. Instead, Congress wrote into Gramm-Rudman II some strict limits on the way OMB could calculate economic and technical assumptions that lead to deficit projections. That was done in an effort to eliminate political manipulation of the numbers. Moreover, Gramm-Rudman II would no longer allow Congress to sell government assets—loan portfolios, for instance—as a means to reduce the deficit. Such sales would not count in calculations of whether Congress had met the deficit target; instead "real," permanent changes in spending patterns and revenues were required. This crackdown was in part aimed at the Reagan administration, which favored use of such gimmicks, but it would also make life more difficult for Democrats in Congress.

Democrats also won their desired changes in annual deficit targets. They were revised upward to $144 billion in fiscal 1988, $136 billion in fiscal 1989, $100 billion in fiscal 1990, $64 billion in fiscal 1991, $28 billion in fiscal 1992, and zero, or a balanced budget, in fiscal 1993.

The changes reflected the understanding that there was no way Congress could adhere to the previous, steeper path toward eliminating deficit spending. That goal was put back two years, from 1991 to 1993, but the net change in the deficit required year to year was little changed. Over the term of Gramm-Rudman II, the deficit still would have to be reduced by about $36 billion a year; and Congress would still be entitled to miss the target by up to $10 billion a year, except for fiscal 1993, before automatic cuts would be triggered.

For fiscal 1988, however, there were a few twists. For example, the target was increased from $108 billion—widely acknowledged to be impossible to achieve—to $144 billion. Sponsors of Gramm-Rudman II did not go around admitting it, but that change made the deficit target for fiscal 1988 identical to that for fiscal 1987. But actually the fiscal 1988 deficit target was relevant only for political reasons. The new law did not take the target or the anticipated deficit into account when calculating whether automatic cuts would be needed. Instead, the new law required $23 billion in automatic cuts unless Congress voted to reduce the deficit by that amount before November 20. (A separate provision limited automatic cuts for fiscal 1989 to $36 billion less any amount by which Congress voted to reduce the deficit before October 20.)

Market Crashes

There are probably more reasons for why the bottom dropped out of the stock market in October 1987 than can be counted: greatly overvalued stocks, an unstable dollar made worse by severe trade deficits, and expectations of inflation and rising interest rates, among others. But the budget deficit was clearly one of the reasons, because of renewed concerns that it was increasing, because negotiations to reduce it were leading nowhere, and because the White House seemed determined to force a confrontation with Congress.

That brewing confrontation was even troubling some on Capitol Hill. Domenici, for example, a long-time supporter of Gramm-Rudman and an early sponsor of proposals to restore the automatic cuts, became an opponent of that effort toward the end, just before Gramm-Rudman II was enacted. Disillusioned at the unlikely prospect of Reagan agreeing to new taxes to reduce the deficit, he feared that the automatic cuts would be triggered and believed that would be a disaster. The whole purpose of Gramm-Rudman was to force a compromise, but the compromise looked less palatable to Reagan than the nasty alternative, Domenici believed.

Reagan himself did little to disabuse anyone of that notion. During the White House ceremony where he signed Gramm-Rudman II into law, he said "nuts" to taxes and defense cuts as a means to deficit reduction.

And there were also those in Congress who viewed the idea of automatic cuts as less troubling than trying to enact a tax increase over Reagan's objections. The terms of Gramm-Rudman II had limited the automatic cuts in 1987 for fiscal 1988 to $11.5 billion for defense and $11.5 billion for nondefense programs. That was twice as large as the automatic cuts that took effect in March 1986. But for some liberal advocates of defense cuts—whose favored social programs were mostly protected from the cuts—that did not seem such a bad deal, even if it looked like an abdication of responsible budgeting to those outside Washington.

In any event, on Monday, October 19, the world's financial markets convulsed. The Dow Jones Industrial Average fell 508 points or 22.6 percent. It was the largest one-day fall in either absolute or percentage terms, almost twice as large in percentage terms as the 12.8 percent drop on Black Tuesday, October 28, 1929, which signaled the start of the Great Depression.

The market had in fact been slipping for weeks and had dropped suddenly the week before. And although it recovered somewhat from Monday's collapse during the balance of the week, the market remained very unstable.

Reagan's first response was that "everyone is a little puzzled" by the crash, and he referred to it as merely a "correction," financial market lingo for changes that bring stock prices more in line with perceived real values.

But especially in the parochial eyes of many members of Congress, the crash had a bigger meaning. It was widely known that $23 billion in automatic cuts would be triggered October 20, and there were no signs that Congress and the president would act to roll them back or offset them with more rational policy choices before they became permanent November 20. Some, like Bob Dole, who was by then Senate minority leader since the Democrats had taken control of the chamber after the 1986 elections, focused their attention on the White House. Dole was a battle-scarred veteran of congressional-White House budget battles. But like others on Capitol Hill, he viewed the crash as the best possible lever to make Reagan come to the table to compromise on reducing the deficit.

And the day after the crash Reagan agreed, reluctantly, to negotiate. Two days later, he told a televised press conference, his first in more than four months, "I'm putting everything on the table with the exception of Social Security, with no other preconditions." It was a vague, if significant, step back from his earlier refusals to talk about taxes.

The Economic Summit

Getting Reagan to agree to negotiate with Congress was hard enough. Actually cutting a deal and getting it enacted into law proved to be nearly impossible, reflecting how often this approach to deficit reduction had failed in the recent past.

Reagan himself was not a negotiator. But chief of staff Howard H. Baker, Jr., Treasury secretary James Baker, national security adviser Frank C. Carlucci, and budget director James C. Miller III were. Representing Congress were the Democratic chairmen and ranking Republicans on the Appropriations, Budget, and tax-writing committees, as well as senior Senate Appropriations member J. Bennett Johnston, D-La. (1972-), House Democratic whip Foley, and House Republican whip Lott.

It took almost two months of ongoing negotiations from the time formal talks began October 27 to seal the deal. But on December 22 Reagan signed into law two enormous bills—one, the largest continuing appropriations resolution ever; the other a deficit-reducing reconciliation bill. Together they promised to reduce the fiscal 1988 deficit by $33.3 billion and the fiscal 1989 deficit by $42.4 billion. At the end of fiscal 1988, the year's deficit was calculated at $155.1 billion, roughly what had been expected at the time of the summit agreement. (See Table 7-1.)

The two-year deal was a formidable achievement and went farther than most

Table 7-1   Deficit Reduction from Economic Summit Agreement (in billions)

	Summit agreement		Enacted [a]	
	1988	1989	1988	1989
Revenues	$11.0	$17.3	$11.4	$17.4
Taxes	9.0	14.0	9.1	14.1
Internal Revenue Service compliance (net)	1.6	2.9	1.6	2.9
User fees	0.4	0.4	0.7	0.4
Spending cuts	19.2	28.6	22.0	25.1
Appropriations	7.6	14.0	7.7	14.0
Defense	5.0	8.2	5.1	8.2
Nondefense discretionary	2.6	3.4	2.6	3.4
2 percent pay raise cap	0.0	2.4	0.0	2.4
Entitlements	4.0	6.0	4.1	6.0
Medicare	2.0	3.5	2.1	4.0
Farm price supports	0.9	1.6	1.0	1.5
Guaranteed student loan balances	0.3	0.0	0.3	0.0
Federal personnel savings	0.9	0.9	0.9	0.9
Medicaid [b]	—	—	−0.1	−0.2
Income security [b]	—	—	−0.1	−0.2
Additional savings	2.6	5.1	2.6	5.1
Debt service	1.2	3.5	1.2	3.5
Pension Benefit Guaranty Corporation premiums	0.4	0.4	0.4	0.4
Veterans Administration loan origination fee extension	0.2	0.2	0.2	0.2
Veterans Administration loan guarantee	0.8	1.0	0.8	1.0
Asset sales	5.0	3.5	7.7	0.0
Total	30.2	45.9	33.3	42.4

Source: Senate Budget Committee.

Note: Totals may not add due to rounding.

[a] Provisions making these savings were contained in the full-year continuing appropriations resolution for fiscal 1988 (PL 100-202) and the fiscal 1988 omnibus reconciliation bill (PL 100-203).
[b] Additional spending for Medicaid (the federal health program for the poor) and for other benefits for the poor and disabled was not contemplated in the budget summit agreement but was included in the reconciliation bill.

observers or participants expected that it would when the idea of a summit was first accepted. To begin with, a one-year deficit-reduction agreement was all that was envisioned at first. Moreover, most believed that the negotiators would have enough trouble agreeing on $23 billion in cuts for fiscal 1988. That was the amount of automatic cuts called for by Gramm-Rudman, and for weeks negotiators had hoped merely to enact savings equal to those cuts, so they

would be negated. But the automatic cuts were to become permanent by November 20, and the negotiators raised their sights, agreeing on the broad outlines of the agreement the same day. Those outlined savings were basically copied into law through the continuing appropriations resolution and the reconciliation bill. And, the automatic cuts were repealed.

The two-year package required compromises on all sides. Democrats accepted a smaller tax increase—$9 billion the first year and $14 billion the second—than they wanted. In fact, the tax increase was half the size of that anticipated in the by-then forgotten budget resolution for fiscal 1988 that had been adopted in June. It was even less than the $12 billion tax increase that was in a reconciliation bill the House passed by a one-vote margin October 29. That bill was forced onto the floor by House Democrats to put pressure on the summit negotiators, but there was plainly no way that its tax increase was going to become law. In fact, conservative House Republicans were so antagonistic toward a tax increase that many wondered why the White House negotiators agreed to it.

Both sides gave some on the question of defense. The agreement allowed for more than House Democrats wanted. But the administration accepted a spending level for fiscal 1988 that was $5 billion less than the amount spent in fiscal 1987, after making allowances for inflation. For fiscal 1989, defense was cut $8.2 billion below an inflation-adjusted increase.

The agreement made some limited cuts in entitlements, including Medicare payments to hospitals and price-support payments to farmers. But it also proposed more than $8 billion in savings from asset sales—the sort of one-shot "savings" that serious budget cutters decried and that Gramm-Rudman would no longer take into account.

Some Senate Republicans wanted to cut the deficit deeper than the summit agreement proposed. Led by Nancy Landon Kassebaum of Kansas (1978-   ), these Republicans proposed a flat spending freeze, coupled with a limit on growth in Social Security and some other entitlement benefits that were indexed to inflation plus the tax increases from the accord. Kassebaum's proposal would have saved $41.7 billion the first year, but it was killed in a Senate floor vote by a 71-25 margin.

The deal cutting went down to the wire. Final negotiations were finished in the evening of December 21, and that night and early the following morning large, bipartisan majorities of the House and Senate approved the bills.

Fiscal 1989 Budget: No Contest

The budget process in 1988 at last provided most of what congressional leaders wanted: deadlines were met (more or less) and budgeting did not get in the way of all other legislative business (as it had in the more recent past). On the other hand, Congress did virtually nothing about the deficit, other than to adhere as nearly as possible to the spending targets agreed to the year before during the budget summit.

And, although Congress and the president missed their Gramm-Rudman deficit target of $136 billion, OMB projections of the fiscal 1989 deficit put it within the $10 billion margin of error. (Not surprisingly, CBO disagreed. The congressional forecasting agency, which almost always projected higer deficits than OMB, said October 10 that the deficit would reach nearly $152 billion, requiring equal $7.9 billion cuts from defense and nondomestic programs. But CBO's estimates did not count.)

OMB director Miller said October 15 that the deficit would be under $146 billion by the relatively small amount of $545 million. That was sufficient to avoid automatic cuts. That was also effectively the end of Gramm-Rudman's demands on fiscal 1989, even though Congress had not yet quit work for the year. Before adjourning, Congress passed an omnibus anti-drug-abuse bill and another measure making technical and other minor changes in the 1986 law overhauling the tax code. It was likely that the net effect of those two bills and other last minute business would add up to a deficit even by OMB's calculations in excess of the target.

The law did provide sufficient political pressure to keep Congress from breaching its deficit target through enactment of additional spending bills. Spending in the drug bill was kept to a modest $500 million for fiscal 1989, even though its sponsors would have preferred three or four times that amount. However, after October 15 there was no longer a threat of automatic cuts if Congress did exceed the target.

By far the most significant achievement of the year was that Congress completed work on all thirteen individual appropriations bills before the new fiscal year began, if only barely. The last one was finished a minute before midnight September 30, however, so they were not all signed into law on time. But meeting that deadline was symbolically important and marked the first time since 1954 that Congress did not have to resort to a stopgap continuing appropriations resolution to keep the government running while it debated spending bills. After the public opprobrium Congress received for having lumped all appropriations actions into single bills in 1986 and 1987, the accomplishment of 1988 was all the more evident.

Reagan had threatened to veto another monster, omnibus continuing appropriations resolution like the ones he was sent in 1986 and 1987. But with an election on, Democrats in Congress wanted to show that they, too, could govern responsibly. Congressional leaders made an early promise in 1988 to enact all thirteen appropriations bills separately. And they kept that promise.

Because the year's budget actions were relatively painless, there was renewed pressure for permanent adoption of a two-year budgeting cycle. The idea had been proposed off and on for several years, and one of its leading champions was Sen. Wendell H. Ford, D-Ky. (1974-   ). Ford sponsored a bill to establish a two-year budget process, in which budget resolutions and most authorizing and appropriations decisions would be made once every two years, on a staggered cycle. Under the proposal, additional spending could be authorized or appropriated at any time, if it were necessary, so long as it conformed to the budget resolution in force and Gramm-Rudman deficit targets.

Ford drew the support of Comptroller General Charles Bowsher, Reagan's budget director James C. Miller III, Domenici, and others. But there were also concerns that it would prove to be unworkable in a changing world. The bill never came to the floor for a vote, but Ford indicated that he would use the experience of 1988 to press his case in the future. As he put it October 21: "It was an experiment in biennial budgeting, and if the results are any indication of what we can expect from moving to a two-year budget, the time has come to do so."

But if the 1987 budget summit—by making the decisions a year in advance—had given Congress the political impetus it needed to finish work on its appropriations bills more or less on time, it also provided political cover to do nothing more on the deficit than previously announced. The fact that Gramm-Rudman II assumed only an $8 billion improvement in the deficit from fiscal 1988 to 1989 did not hurt either. It made reaching the 1989 target a near cinch.

Unfortunately, it also left Congress facing a $100 billion deficit target in 1989 for fiscal 1990—$110 billion adding in the allowed margin of error. But the deficit was on anything but a downward path that would lead to that target. And the day of reckoning had been successfully put off for another year, to confront a new president and a new Congress.

Appendix A: The Budget Process

The process by which the federal government annually adjusts spending and tax policies was established by the Budget and Accounting Act of 1921, and the 1974 Congressional Budget and Impoundment Control Act (PL 93-344), which was amended by the Balanced Budget and Emergency Deficit Control Act of 1985 (Gramm-Rudman—PL 99-177) and repaired by the Balanced Budget and Emergency Deficit Control Reaffirmation Act of 1987 (Gramm-Rudman II—PL 100-119).

The process prescribes a detailed, yet evolving, choreography for Congress and the president to follow each year as they decide how much to spend and on what, who to tax and by how much, and how much to borrow to offset the difference.

There are five basic components of the budget process: the president's budget request, Congress's budget resolution, authorizations and appropriations, reconciliation (making existing laws match the budget resolution), and sequester (the end-of-the-line automatic cuts to meet the deficit target). Presumably, and according to a twice-revised calendar that was adopted as part of Gramm-Rudman I and II and House and Senate rules, the five steps will happen more or less in the order described. (See Table A-1.)

Calendar years and fiscal years do not overlap exactly, leading occasionally to confusion, when, for example, deficits for fiscal year 1990 are forecast in calendar year 1989. The fiscal year begins October 1—the real target date for all budget action on Capitol Hill. The fiscal year ends the following September 30 and is numbered by the calendar year in which it ends. For Congress's purposes, budget writing begins on January 1 before the start of the fiscal year. For administration officials who prepare the president's budget submission, planning begins months earlier than Congress's January start, even before the books are closed and audited on the previous budget cycle.

In no two years from 1975, when the process was first used, through 1987 did events develop quite in the same way; nor were most of the deadlines met. Partly in response to procedural failure and partly because the deficit continued to grow, Congress enacted Gramm-Rudman in 1985 to streamline the process and increase procedural controls. And, although deadlines were missed under the original law, Gramm-Rudman moved most of them ahead. Despite complaints, however, the process does get used in the main, and each of the five chief components has a role in the outcome.

Table A-1   Budget Deadlines under the Gramm-Rudman Antideficit Law, as Amended

Deadline	Action
First Monday after January 3	President's budget request for the fiscal year beginning October 1 is due to Congress.
February 15	Congressional Budget Office (CBO) reports to Congress on the nation's economic outlook, spending and revenue options, and the president's budget request.
February 25	Congressional committees report to the Budget committees their "views and estimates" of spending and revenues for programs under their jurisdiction for the coming fiscal year.
April 1	Senate Budget Committee reports its budget resolution to the Senate floor (no comparable deadline for the House Budget Committee).
April 15	Congress adopts its budget resolution, including "reconciliation instructions" to congressional committees on spending cuts and revenue increases needed to meet the deficit projected in the budget.
May 15	Annual appropriations bills may be considered on the House floor, even if there is no adopted budget resolution.
June 10	House Appropriations Committee reports the last annual appropriations bill to the floor.
June 15	Congress completes action on the reconciliation bill making changes in exisiting laws to accomplish spending cuts and revenue increases called for in the budget.
June 30	House completes action on last annual appropriations bill (no comparable deadline for the Senate or for conference action).
July 15	President submits his midsession review of the budget to Congress, along with a revised deficit estimate.
August 15	CBO and the Office of Management and Budget (OMB) take a "snapshot" of the economy and the budget deficit; the president also reports whether he intends to adjust future automatic cuts to protect military personnel or other accounts.
August 20	CBO issues its initial report on the projected deficit and the size of automatic spending cuts needed to bring the deficit in line with the Gramm-Rudman targets.
August 25	OMB issues its initial report on the deficit and the size of needed automatic cuts; the president issues order to freeze spending in line with the OMB report.
October 1	Fiscal year begins; the president's freeze order takes effect.
October 10	CBO issues final report on deficit and cuts, revised to account for congressional actions after August 15.
October 15	OMB issues final, revised report; the president issues final order making cuts permanent.
November 15	The General Accounting Office reports to Congress on compliance with the spending cut order.

What follows is a thumbnail sketch of the way, at the beginning of 1989, the law presumed that Congress and the president will act, and a description of the key rules and means of enforcing adherence to that process:

Budget Request

The president is to submit a budget proposal to Congress no later than the first Monday after January 3, the date established by the Constitution for Congress to convene yearly. There is no sanction against missing the deadline, however, and in some years, most recently 1988, the president submitted his budget request well after the stated date.

Somewhat later submission dates had been specified by the Budget and Accounting Act of 1921 and the 1974 budget act. Until enactment of Gramm-Rudman, the budget was due within fifteen days of Congress convening. But often Congress put back until late January its first meeting, which had the effect of delaying the budget submission.

The budget is to include estimates of new budget authority, revenues, outlays, the deficit (or surplus), and the total federal debt. Since Gramm-Rudman (and its 1987 revisions), the budget has been required to meet annual deficit targets: $171.9 billion for fiscal 1986; $144 billion for 1987; $144 billion for 1988; $136 billion for 1989; $100 billion for 1990; $64 billion for 1991; $28 billion for 1992; and zero for 1993.

The budget is to estimate the cost of tax expenditures—revenues that would be collected under existing tax laws, except for special deductions, credits, and exemptions in those laws. And it is to project costs of federal spending for five years.

The law directs that the budget figures be presented in terms of national needs, agency missions, and basic programs. And the budget must contain an estimate of the cost of "current services," which is what

government programs would cost in future years with no changes in policy.

Originally, the current services budget was due November 10, before the budget request in January, so Congress's Joint Economic Committee could review it and issue a report by January 1. That requirement was clearly unrealistic, due to the slowness of enacting appropriations upon which any current services budget must be based. And soon Congress and the administration agreed informally that the current services budget would be submitted with the January request. Gramm-Rudman formally eliminated the earlier date. And the Joint Economic Committee report was pushed back to March 1.

Other laws have further refined the president's budget submission. For example, since 1984, the president has had to include an estimate of proposed capital improvement expenditures and a comparison of spending for long-term investment with that for operating costs. And under Gramm-Rudman, the president's budget request is not supposed to project a deficit that exceeds the target for the year, although, again there is no penalty should it fail to do so, save political embarrassment for the administration.

Budget Resolution

After reviewing the president's budget proposals—and considering the advice of the Congressional Budget Office (CBO) and all interested committees—the House and Senate Budget committees draw up a concurrent resolution outlining Congress's own budget, which, once adopted, is to guide congressional action on entitlement and other backdoor spending authorizations, appropriations, and tax bills for the rest of the year. Where necessary, the budget resolution may dictate congressional action to bring spending and revenue measures or existing laws into line.

And the budget is required by Gramm-

Rudman to project a deficit within the target for the year.

Under the 1974 budget act, this concurrent resolution, which does not go to the president for approval and therefore does not have the force of law, was to be but the first of two or more adopted during the course of the year. In fact, the first resolution was not supposed to be binding. A later resolution was to set revised, binding limits on congressional action.

Since President Reagan took office, however, Congress has not managed to adopt a second resolution prior to start of the fiscal year. (There have been revisions adopted later, as part of the budget for the following year.) It became the practice that the first resolution would become binding if a second were not adopted by the start of the fiscal year. And Gramm-Rudman changed the procedure to eliminate the requirement for a second resolution and make the first binding—insofar as Congress ever allows itself to be bound by prior votes. The law spells out the circumstances under which the budget is to be binding, and how the House or Senate can vote to waive the rules.

CBO is to report to Congress no later than February 15 its analyses of the budget and economic outlook, the president's request, and options for spending cuts and revenue increases. Within the following ten days, congressional committees are supposed to forward their recommendations to the Budget committees.

By April 1, the Senate panel is to report its budget resolution to the floor. (There is no deadline for the House committee. It is often the case on budget matters that rules governing procedures in the two chambers are different; Senate rules tend to be more specific and require stricter adherence to budget limits.) By April 15—which originally had been the deadline for the committees to report—Congress is to finish action on the budget, to give authorizing

and Appropriations committees ample time to do their work.

The law specifies time limits for consideration of the budget resolution in each chamber and even in the House-Senate conference committee that melds differing versions for final action. These limits are especially important in the Senate, where ordinarily debate is unlimited.

Budget resolutions must be "mathematically consistent." And Congress also decided in Gramm-Rudman II that they must rely on a single set of economic assumptions, the numbers relating to economic growth, inflation, interest rates, unemployment, and the like that form the basis of budget projections. This decision followed closely the adoption of the fiscal 1988 budget, which used sleight-of-hand techniques—in particular, an amalgam of differing economic and technical assumptions—to produce a budget that seemed to meet the deficit target for the year.

The budget resolution breaks down spending into specific budget authority and outlay totals along broad functional lines, which correspond to the myriad spending accounts maintained by the Office of Management and Budget (OMB).

In 1988 there were twenty such functions—national defense; international affairs; general science, space, and technology; energy; natural resources and environment; agriculture; commerce and housing credit; transportation; community and regional development; education, training, employment, and social services; health; Medicare; income security; Social Security; veterans' benefits and services; administration of justice; general government; net interest; allowances; and undistributed offsetting receipts. With the expiration of general revenue sharing in 1987, a twenty-first budget function—general purpose fiscal assistance—was dropped.

The functions overlap departments and range in scope from single, but expensive, programs like Social Security to vast parts of the government. They also change from time to time; for example, Medicare was at one time included under the health function.

One adverse consequence of the functional breakdown, however, is that it is exceedingly difficult to compare budget resolution totals with departmental budgets or appropriations bills, because they are divided up differently.

As part of the resolution's binding nature, it is to specify in dollar terms how existing laws must be reconciled with spending and revenue totals in the budget. These reconciliation instructions are to be broken down by committee. They do not require any particular action to achieve the necessary savings; although often there are assumptions about such actions, the decisions are left up to the legislative committees.

The budget resolution also specifies how much the ceiling on the federal debt will need to be increased. (A debt-limit procedural change, called the Gephardt rule after Richard A. Gephardt, D-Mo., its author, was adopted by the House in 1979. As a result, final adoption of a budget resolution in the House is simultaneously deemed to be passage of a bill increasing the debt ceiling. No such procedure exists in the Senate.)

Authorizations and Appropriations

The budget act assumes that authorizations will be enacted well in advance of appropriations and originally set May 15 as the deadline for completion of work on all authorizations not creating new entitlements. Gramm-Rudman eliminated the authorization bill deadline, which was not effective anyway, and it strengthened budget act requirements that authorizations creating new spending or credit authority must be subject to the appropriations process.

Bills creating new entitlements, increasing or reducing revenues, or appropri-

ating new budget authority for the upcoming fiscal year are not supposed to be considered on the floor of either chamber until a budget resolution for that year is in place. An exception exists for appropriations bills in the House after May 15, to allow the Appropriations committees to get on with their work even if the budget has not been adopted.

Once adopted, the budget resolution's spending totals are divided by the Budget committees among the legislative committees, into so-called section 302(a) allocations. These are budget authority and outlay limits on new entitlement authority, new credit authority, and appropriations. In turn, the committees are to further divide their totals into so-called 302(b) allocations for their subcommittees. As a practical matter, since budgets in the 1980s have rarely provided much new entitlement or credit authority, these allocations have the most impact on the Appropriations committees. In effect, the 302(b) allocations for the thirteen Appropriations subcommittees become the spending limits for the thirteen regular appropriations bills.

In general, it is not in order for either the House or Senate to consider bills creating new entitlements or appropriating new budget authority that exceed the committee and subcommittee targets. The rules, however, are somewhat different in each chamber.

The law requires the House Appropriations Committee to have reported all the regular appropriations bills for the upcoming year to the floor by June 10, and for the House to complete action on all of them by June 30. There is no appropriations deadline in the Senate.

Previously, all appropriations bills were to have been finished by no later than the seventh day after Labor Day. And the House committee was strongly encouraged not to report any appropriations measure until all were ready to go to the floor, in an effort to ensure that spending limits would not be breached. Both requirements were dropped in Gramm-Rudman.

Reconciliation

Originally conceived in the budget act as a process for fine-tuning spending and revenues to conform to the budget, reconciliation has become the chief tool for deficit reduction. It was first used in 1980, for the fiscal 1981 budget. And a year later the Reagan administration's widespread domestic program cuts were enacted not piecemeal but instead through reconciliation, making it—along with huge continuing appropriations resolutions—one of the chief policy-making instruments of government.

Reconciliation has been employed to cut entitlement spending, alter discretionary programs, sell government assets, enact fees for users of government services, and increase taxes. The budget act even presumes that it could be used to reduce appropriations. But that has never occurred, because appropriations have never been enacted long enough in advance of reconciliation to make such changes necessary or possible. (In 1981, the budget resolution included reconciliation instructions to the Senate Appropriations Committee to make cuts in fiscal 1981 appropriations. Those cuts were included in a supplemental appropriations bill, however, and were not included in the reconciliation measure.)

By and large, the contents of reconciliation bills are dictated by the authorizing committees. Responding to the reconciliation instructions in the budget resolution, they draft legislative proposals that are forwarded to the Budget committees. Under specific procedures established under the budget act, these legislative proposals are usually rolled into one bill for floor action.

There is nothing in the law or in congressional rules that requires authorizing committees to follow the assumptions about program changes that guided the Budget committees' earlier work. And the Budget committees may not change the legislative proposals that were packaged together for floor action. The effect is that authorizing committees can, and do, propose different methods of achieving the required savings—asset sales instead of program cuts, for instance. And, in fact, there is no penalty for a committee's failure to meet its savings target. Moreover, authorizing committees have managed through reconciliation to make changes in some programs that increased, not reduced, spending. Medicaid, the federal health program for the poor, is one such program. In the House, however, the Rules Committee may allow floor amendments to be offered to make a committee's recommendations conform with its savings target.

Occasionally, for example when the House Ways and Means Committee has responsibility for savings in Medicare (the federal health program for the elderly) and a tax increase, committee proposals will go to the floor separately. If several reconciliation bills are reported to the floor in one session of Congress, they can be combined in a conference committee into one measure.

The budget act first set September 25 as the deadline for completing reconciliation action, since reconciliation originally was to be triggered by a second budget resolution adopted late in the budget cycle. But Gramm-Rudman pushed the deadline ahead to June 15, principally because the sequester process begins August 15. That procedure is designed to force automatic spending cuts if Congress has not acted to reduce the deficit sufficiently.

And just as it does for budget resolutions, the law sets limits on floor debate for reconciliation bills to expedite their consideration and prevent Senate filibusters.

Sequester

The key innovation of Gramm-Rudman was a process by which most discretionary government outlays (actually only about a fourth of all spending) would be cut—"sequestered"—by a uniform percentage to achieve annual deficit targets, unless Congress and the president succeeding in doing so through traditional legislative means.

As originally conceived in 1985, CBO and the White House Office of Management and Budget would each make projections of the anticipated deficit. Those numbers would be averaged and reviewed by the General Accounting Office (GAO), Congress's auditing arm. The GAO would then make a final decision on the size of automatic cuts needed to make the deficit agree with its target, and the president would issue the GAO report as an order making the cuts.

Opponents of the process convinced the Supreme Court in 1986 that the procedure violated the Constitution's "separation of powers" doctrine—the GAO cannot bind the president—and the procedure was thrown out.

As revived by Gramm-Rudman II, the GAO and, for practical purposes, CBO are eliminated from the process. Both still have advisory roles, however. On August 15, under the law, CBO and OMB take a "snapshot" of the economy and bills enacted from January 1 to date aimed at reducing the deficit.

CBO reports on the size of the anticipated deficit on August 20, and OMB follows suit August 25, explaining any differences with the CBO report. If the OMB report projects a deficit that exceeds the target by more than $10 billion, the president simultaneously issues a sequester order detailing necessary reductions in budget authority that will produce outlay cuts to achieve the deficit target for the coming year. That order will take effect October 1, temporarily freezing budget authority at levels specified in the order (except for a few select programs). CBO will follow up with a second report October 10, and OMB will do so October 15, taking account of bills enacted since August 15. If necessary, based on the OMB report, the president will issue a final, revised order October 15 permanently canceling budget authority to achieve the required deficit reduction.

One change made by Gramm-Rudman II was to disallow sales of government assets in calculating whether Congress and the president succeeded in meeting the annual deficit target. Although asset sales do produce revenue in the year of the sale, they also typically lose money. For instance, the sale of a portfolio of federal loans would cost the government the interest payments that it would have received from those loans. Prior to 1988, asset sales were a popular means of deficit reduction.

Exempted from the cuts are Social Security, most other entitlements, signed contracts, most government insurance programs, and a host of programs for low-income persons, including Medicaid, Aid to Families with Dependent Children, child and infant nutrition programs, and food stamps. Some programs that have built-in inflation increases may be cut only by the amount of that inflation increase.

The law specifies that half of the required outlay cuts must come from defense programs, and half from nondefense programs. Different percentage cuts can result for each, since the amounts of available new budget authority are likely to be different for the two segments of the budget, and the rates of converting that budget authority into outlays may also differ.

And, although the law requires outlays in each individual program within the broad categories of defense and nondefense spending to be reduced by the same amount, it allows the president to make limited adjustments in defense programs to exempt uniform personnel. The president may also propose adjustments in defense spending cuts to protect certain weapons programs, but Congress must approve those changes.

In any event, the changes must not alter the overall required spending reduction.

The law creates an expedited procedure for enacting an alternative scheme of deficit reduction to replace the sequester order. And it also creates an expedited procedure for enacting a law suspending automatic cuts in the event of a severe economic downturn, but not necessarily a recession.

Procedural Controls

The only sanction available in the budget act for failure to meet any of its requirements is a parliamentary device to prevent floor action on a bill or budget resolution that somehow does not conform and is "not in order."

Any member in either chamber can raise a point of order that the budget act is being violated, and the presiding officer can rule that the anticipated floor action cannot go on. In that case the members can vote to waive the rule or sustain the decision, and some waivers require more than a simple majority vote. The rules generally do not apply in time of war.

Following are the major points of order, most of which have been successfully raised, and most of which have been waived from time to time (except where noted a simple majority vote is all that is necessary to waive the rule):

● Exceeding Deficit Targets. No budget resolution may be considered in either chamber that would yield a deficit in excess of the target for the year. A three-fifths majority of those voting in the House and a three-fifths majority of the Senate membership would be required to waive the rule.

● Before a Budget Is Adopted. No bill or amendment may be considered in either chamber that would increase budget authority, increase or decrease revenues or the federal debt, or create a new entitlement, until a budget resolution for the year is in effect. The rule does not apply if the change would not take effect until two fiscal years after the ongoing year.

● After a Budget Is Adopted. No bill or amendment may be considered in either chamber that would increase budget authority or outlays above the budget resolution's totals, or decrease revenues below the budget's totals. A three-fifths majority of the Senate is required to waive the rule. In the House, the rule does not apply if the bill would not breach the 302(b) allocations of discretionary new budget authority or entitlement authority.

A separate point of order prohibits consideration of bills (chiefly appropriations measures) from exceeding 302(b) allocations. In the House the rule applies to discretionary new budget authority and new entitlement authority. In the Senate, it applies to all new budget authority, outlays, and new entitlement authority. And in the Senate a three-fifths vote is required to waive the rule.

● Economic Assumptions. In the Senate, no budget resolution may be based on more than one set of economic assumptions, and its totals must be "mathematically consistent."

● Reconciliation Amendments. It is not in order in either chamber to consider amendments that would increase total outlays above those originally provided for in the bill or reduce revenues, without including offsetting provisions that make the amendment "deficit-neutral." In addition, it is not in order to use a reconciliation bill to make any changes in the Social Security program. Waiver of these rules requires a three-fifths majority in the Senate.

Two points of order also are available in the House to prevent Congress from taking its traditional one- or two-week July 4 recess unless the House has completed action beforehand on all appropriations and required reconciliation bills. As with most other points of order in the House, these may be waived by majority vote; neither has ever been successfully raised.

Appendix B: Glossary

This glossary of budget and economic terms was adapted from the General Accounting Office's Terms Used in the Budgetary Process, *March 1981.*

Appropriations Bill—Grants the actual money approved by authorization bills, but not necessarily to the total permissible under the authorization bill. An appropriations bill must, under the Constitution, originate in the House and normally is not acted on until its authorization measure is enacted. The 1985 Gramm-Rudman-Hollings antideficit law set June 30 as the deadline for House passage of regular (annual) appropriations bills, but no deadline for the Senate; in recent years there have been thirteen such bills, mostly identified with single cabinet-level agencies or groups of related agencies. Under the 1974 budget act, annual appropriations were supposed to be enacted by the seventh day after Labor Day before the October 1 start of the fiscal year to which they applied, but this rarely happened. In fact, for decades appropriations often have not been final until well after the fiscal year begins, requiring a succession of stopgap bills to continue the government's functions. In addition, much federal spending—actually, about half of all budget authority, notably that for Social Security and interest on the federal debt—does not require annual appropriations; those programs exist under permanent appropriations. *See also* Continuing Appropriations and Supplemental Appropriations.

Authorization Bill—Authorizes a program, specifies its general aim and conduct, and, unless "open-ended," puts a ceiling on money that can be used to finance it. Usually enacted before the related appropriations bill is passed. *See also* Contract Authority.

Automatic Stabilizer (Built-in Stabilizer)—A mechanism having a countercyclical effect that automatically moderates changes in incomes and outputs in the economy without specific decisions to change government policy. Unemployment insurance and the income tax are among the most important of the automatic stabilizers in the United States.

Backdoor Spending Authority—Budget authority provided in legislation outside the normal appropriations process. The most common forms of backdoor authority are borrowing authority, contract authority, entitlements, and loan guarantees that commit the government to payments of principal and interest on loans—such as Guaranteed Student Loans—made by banks or other private lenders. Loan guarantees only result in actual outlays when there is a default by the borrower.

Balanced Budget—A budget where the receipts are equal to or greater than outlays.

Balance of Payments—The relationship between total flows of assets into or out of a country, including not only trade but also transfers of capital, defense spending, foreign aid, and transfers of monetary reserve assets such as gold. Although the balance of payments technically should be zero, this term is sometimes used to mean the balance on current account. The current account surplus or deficit is essentially the same measure, minus monetary transfers, and thus is an indication of how much a country lends or borrows abroad.

Balance of Trade—Typically, this refers to the relationship between a nation's total exports and imports of manufactured goods, with an excess of exports producing a trade surplus and an excess of imports a trade deficit. When trade in services is included, the measure most commonly used is the balance on current account.

Balance on Current Account—*See* Balance of Payments and Balance of Trade.

Borrowing Authority—Budget authority that permits a federal agency to incur obligations and make payments for specified purposes with borrowed money.

Budget Act—Common name for the Congressional Budget and Impoundment Control Act of 1974, which established the current budget process and created the Congressional Budget Office. It also put limits on presidential authority to refuse to spend appropriated money. *See also* Gramm-Rudman.

Budget Authority (BA)—Authority to enter into obligations that will result in outlays of federal money. The basic forms of budget authority are appropriations, contract authority, and borrowing authority. BA is divided into new obligational authority and loan authority.

Budget Outlays—The actual spending of money as distinguished from the appropriation of it. Outlays, also called expenditures, are made by the disbursing officers of the administration; appropriations are made only by Congress. The two are rarely identical in any fiscal year; outlays may represent money appropriated one, two, or more years previously; likewise, budget authority may be held over for future years, as in the case of Defense Department contracts for construction of ships. Total budget outlays for a fiscal year exclude outlays for off-budget federal entities. *See* Off-Budget Outlays.

Budget Resolution—A concurrent resolution adopted by both houses of Congress, which does not require the president's signature, that sets forth, reaffirms, or revises the congressional budget for the federal government for a fiscal year. The budget resolution specifies budget authority, outlays, and loan authority for each of twenty "functional" spending categories that do not necessarily correspond to agencies or the thirteen regular appropriations bills. The 1974 budget act presumed several budget resolutions during the course of a year, the second and subsequent of which would be binding on total budget authority and outlays, and a floor under receipts. The Gramm-Rudman antideficit law in 1985 accelerated the budget process somewhat, eliminated the presumption of multiple budget resolutions and made the first resolution (scheduled to be adopted by April 15) binding. Revised budget resolutions updating the budget levels may be adopted at any time.

Budget Surplus or Deficit—The difference between budget receipts and outlays.

Business Cycle—The recurrent phases of expansion and contraction in overall business activity, as indicated by fluctuations in measures of aggregate economic activity, especially real (inflation-adjusted) gross national product. Although business cycles are recurrent, both the duration and the magnitude of individual cycles vary considerably. The National Bureau of Economic Research, a private organization in Cambridge, Mass., is the designated arbiter of when a business cycle begins and ends.

Capital—In addition to land and labor, the third major factor of production. Capital refers either to physical capital, such as plant and equipment, or to the financial resources required to purchase physical capital.

Capital Gain—Profit from the sale of capital investments, such as stock and real estate.

Constant Dollar—A dollar value adjusted for changes in prices. Constant dollars are derived by dividing current dollar amounts by an appropriate price index ("deflating"). The result is a dollar value that would exist if prices and transactions were the same in all prior and subsequent years as in the base year. Any changes therefore reflect only changes in the real volume of goods and services produced.

Consumer Price Index (CPI)—Actually several measures of the price change of a fixed "market basket" of goods and services typically purchased by urban consumers. CPI-U is based on a market basket determined by expenditure patterns of all urban households, while the market basket for CPI-W is determined by expenditure patterns of urban wage-earner and clerical-worker families. The level of the CPI indicates the relative cost of purchasing the specified market basket compared with the cost in a designated base year, while the current rate of change in the CPI measures how fast prices are rising or falling. Although the consumer price index is often used as the "cost-of-living index," the CPI measures only price changes, which are just one of several important factors affecting living costs. The CPI is published monthly by the Labor Department's Bureau of Labor Statistics.

Continuing Appropriations—Legislation, virtually always in the form of a joint resolution (which is effectively no different from a bill, since it must be signed into law by the president), enacted to provide budget authority for specific on-going activities in cases where regular appropriations have not been enacted by the beginning of the fiscal year. The continuing appropriations resolution usually specifies a maximum rate at which the agency may incur obligations, based on the rate of the prior year, the president's budget request, or an appropriations bill passed by either or both houses of Congress but not yet enacted. In recent years, most regular appropriations have not been enacted at all, and a full-year continuing resolution (CR) has taken their place. In fact, in fiscal 1987 and fiscal 1988, Congress made no effort to enact separate appropriations bills, instead it rolled all thirteen regular appropriations bills into one continuing resolution. *See* Appropriations.

Contract Authority—Budget authority that permits the federal government to let contracts or obligate itself for future payments from money not yet appropriated. The assumption is that money will be available for payment when contracted debts come due.

Controllability—The ability of Congress and the president to increase and decrease budget outlays or budget authority without changing the basic law authorizing the program. Relatively uncontrollable spending is that which the government cannot increase or decrease without changing existing substantive law. Uncontrollable spending includes outlays for open-ended programs and fixed costs such as interest on the public debt and Social Security benefits. More and more spending for federal programs has become uncontrollable or relatively uncontrollable.

Cost-Benefit Analysis—An analytical technique that measures the costs of a proposed program or policy action against its presumed benefits, stated in terms of dollars.

Countercyclical—Deliberate government actions aimed at smoothing out swings in economic activity, including monetary and fiscal policy (such as countercyclical revenue sharing or public jobs programs). *See also* Automatic Stabilizer.

Current Dollar—The dollar value of a product or service in terms of prices existing at the time the product or service was sold.

Current Services Estimates—Estimated budget authority and outlays for the upcoming fiscal year based on continuation of existing levels of service without policy changes. These estimates, accompanied by the underlying economic and programmatic assumptions upon which they are based, are transmitted by the president to Congress when the budget is submitted.

Deferral of Budget Authority—Any action or inaction by an employee of the United States that withholds, delays, or effectively precludes the obligation or expenditure of budget authority. The 1974 budget act requires a special message from the president to Congress reporting a proposed deferral of budget authority. Deferrals may not extend beyond the end of the fiscal year in which the message reporting them is transmitted. Congress can and has prohibited proposed deferrals by enacting a law doing so; most often cancellations of proposed deferrals are included in appropriations bills.

Deflation—A decrease in the general price level, usually accompanied by declining levels of output, increasing unemployment, and a contraction of the supply of money and credit. Declines in output with increases in unemployment are sometimes referred to as deflationary changes.

Devaluation—The lowering of the value of a country's currency in relation to gold, or to the currency of other countries, when this value is set by government intervention in the exchange market. Devaluation usually refers to fixed exchange rates. In a system of flexible rates, if the value of the currency falls, it is referred to as depreciation; if the value rises, it is called appreciation.

Discount Rate—The interest rate that a commercial bank pays when it borrows from a Federal Reserve bank. The discount rate is one of the tools of monetary policy used by the Federal Reserve System to affect economic conditions. The Fed raises or lowers the discount rate to signal a shift toward restraining or easing its money and credit policy.

Disposable Personal Income—Personal income less personal taxes and nontax payments to the federal government. It is the income available for consumption or saving.

Economic Growth—An increase in a country's productive capacity leading to an increase in the production of goods and services. Economic growth is measured by the annual rate of increase in real (inflation-adjusted) gross national product.

Economic Indicators—Sets of statistics issued by the government that have had a systematic relationship to the business cycle. Each indicator is classified as leading, coincident, or lagging, depending on whether the indicator generally changes direction in advance of, at the same time as, or after changes in the overall economy. Taken as a whole, the economic indicators are valuable tools for identifying and analyzing changes in business cycles.

Employment—In economic statistics, employment refers to all persons who, during the week when the employment survey was taken, did any work for pay or profit, or who worked for fifteen or more hours without pay on a farm or in a business operated by a member of the person's family. Also included as employed are those people who did not work or look for work, but had a job or business from which they were temporarily absent during the week.

Entitlement Program—A federal program that guarantees a certain level of benefits to persons who meet the requirements set by law. It thus leaves no discretion to Congress as to how much money to appropriate, and some entitlements carry permanent appropriations. Entitlement programs include Social Security, farm price supports, and veterans' benefits.

Expenditures—*See* Budget Outlays.

Federal Debt—The federal debt consists of public debt, which occurs when the Treasury or the Federal Financing Bank (FFB) borrows money directly from the public or another fund or account, and agency debt, which is incurred when a federal agency other than Treasury or the FFB is authorized by law to borrow money from the public or another fund or account. The public debt comprises about 99 percent of the gross federal debt.

Fiscal Policy—Federal government policies with respect to taxes, spending, and debt management, intended to promote the nation's economic goals, particularly with respect to employment, gross national product, price level stability, and equilibrium in balance of payments.

Fiscal Year—Financial operations of the government are carried out in a twelve-month fiscal year, beginning on October 1 and ending on September 30. The fiscal year carries the date of the calendar year in which it ends. (Prior to fiscal 1977, the federal fiscal year began on July 1 and ended on June 30. The period June 30 through September 30, 1976, is usually included as a separate accounting period commonly referred to as the transition quarter.)

Functions—Categories of spending established for accounting purposes to keep track of specific expenditures. As of 1988 there were twenty such functional categories, including national defense; international affairs; and general science, space, and technology. These functions do not correspond directly with appropriations or with the budgets of individual agencies. In 1987, the general revenue sharing program expired, and the budget function that contained revenue-sharing expenditures—general purpose fiscal assistance—was elim-

inated. Several smaller programs that were included in that function were rolled into the general government function.

Gramm-Rudman (or Gramm-Rudman-Hollings)—Common name for the 1985 and 1987 amendments to the 1974 budget act authored by Sens. Phil Gramm, R-Texas, Warren B. Rudman, R-N.H., and Ernest P. Hollings, D-S.C. The 1985 law, titled the Balanced Budget and Emergency Deficit Control Act, established a series of declining deficit targets—leading to a balanced budget by 1991—and set up a system for exacting automatic, uniform reductions in federal spending to achieve those deficit targets, if ordinary legislative processes failed to do so. After the Supreme Court declared the method for automatic cuts to be unconstitutional, further amendments were enacted in 1987 to restore the automatic process and to relax the deficit targets, pushing back by two years the date for achieving a balanced budget.

Gross National Product (GNP)—The market value of all final goods and services produced by labor and property supplied by residents of the United States in a given calendar or fiscal year. Depreciation charges and other allowances for business and institutional consumption of fixed capital goods are subtracted from GNP to derive net national product. GNP comprises the purchases of final goods and services by persons and governments, gross private domestic investment (including the change in business inventories), and net exports. GNP can be expressed in current dollars or in constant, inflation-adjusted dollars ("real GNP").

Implicit Price Deflator (GNP Deflator)—A price index for all final goods and services produced in the economy, derived by calculating the ratio of the gross national product in current prices to the gross national product in constant prices. It is a weighted average of the price indexes used to deflate the component of current-dollar

GNP, the implicit weights being expenditures in the current period.

Impoundment—A term applied to action or inaction by an employee of the United States that precludes the obligation or expenditure of budget authority provided by Congress. The Congressional Budget and Impoundment Control Act of 1974 was enacted after frequent use of impoundments by President Richard Nixon. In addition to creating the budget process currently used, the 1974 law established procedures for congressional approval or disapproval of temporary or permanent impoundments, which are called deferrals and rescissions. *See* Deferral of Budget Authority and Rescission of Budget Authority.

Indexing—The practice of adjusting (wages, interest rates, Social Security benefits, tax rates) automatically to reflect changes in the cost of living.

Inflation—A persistent rise in the general price level that results in a decline in the purchasing power of money. Frequently defined as "too much money chasing too few goods."

Labor Force—Those persons who are employed plus those who are seeking work but are unemployed. The total U.S. labor force consists of civilians plus members of the armed forces stationed at home or abroad.

Marginal Tax Rate—The tax rate imposed on the last dollar of income.

Monetary Policy—Policies, which affect the money supply, interest rates, and credit availability, that are intended to promote national economic goals—particularly with respect to employment, gross national product, price level stability, and equilibrium in balance of payments. Monetary policy is directed primarily by the Board of Governors of the Federal Reserve System and its Federal Open Market Committee. Monetary policy works by influencing the cost and availability of bank reserves. This is accomplished through open-market operations (the purchase and sale of securities, primarily government securities), changes in the ratio of reserves to deposits that commercial banks are required to maintain, and changes in the discount rate.

Money Supply—The amount of money in the economy. There are several definitions of money. M1-A consists of currency (coin and paper notes) plus demand deposits at commercial banks, exclusive of demand deposits held by other domestic banks, foreign banks, official institutions, and the U.S. government. M1-B is M1-A plus other checkable accounts, including negotiable orders of withdrawal and automatic transfers from savings accounts at commercial banks and thrift institutions, credit unions share draft accounts, and demand deposits at mutual savings banks. M-2 consists of M1-B plus savings and small denomination time deposits at all depository institutions, overnight repurchase agreements at commercial banks, overnight Eurodollars held by U.S. residents other than Caribbean branches of member banks, and money market mutual fund shares. M-3 is M-2 plus large denomination time deposits at all depository institutions and term repurchase agreements at commercial banks and savings and loan associations.

Off-Budget Outlays—Transactions of certain federally owned or controlled agencies that have been excluded from the budget totals under provisions of law even though these outlays are part of total government spending. Spending activities of off-budget entities, such as the Federal National Mortgage Association, are not included in outlay totals but are presented in a separate part of the budget and as memorandum items in various tables in the budget. Gramm-Rudman required that the Social Security system be moved off budget. But the law specified that Social Security receipts and outlays be counted as part of the unified budget, along with those of other off-budget entities, for purposes of

Gramm-Rudman deficit and sequester calculations. *See* Budget Outlays.

Prime Rate—The rate of interest charged by commercial banks for short-term loans to their most creditworthy customers.

Producer Price Index (PPI)—A measure of average changes in prices received in all stages of processing by producers of commodities in the manufacturing, agriculture, forestry, fishing, mining, gas and electricity, and public utilities sectors. Published monthly by the Labor Department's Bureau of Labor Statistics. (Formerly known as the wholesale price index.)

Recession—A decline in overall business activity that is pervasive, substantial, and of at least several months' duration. Historically, a decline in real (inflation-adjusted) gross national product for at least two consecutive quarters has been considered a recession.

Reconciliation—The process used by Congress to reconcile taxation and spending activities for a given fiscal year with the ceilings enacted in the budget resolution for that year. Changes to existing laws, as required to conform with the binding totals for budget authority, outlays, revenues, and the public debt, are incorporated into a reconciliation bill. Although reconciliation theoretically could apply to the appropriations process, in practice it has been used only to make changes in program authorizations and tax laws. Other rules are used to keep appropriations in line with the budget resolution. Orders to congressional committees to report recommendations for reconciliation bills are written into budget resolutions. These reconciliation instructions are not binding, but Congress must meet annual Gramm-Rudman deficit targets to avoid the automatic spending cuts of sequestration, which means it must also meet the goal of reconciliation. *See* Appropriations, Budget Resolution, and Sequester.

Rescission of Budget Authority—An item in an appropriations bill rescinding, or canceling, money previously appropriated but not spent. Also, the repeal of a previous appropriation by Congress at the request of the president to cut spending. Congress must approve such proposed rescissions under procedures in the 1974 budget act for them to take effect.

Reserve Requirements—The percentage of deposit liabilities that U.S. commercial banks are required to hold as a reserve at their Federal Reserve bank, as cash in their vaults or as directed by state banking authorities. The reserve requirement is one of the tools of monetary policy. Federal Reserve officials can control the lending capacity of banks (thus influencing the money supply) by varying the ratio of reserves to deposits that commercial banks are required to maintain.

Sequester—The term used to describe automatic spending cuts put into place by order of the president, as required by the Gramm-Rudman-Hollings antideficit law.

Stabilization—The maintenance of high-level economic activity with an absence of severe cyclical fluctuations. Stability is usually measured by an absence of fluctuations in production, employment, and prices, three aspects of economic activity that tend to change in a cyclical fashion.

Stagflation—Simultaneous high unemployment (resulting from stagnant economic growth) and high inflation.

Supplemental Appropriations—Normally, these are passed after the regular (annual) appropriations bills, but before the end of the fiscal year to which they apply. They allow an agency to continue functioning if its costs will exceed the amount previously appropriated. Recently they have been needed particularly to cover shortfalls in farm price-support programs, which increased in cost tenfold from the late 1970s until the late 1980s. In years past, such midyear bills were sometimes called deficiency appropriations.

Tax Credits—Tax credits include any special provision of law that results in a dollar-for-dollar reduction in tax liabilities that would otherwise be due.

Tax Expenditures—Revenue losses attributable to provisions of the federal income tax laws that allow a special exclusion, or deduction from gross income, or that provide a special credit, preferential tax rate, or deferral of tax liability. Tax expenditures may be considered federal government subsidies provided through the tax system to encourage certain activities and to assist certain groups. The U.S. Treasury forgoes some of the receipts that it otherwise would have collected, and the beneficiary taxpayers pay lower taxes than they would otherwise have had to pay.

Trust Funds—Money collected and used by the federal government for carrying out specific purposes and programs according to terms of a trust agreement or statute, such as the Social Security and unemployment compensation trust funds. Trust funds are administered by the government in a fiduciary capacity and are not available for the general purposes of the government.

Unemployment Rate—The number of unemployed persons expressed as a percentage of the civilian labor force. Unemployed persons are those who, during a specified week, had no employment but were available for work and had sought employment within the past four weeks, were laid off from a job, or were waiting to report to a new job within thirty days. The unemployment rate is published monthly by the Labor Department's Bureau of Labor Statistics and is released at a hearing of the Joint Economic Committee.

Bibliography

Books

Aaron, Henry J., and Michael J. Boskin, eds. *The Economics of Taxation.* Washington, D.C.: The Brookings Institution, 1980.

Bell, Daniel, and Lester Thurow. *The Deficits: How Big? How Long? How Dangerous?* New York: New York University Press, 1985.

Birnbaum, Jeffrey H., and Alan S. Murray. *Showdown at Gucci Gulch: Lawmakers, Lobbyists, and the Unlikely Triumph of Tax Reform.* New York: Random House, 1987.

Burns, Arthur F., and Paul A. Samuelson. *Full Employment, Guideposts, and Economic Stability.* Washington, D.C.: American Enterprise Institute for Public Policy Research, 1967.

Butler, Stuart M., Michael Sanera, and W. Bruce Weinrod, eds. *Mandate for Leadership II: Continuing the Conservative Revolution.* Washington, D.C.: The Heritage Foundation, 1984.

Cagan, Phillip, ed. *Contemporary Economic Problems: Deficits, Taxes, and Economic Adjustments.* Washington, D.C.: American Enterprise Institute for Public Policy Research, 1987.

———. *Essays in Contemporary Economic Problems: The Impact of the Reagan Program.* Washington, D.C.: American Enterprise Institute for Public Policy Research, 1986.

Collender, Stanley E. *The Guide to the Federal Budget, Fiscal 1989.* Washington, D.C.: The Urban Institute Press, 1988.

Destler, I. M. *Making Foreign Economic Policy.* Washington, D.C.: The Brookings Institution, 1980.

Eisner, Robert. *How Real Is the Federal Deficit?* New York: The Free Press, 1986.

Feldstein, Martin. *The American Economy in Transition.* Chicago, Ill.: University of Chicago Press, 1980.

Fenno, Richard F., Jr. *The Power of the Purse: Appropriations Politics in Congress.* Boston: Little, Brown & Co., 1966.

Fisher, Louis. *Presidential Spending Power.* Princeton, N.J.: Princeton University Press, 1975.

Gilder, George. *Wealth and Poverty.* New York: Basic Books, 1981.

Harrington, Michael. *Decade of Decisions.* New York: Simon & Schuster, 1980.

Harriss, C. Lowell, ed. *Control of Federal Spending.* New York: The Academy of Political Science, 1985.

Havemann, Joel. *Congress and the Budget.* Bloomington: Indiana University Press, 1978.

Heller, Walter. *New Dimensions of Political Economy.* Cambridge, Mass.: Harvard University Press, 1966.

Hulten, Charles R., and Isabel V. Sawhill, eds. *The Legacy of Reaganomics: Prospects for Long-Term Growth.* Washington, D.C.: The Urban Institute Press, 1984.

Laffer, Arthur B., and Jan P. Seymour. *The Economics of the Tax Revolt.* New York: Harcourt Brace Jovanovich, 1979.

McAllister, Eugene J. *Agenda for Progress: Examining Federal Spending.* Washington, D.C.: The Heritage Foundation, 1981.

Mills, Gregory B., and John L. Palmer. *The Deficit Dilemma: Budget Policy in the Reagan Era.* Washington, D.C.: The Urban Institute Press, 1984.

———, eds. *Federal Budget Policy in the 1980s.* Washington, D.C.: The Urban Institute Press, 1984.

Oleszek, Walter J. *Congressional Procedures and the Policy Process.* 3d ed. Washington, D.C.: CQ Press, 1989.

Owen, Henry, and Charles L. Schultze, eds. *Setting National Priorities: The Next Ten Years.* Washington, D.C.: The Brookings Institution, 1976.

Palmer, John L., ed. *Perspectives on the Reagan Years.* Washington, D.C.: The Urban Institute Press, 1987.

Pechman, Joseph A. *Federal Tax Policy.* 5th ed. Washington, D.C.: The Brookings Institution, 1987.

———, ed. *Setting National Priorities: Agenda for the 1980s.* Washington, D.C.: The Brookings Institution, 1980.

Penner, Rudolph G., ed. *The Congressional Budget Process after Five Years.* Washington, D.C.: American Interprise Institute for Public Policy Research, 1981.

Rivlin, Alice M., ed. *Economic Choices 1984.* Washington, D.C.: The Brookings Institution, 1984.

Savage, James D. *Balanced Budgets and American Politics.* Ithaca, N.Y.: Cornell University Press, 1988.

Sawhill, Isabel V., ed. *Challenge to Leadership: Economic and Social Issues for the Next Decade.* Washington, D.C.: The Urban Institute Press, 1988.

Schick, Allen. *Crisis in the Budget Process: Exercising Political Choice.* Washington, D.C.: American Enterprise Institute for Public Policy Research, 1986.

———, ed. *Making Economic Policy in Congress.* Washington, D.C.: American Enterprise Institute for Public Policy Research, 1983.

Silk, Leonard S. *Nixonomics: How the Dismal Science of Free Enterprise Became the Black Art of Controls.* New York: Praeger Publishers, 1973.

Stockman, David A. *The Triumph of Politics: Why the Reagan Revolution Failed.* New York: Harper & Row, 1986.

West, Darrell M. *Congress and Economic Policymaking.* Pittsburgh, Pa.: University of Pittsburgh Press, 1987.

Wildavsky, Aaron. *The Politics of the Budgetary Process.* 4th ed. Boston: Little, Brown & Co., 1984.

Government Documents

Executive Office of the President. *Economic Report of the President,* with the *Annual Report of the Council of Economic Advisers.* Washington, D.C.: Government Printing Office, annually in January or February.

Executive Office of the President and Office of Management and Budget. *Budget of the United States Government.* In several volumes: *Budget, Budget in Brief, Appendix, Special Analyses,* and *Historical Tables.* Washington, D.C.: Government Printing Office, annually in January.

Congressional Budget Office. *An Analysis of the President's Budgetary Proposals.*

Washington, D.C.: Government Printing Office, annually in January or February.

———. *Reducing the Deficit: Spending and Revenue Options.* Washington, D.C.: Government Printing Office, annually in January or February.

———. *The Economic and Budget Outlook.* Washington, D.C.: Government Printing Office, annually in January or February.

———. *The Economic and Budget Outlook: An Update.* Washington, D.C.: Government Printing Office, annually in August.

Index